Scottish Universities:
Distinctiveness and Diversity

Edited by
JENNIFER J. CARTER
and
DONALD J. WITHRINGTON

JOHN DONALD PUBLISHERS LTD
EDINBURGH

ISBN 0 85976 375 7

British Library Cataloguing in Publication Data

A catalogue record for this book
is available from the British Library.

Phototypeset by The Midlands Book Typesetting Co.
Printed and bound in Great Britain by Hartnolls Ltd., Bodmin, Cornwall.

Contents

Contributors

Robert D. Anderson
Reader in History, University of Edinburgh

Deborah Brunton
Science Studies Unit, University of Edinburgh

Jennifer J. Carter
Senior Lecturer in History, University of Aberdeen

John M. Fletcher
Reader in the History of European Universities, University of Aston

David A. R. Forrester
Lecturer in Accountancy and Finance, University of Strathclyde

Marjory Harper
Lecturer in History, University of Aberdeen

Winifred Bryan Horner
Professor of Rhetoric, Texas Christian University, Fort Worth

Iain G. C. Hutchison
Lecturer in History, University of Stirling

A. Allan Maclaren
Senior Lecturer in History, University of Strathclyde

Colin A. McLaren
University Archivist and Keeper of Special Collections,
University of Aberdeen

Lindy Moore
Independent Scholar

Carolyn Pennington
Honorary Research Fellow, Quincentenary History Project,
University of Aberdeen

Sheldon Rothblatt
> Professor of History, and Director of the Center for Studies in Higher Education, University of California at Berkeley

Christine Shepherd
> Tutor, The Open University in Scotland

Lawrence Williams
> Lecturer in History, University of Dundee

David B. Wilson
> Professor of History, Mechanical Engineering and Philosophy, Iowa State University

Donald J. Withrington
> Senior Lecturer in Scottish History, University of Aberdeen

Introduction

Jennifer J. Carter and Donald J. Withrington

When the conference on Scottish universities, at which the papers in this book were given, took place in July 1990, the future of Scottish higher education was already much in debate. The Howie Committee had been appointed to reconsider the schooling of the 16 to 18 years old age group, and to make recommendations about the Highers, the Scottish Certificate of Education school-leaving examination which qualifies young Scots for entry into higher and further education. After a decade of funding problems for all British universities, with current problems of exceptional magnitude for some, especially in Scotland, and with the long-term viability of the still new Universities Funding Council unclear, universities worried about which way to go in future. Together with the universities, Scottish central institutions (the Scottish equivalent, more or less, to polytechnics) and further education colleges, and the wider public interested in higher education (including that part of it which stressed the especially national character of Scottish education) were debating the shape of things to come — a shape since revealed, in part, by the government's White Paper published in April 1991. The European dimension too was more prominent in the educational debate than is usual in Britain, because of the political anxieties as well as the idealism embodied in the intended closer union of European states in 1992. Economic difficulties in Britain also prompted comparison of our education system with those in (for example) America and Japan.

At such a time it was particularly appropriate that a group of historians interested in higher education should meet to examine the nature of Scottish universities — their distinctiveness, in the sense of differences from the university systems of other countries, especially England; and their diversity from one another.

It was the distinctiveness of the Scottish university system, the very fact that over four centuries and more its universities could be seen to constitute a system, which emerged most strongly from three days of papers and discussion at the Aberdeen conference. From its very beginning, in its medieval foundations, there was distinctiveness. Uniquely in Britain, though not in Europe, the characteristic foundation in Scotland was the college-university: an institution which combined in one administrative unit the rights and functions of a residential community of teachers and students and the degree-granting

1

powers of the *universitas*. By contrast, England's two ancient universities of Oxford and Cambridge were federations of colleges, in which the responsibilities of college and university were to be clearly distinguished. Dublin may have been intended to have a similar federal structure but, somewhat mysteriously, this was lost to view and Trinity College indiscriminately exercised both university and collegiate powers — in much the same way as did the older Scottish college-universities. Of them, it is true, St Andrews, had by the time of the Reformation three colleges, but two of these, St Salvator's and St Mary's, had independent papal licences to grant degrees; by the mid eighteenth century the monastic-hospital foundation, St Leonard's College, had united with St Salvator's and St Mary's taught only divinity — and St Andrews in effect was confirmed as part of the Scottish structure of college-universities.

The post-Reformation foundations in Scotland followed the same pattern: to the college-universities which already existed in St Andrews, Glasgow and in Old Aberdeen (St Mary's, later King's College and University) were added Edinburgh and Marischal College and University in New Aberdeen. The two newer institutions brought one novelty with them, for in both some control of university affairs was shared (and was in time to be much fought over) with the local town council. In all five of the Scottish university sites, the body of the teachers — variously, as a body, called the Faculty or the Senatus Academicus — came to wield much greater power than was allowed in England to academic staff, the more so as college fellows and tutors in England came to usurp the positions intended for the university professoriate. London's first two colleges, University College and King's College, did not have officially-sanctioned degree granting powers: in 1836 they were subsumed in the royally-chartered University of London, a novel type of federal structure within which, for the remainder of the nineteenth century, university teachers had little or no say in matters of academic planning and examining. Durham, founded in 1832, followed the collegiate model of Oxbridge. Not until Birmingham University was chartered in 1900 did England gain a college-university on something like the Scottish pattern. Earlier, in England and Wales there developed a clutch of 'redbrick' or 'provincial' university colleges (not college-universities) which, in the later nineteenth century, offered teaching for degrees which were conferred elsewhere — by London University from 1836 onwards, by the federal Victoria University in Manchester from 1880 onwards, and by the new federal University of Wales from 1893. When in Scotland one, and only one, similar 'satellite' university college developed in Dundee, it was closely associated with the neighbouring degree-granting university in St Andrews.

The identification of university and college in Scotland, and the merging of duties and responsibilities under these two headings, gave peculiarly wide powers to the Senatus — over property and finances, over appointments and salaries, as much as over curriculum and discipline. A major exception, however, was Edinburgh, where the town council rather than a royal or papal or noble patron had acted as midwife in the emergence of the college and, being constantly at hand, exercised oversight and was ready to interfere in order to secure its own interests. In the era of high patronage, in the early and middle decades of the eighteenth century, town council intervention was often acceptable, coming at a time of growth directly aided by the council when increased numbers of students, and hence fatter salaries from increased fee income, were a boon to the university's teachers. But trouble was never far away: soon complaints about the council's meddling in matters of curricula, discipline and in appointments not directly in council patronage came to the fore, as did complaints about the council's mishandling of university finances. These complaints surfaced in a period when university teachers were beginning to develop a new professionalism in order to attract still more students, when they had philosophical as well as selfish reasons for wishing to extend and reorder the curriculum, when for instance the college medical teachers were desperately trying to hold their own ground and were looking for support against extra-mural lecturers, and when patronage did not always seem to be in the best interests of the college. In such a situation, conflict between patron's rights and teachers' rights could easily burst out. In New Aberdeen the relationship between Marischal College and town council was generally smoother in the late eighteenth and early nineteenth centuries, partly because the council had fewer direct powers of oversight or control, mostly because there was always a greater identity of interest between a small academic institution and its sponsoring small-town oligarchy. There would be confrontation at times in the nineteenth century but this was tempered by a shared antagonism to the older rival, barely a mile away in Old Aberdeen, the self-righteous, Church-dominated and 'corrupt Tory corporation' of King's College. In difficult dealings with its neighbour in the nineteenth century, as government and public pressure increased for the union of the two Aberdeen universities, Marischal widened the backing it received from the town council and the Senatus, and the councillors took some care in claiming rights or asserting privileges where these were in some doubt.

In the early nineteenth century, the 'university question' in Scotland was not one dominated by the internecine struggles of university factions or by confrontations between academia and town councils or noble patrons. Newspapers and journals show clearly that there was widespread public and national concern over the declining status of the Scottish colleges; over indolence and corruption which inhibited their meeting the changing demands of a changed society; over national institutions apparently converted into private, secretive corporations; and over a national heritage so poorly cared for that buildings were crumbling, teaching was outdated and often perfunctory, the curriculum was too limited, and remarkably few students bothered to go through the full 'gowned' course and graduate. There were certainly in the 1810s and 1820s anxieties about particular universities — evidence of open nepotism and flagrant corruption in St Andrews and Aberdeen, and of their generally debilitated state; inter-faction rivalries in the Glasgow professoriate which badly weakened the college; increasingly sharp exchanges between Senatus and town council in Edinburgh leading to embittered lawsuits in the Court of Session. When at last government acted in 1825–26 to set up a royal commission of enquiry, it was widely welcomed as a long-needed investigation into the national educational structure on behalf of the public. What it is important to note is that the commission's task was to enquire into *all* the Scottish universities (and also their relationship with their 'feeder' schools) and, when it reported, that it emphasised time and again that these universities were public institutions to be regulated together in the national and public interest.

This was no new concept. In 1560, in the Book of Discipline, the Scottish reformers had planned a national educational system with the universities at its apex. Throughout the seventeenth century their shared national standing was confirmed in a succession of government and church commissions which, *inter alia*, attempted to secure teachers of particular known and safe religious and political views, and in the 1690s endeavoured to establish directly a national curriculum in the five universities — which, however, at the end of the day may have come about more out of agreed, shared practice than through government fiat. It is curious that St Andrews alone seems to have offered any strenuous objection to the government attempts in the 1690s to control teaching styles and the subject matter of the courses: we are left wondering what, if anything, it had to gain by so doing. There is no doubt that in seventeenth-century Scotland it was generally accepted that prevailing civil and religious governments should demand political and religious conformity, and there was nothing out of the way in government using its patronage or influence in making and unmaking university appointments. There is no Scottish equivalent to the fellows of Magdalen College, Oxford, who became national heroes in 1688 by active resistance to government attempts to take over control and who, after the Revolution, were restored to the offices from which King James had driven them. But, then, compared to their counterparts in England, the Scottish college-universities were relatively very poor and, to varying extents, looked to government for financial support. They sought handouts from the state for additions to salary, for grants in aid of building repairs, for the founding of new posts, in the centuries both before and after the Union of 1707. In Scotland the piper's tune was heard very loud and clear. Moreover, Scottish universities, unlike Oxford and Cambridge, enjoyed no rights of electing MPs until the nineteenth century. When a Scottish university happened to choose the wrong side in the ever-changing religious politics of the country, then it would expect to suffer. It was only to be anticipated that, when victorious Hanoverians drove out Jacobitism from its last university strongholds in Scotland, there was an almost clean sweep of the teaching staffs in both King's and Marischal, with Marischal being closed down for two years.

Not only were the poorly-endowed Scottish universities sensitive to the demands, and hoped-for support, of national church and national government, they were forced to be sensitive to their customers and their parents: fee-income was a vital consideration to teachers whose stipends from endowment rarely produced a satisfactory income. If a college lost student support it would certainly weaken and might wither away. Thus the need to offer ready access to its customers ate steadily away at demands for entrance qualifications; the need to keep university education as cheaply attractive as possible kept fees low, led to shortened sessions, reduced and then removed expensive residential requirements, made graduation a relatively expensive option which few took. Meanwhile the college buildings were often spare and comfortless, communal space was limited, classrooms were bare and generally ill-fitted, libraries were modest and generally not intended for undergraduate use — all in very marked contrast to the spacious residences, the handsome common rooms and the rich living of Oxford and Cambridge. Scottish university education developed distinctively, therefore, with its own special flavour, which by the early nineteenth century was to be characterised as plain living and hard learning — and open to a very wide social clientele.

In the early nineteenth century, clearly visible in the royal commission's report of 1830, it was the Scottish universities' nationality — and their widely accepted national importance as part of an educational structure intended to serve the whole community — which provided the best and most readily-available means of attacking entrenched professional rights and, in the case of Edinburgh in particular, of breaking town council control. Government commissioners and individual reformers alike could argue that the selfish interest of the professoriates, for example in 'stealing' young classical students from burgh and parochial schools, was hindering the development of good 'secondary' school provision and also restraining the development of more advanced learning in the universities, working both against public demand and national interest. It was easy to play the card of national progress against the self-seeking of individuals or groups, and to demand the rights of public scrutiny not only in supervising financial dealings, in resisting temptations to corrupt management of funds, in introducing more 'open' systems of academic appointments and of apportioning student bursaries, but also in course-structures, the allocation of additional teaching support and development in depth or in widening subject-choice of the curriculum. What was agreed was the need for some system of closer control, balancing professorial interests against some form of outside supervision. The 1830 commission outlined a structure of rectorial or university courts to act alongside the Senatus system, but this was not to be enforced until 1858. There was another mechanism for control which, in many respects, could be seen as particularly fitting in Scotland — and in the 1840s and 1850s this was pressed with some vigour. This was to reconstruct the system to be even more obviously national, by erecting a federal structure, a National University with four constituent colleges (it being generally accepted that King's and Marischal must be united) which would then be effectively regulated by a central supervisory council which, it was often argued, should secure and improve standards in all the colleges by controlling a common examination for all degrees in Scotland. By the mid nineteenth century, indeed, there were British models for federations of colleges: not so obviously, perhaps, in the curiously-structured London University (an examining body only) and its very varied affiliated colleges, but certainly in the new government-funded Queen's University in Ireland with its carefully planned structure of constituent colleges in Belfast (based on a Scottish-style institution of long-standing), in Cork and in Galway. Queen's University was established by parliament for the 'national' higher education of Ireland, with the academic appointments in government hands, with strong centrally-controlled and government-influenced teaching and learning systems in the colleges, and with examinations and monitoring of standards firmly given over to the university. In Scotland the federal idea was still in the air at the time of the passing of the 1858 Act, which at last broke legal or presumed professorial privileges and reconstructed university administrations so as to give very large supervisory powers to local university courts with strong representation from local businessmen and professional bodies as well as from town councils and graduates' associations, and from the professors on Senatus. At the same time the union of Marischal and King's as the University of Aberdeen was accomplished. The 1858 Act did not directly federalise the system, nor erect a common examination council, but it ceded to government-appointed commissioners large powers over the extension of curricula, the funding of additional teaching posts at professorial or assistant level and the restructuring of degree-course programmes. It might well be that, if government could have been assured of firmer support in parliament (where MPs who acted as guardians of Oxbridge were always extremely worried about the repercussions for English education, school or university, of any Scottish precedent) and if Edinburgh had been more amenable than it appeared to be, then government might well have pressed for the federated National University that had so often been mentioned. As it was, after 1858, and again after the next major universities' act of 1889, the four Scottish universities were in some degree harnessed together, required to act in sometimes awkward harmony — a kind of federation, kept alive more by suffering acceptance than by inner compulsion, yet nonetheless recognising that there were advantages, for instance in dealings with government and Treasury, if they were seen to march together.

Government dealings with the Scottish universities, viewed from south of the border, always seemed extraordinarily dirigiste, smacking of a quite unacceptable degree of state intervention. What is remarkable is that the self-same governments and parliaments could and did act so differently towards the Scottish and English universities, reflecting their distinctive historical traditions and the level and nature of the concern of the voting public in them. In England the experience of state intervention in its higher education was altogether gentler, more hesitant, and persuasive rather than directive. Oxford and Cambridge, which were examined and reviewed separately by royal commissions, not together as parts of a national structure, were only gradually reformed; and groups of friendly royal commissioners were at great pains to try to work along with moderate reformers within their institutions, prompting emergent internal changes rather than threatening abrupt reconstruction by outside agency.

Meanwhile, government encouraged but did little directly to initiate or press developments elsewhere in England. London University grew in importance and standing, predominantly as an examining body whose degrees were open to a very varied and geographically widespread grouping of colleges, these colleges opting into a loose federation whose basis of connection was limited to their acceptance of uniform curricular regulations and examinations. In the Victoria University of northern England and in the University of Wales, government acted only to give a new legal solidity to, and vital degree-granting rights to, federated colleges which had developed independently of each other and out of local rather than the national interests. In all these federations central academic control was, nonetheless, relatively weak and there was little of that shared responsibility within a national enterprise demonstrated and developed in Scotland.

Much of this diversity of approach by government to higher education reflects the clear distinctions that there were, especially in Scotland and England, in views of the relationship of the state to education and of the state and its role in society. In English education the state was viewed often with deep suspicion, even with dread, and legislation which induced state supervision or state interference was something to be avoided. In Scotland, under its own parliament before 1707 and under the British parliament in the early nineteenth century, the provision of public schooling ('public' in the Scottish sense) was recognised as being secured and given vital financial support in law; there it was expected that government would and should intervene, and there was no hesitation about extending that expectation to university education. England clung to the notion that universities were autonomous corporations, guarded by law against the state, regulated by charter and only meagrely financed by or through the state. When in the early nineteenth century Sir William Hamilton argued for state intervention in Oxford and Cambridge on the grounds that their large endowments were in effect public funds, which therefore required public (i.e. government) monitoring and control to ensure that they were used properly for the public good, such claims not only angered but they bewildered Englishmen who did not share Hamilton's thoroughly Scottish vision. That vision was warmly shared by the royal commissioners on the Scottish universities in 1826–30: it was their declared intention to enhance, and positively to do nothing to weaken, those universities as national and public institutions, not there to serve Church interests or the group interests of any social or economic class but to be so organised that they would be of the greatest utility to all in the national community who had the ability to benefit from them. In Scotland, in extraordinary contrast to England, it was not merely admitted but it was proclaimed that government had both a right and a duty to 'meddle' in the universities.

A further distinctive characteristic of the Scottish universities seems, at first sight, to be a rather surprising one. For all its close interest in post-Reformation education, in the eighteenth and nineteenth centuries the Church of Scotland exerted relatively weak control over the universities and even less influence than might be supposed, especially in comparison with Oxford and Cambridge which remained inextricably connected with the Church of England. Indeed it was in supposedly tolerant England, rather than in a Scotland often described as theocratic, that church influence dominated. Until 1871 almost all university and college teachers at Oxbridge were in holy orders, with a church career in view for them, just as it was for many of their students. Even the passing of the Universities Tests Act in 1871 did not prevent Church influence remaining strong in England: the act abolished official religious tests, but many unofficial practices such as attendance at chapel maintained an Anglican tone in many colleges. Even the foundation of University College in London (the 'godless' college of Gower Street, which had such strong Scottish representation among its founders), in part a reaction against the Anglican monopoly of the ancient English universities, was rapidly matched by the formation of an 'Established Church' College in London (King's), while the University of Durham — founded in 1832 from episcopal revenues — was quite openly intended to promote the education of Anglican clergy in the north of England.

In Scotland, meanwhile, only minimal religious tests were applied to professors on their appointment, although Church connection or sponsorship could be vital in some periods or in some colleges. For example, in the eighteenth and earlier nineteenth centuries, King's in Old Aberdeen and St Andrews both had significantly higher proportions, than did the other universities, of Church licentiates and of parish ministers who simultaneously held professorships. What was even more distinctive in Scotland was that no religious tests were applied to students. As early as the mid-eighteenth century compulsory attendance at the college chapel on Sundays had largely disappeared and did not revive. As we have noted, the royal commissioners in 1830 were in no doubt that the Scottish universities were quite definitely secular institutions. How can this be explained? There were certainly some — if mild — attempts to distance the Scottish universities from church and state, even in the 1690s and 1700s. Partly this stemmed from political affiliation to Scottish Episcopacy and to Jacobitism, partly it seems to have sprung from the attempt to assert greater local control by college Senates, which had even then become accustomed to running their own academic affairs untramelled by dependence on 'outside' agencies which controlled large endowments. There is evidence that, while eighteenth-century Moderatism was highly influential in the Scottish universities, there was little direct Church control: not until the early nineteenth century did Church evangelicals try to assert themselves, only to be brushed aside by university Senates which had grown in self-confidence and by increasing popular antipathy to patronage and 'undue influence' exercised for party, rather than for the public, benefit. Strange to say, even in the teaching of divinity in the Scottish universities, the

Church of Scotland had introduced such relaxations of the regulations about requirements for admission to study, about actual attendance on classes, and about evidence of academic quality in performance, that the general assemblies of the early nineteenth century had the greatest difficulties in regaining control over teaching or standards — with rather more opposition, it should be said, coming from conservative presbyteries than from the teachers in the Divinity Halls. The Church's weakness lay in the fact that it provided hardly any endowment or money-payments for theological instruction in the Scottish universities, and came to depend on candidates for the ministry who were only able to meet the deliberately very modest regulations for entry to the profession through part-time study, frequently while holding full-time posts in schoolteaching. Church influence in universities, as shown in contributions to curricular development or in improving physical or social conditions for students or attempts to raise standards, was already low in the 1820s and 1830s, and was to be weakened still further by the Disruption of 1843. Thus, for economic reasons as well as from principle, the Scottish universities prided themselves on being open to all-comers, of all ages, of all faiths, of all interests and of all career-intentions: for institutions so dependent on fees, and hence on a continuing flow of students, any barrier to university admission was a matter of deep concern, and the colleges had long ceased to be religious communities of any readily perceptible kind.

Yet the Scottish universities remained the essential recruiting-ground for the Church ministry; what is distinctive about them is that, unlike English universities, they were training institutions for all the professions. In England neither lawyers nor many doctors of medicine would enter on their careers by way of the ancient universities; in Scotland the universities monopolised the professional teaching of ministers (until the Free Church set up its own postgraduate colleges in the 1840s and 1850s) and increasingly took over the professional training of lawyers and doctors. More than that, the arts curriculum of the undergraduate degree-course was also, in a very real sense, a vocational training: it was a preliminary general education for lawyers and ministers and doctors; it was the main gateway into schoolteaching; its wide curriculum, which sometimes under the designation of particular philosophies offered much practical science teaching in chemistry, physics, mathematics, natural history; also instruction in economics and rudementary social analysis and psychology, and in English, was available (as a whole package or on a 'cafeteria' basis) to those wishing to enter careers in trade, in land surveying, in the armed services, etc; and, after the 1850s the Scottish universities paid particular attention to the needs of those intending to take Indian or home civil service examinations. In the great debate in the nineteenth century about what constituted 'liberal education', protagonists for the Scottish system put special emphasis on its strong philosophical core, as both useful in itself but also as a fine preparation for those who would enter public life — in Sir William Hamilton's view, for example, much to be preferred to Oxford classics or to Cambridge mathematics. Hamilton's emphasis, indeed, was always on the curriculum, whose content developed as the state of knowledge improved and as it kept pace with changing philosophical ideas; and for him, therefore, liberal education was marked out by the way it released the spirit of enquiry at the same time as it was practically useful in terms of prospective careers. Such a view dominated the Scottish universities and is clearly evident in the report of the royal commission in 1830. This was a definition of liberal education which was a long way away from that developed by John Henry Newman in his ideal of a collegiate, residential higher education, *The Idea of a University*, which so represented, and then was so much to influence, the English universities.

Newman's ideal presupposed collegial residence as an essential element in the gentlemanly (or 'liberal') education offered by universities, but by the middle of the nineteenth century Scotland had in practice long turned its back on residence. And, indeed, the students of London University and of the emergent university colleges of provincial England, just as those in the Scottish universities, lived at home or in lodgings. The university community was defined by teacher-learner relationships confined to periods of direct instruction, not by the communal living of Oxbridge colleges. The cheapness of the non-residential Scottish universities underlined the principle of accessibility and of the 'democratic intellect'. That principle, the lecture system of teaching and the deliberately low cost of that instruction, all produced the myth of the 'lad o' pairts' (the poor scholar who makes his way in the world, through education, particularly through making good at university) — myth in the sense that it has been overstated and over-valued, not in the sense that the phenomenon did not exist at all. At any rate, these characteristics — carefully nurtured throughout the nineteenth century — powerfully affected perceptions of the Scottish universities, within Scotland as well as outside. What is not to be denied is that substantially more students from modest and even from very humble social backgrounds could reach the nineteenth-century Scottish universities than could reach, or even contemplate the possibility of reaching, either Oxford or Cambridge.

Thus, it is plainly evident that Scottish universities can be said to constitute a recognisable 'system' of higher education; and that, certainly in comparison with England, that system was remarkably distinctive. Yet within that shared structure of consciously national provision, confirmed and supported by royal commissions and legislation in the nineteenth century and earlier, there was room for diversity. Shared ideals did not always bring uniformity or conformity, not least when the development of individual college-universities could depend so much and so immediately on their customer orientation. In the course of the eighteenth century, partly from their accessibility and partly from the renown of some of their teachers, Glasgow and Edinburgh in particular drew substantial numbers of students from outwith Scotland, from English dissenting families (but not only dissenters from England), from Ireland, from America, and expatriate Scots from America, the West Indies, Asia, anywhere. St Andrews and the Aberdeen colleges remained more Scottish and indeed more notably local. The great improvement of road travel and later ferry and coastal shipping communications, and in due course the coming of the railways, made Edinburgh and Glasgow more and more accessible to home students from widening areas of recruitment. These developments had much less effect on King's and Marischal, which still retained the attachment of north-east and northern families, than they had on St Andrews which suffered serious decline as more and more Fife students went to Edinburgh and students from Angus opted to travel north.

But it was earlier, in the eighteenth century, that the impact of student choice and the variations in student numbers began to bring significant diversity among the five universities, at a time when they were threatened by the emergence of an attractive alternative to university education: modern subjects, vocationally oriented to new employments in merchanting, land-factoring and the like, were increasingly taught in parochial and burgh schools to pupils who might otherwise have gone on to university, and in mid-century private academies were established in some of which there was developed a highly-structured modern curriculum (intensive two-year courses including practical sciences, the 'useful' parts of mathematics, logic and English grammar, bookkeeping, mensuration, surveying) intended to be a direct and preferred substitute for four years of ill-supervised, drawn-out, antiquated, college education useful only for the old professions. What was a saving factor, particularly for the smaller universities in St Andrews and Aberdeen, was one feature of those developments, namely that the modern subjects and the curriculum-packages offered in academies were relatively expensive in fee-payments (and they often offered expensive boarding, although they were not necessarily residential). The fees for classical subjects in parish and burgh schools were, on the other hand, kept deliberately very low, in order to serve the requirements of the able poor who needed cheap and bursary-assisted university studies to make their way in the world.

The smaller universities depended to a greater extent on their bursary students than did Edinburgh or Glasgow, and this in turn kept their graduating courses a more important feature of the learning and teaching in St Andrews and in Old and New Aberdeen. The smaller universities, more locally or regionally dependent for their students, were more directly Church-connected, with higher proportions of their professoriates being also the ministers of local parishes; as a whole they were more influenced by Moderate policies and practices. Edinburgh and Glasgow, much larger, were still local institutions drawing on their own 'captive' urban populations which tended to use the universities only in so far as their studies seemed relevant and useful to their own merchanting and commercial careers, and not in the main for the 'full' education of the graduating course. As a result they drew steadily away from the traditional character that had earlier drawn all five Scottish colleges together: not only in numbers and in wealth (if not as institutions, at least in the incomes which could be derived by successful teachers from attracting large classes to them), but in character and in customer dependence. They were in effect less susceptible to Church domination and much less influenced by movements for reform, whether this was in changing the curriculum or in introducing entrance examinations, or in imposing greater regulation in course-choice and in teaching structures. The proposals of the reforming royal commission of 1826–30 for internal changes in curricula or teaching were generally welcomed in Aberdeen and St Andrews whereas the threat of loss of Church influence in university management was fiercely opposed. In Edinburgh and Glasgow on the other hand, the attempts to introduce greater regulation in attendance and in course-choice were deeply suspected, not for educational reasons but because they were likely to diminish professorial incomes. That royal commission made recommendations for reform of a national system which, since the mid-eighteenth century, had seen its constituent colleges grow apart and become notably less national in character. It was left to later nineteenth-century commissions and two acts of parliament (in 1858 and 1889) to attempt, rather too late in the day as it turned out, to impose a more systematic and shared organisation on all the universities (four in number with the union of the Aberdeen colleges in 1860) and also to reintroduce greater coherence in university studies, all in the name of a national and traditional structure.

It is no coincidence that, in the later nineteenth century, it was the weakest of the four universities, St Andrews, which seems — along with Aberdeen, still the most regional and most inherently traditional of them all — to have stressed the national character of the universities and to have emphasized their role in national education, in both instances seen as vitally and essentially distinctive within Great Britain. Whereas Edinburgh, and to a lesser extent Glasgow, found it inhibiting, or potentially inhibiting, to be tied down — and to be tied to Aberdeen and St Andrews with which they felt they had little inherent connection, for St Andrews in particular there was added strength in promoting such connectedness. There was no question about Aberdeen's viability after 1860, but St Andrews had virtually lost its old regional recruiting ground; it did not share Aberdeen's great strength in bursaries (nor the university-related teaching of secondary schools whose graduate masters enjoyed the fruits of the Dick and other north-east bequests); its endowments could not support the new buildings it needed or the addition of new, more attractive subjects. There is no surprise, therefore, in the readiness of St Andrews to encourage the attendance of women students in its licentiate courses (or, in the suggestion, not to be taken up, that St Andrews should become the women's university of Scotland) or to wish to develop supervised student residences on an English college pattern to add to its attractive distinctiveness. Yet what St Andrews still wanted was to retain its place in a strong national system, a fact emphasised again and again in the 1880s and 1890s by Principal James Donaldson who became, indeed, something of a spokesman for the national heritage of the Scottish universities. Aberdeen epitomised the old traditional Scottish university; St Andrews proclaimed the importance of the Scottish tradition as an argument for its survival (not least in the 1880s when there was every likelihood that it would be closed down altogether); Edinburgh seldom, Glasgow more often, supported the concept of a national system and stressed its advantages, but only when it suited them. Indeed, it may be said that it was the 'attacks' on the Scottish universities in the 1880s by the Treasury, when it attempted to buy them out and convert them into private rather than public institutions, which did more than anything else to draw the four institutions together and to prompt them to find good reasons — financial ones — for defending their distinctive Scottishness. Otherwise, they might have drifted still further apart — with St Andrews and its satellite college in Dundee taking on a still more untraditional character. Treasury ignorance of Scottish traditions, of the nature of student recruitment into the universities, of the weight of professional training which characterised the ancient Scottish colleges and made them so different from Oxford and Cambridge, ignorance of the wide public interest in the Scottish universities and of their part in a capacity-catching educational system, came in the end to force the Scottish universities into joining to defend themselves and those traditions. Their patterns of student recruitment (from more or less defined 'provinces'), their size and the differing emphases in the advanced studies they offered, might together make the four Scottish universities different from each other, but such diversity was as nothing compared to the divide which separated them as a homogenous grouping from those south of the border.

In the twentieth century a number of factors have further weakened the sense of shared Scottishness within the universities, at the same time as much of that distinctiveness has been maintained in practice — for example, in collaborative enterprises like the old Scottish Universities Entrance Board and its successor, the Scottish Universities Council on Entrance; in maintaining faculty rather than departmental or course entry systems; in four-year Honours programmes which retain the first two years for advanced general rather than specialist education, etc. Much has happened to submerge the earlier, more visible distinctiveness: the accession in the 1960s of four more universities in Scotland, which did not so clearly in policies or structures define themselves as 'Scottish'; UK-wide policies applied by the UGC which took relatively little account of Scottish distinctiveness; the vastly greater mobility of university teachers in the decades of expansion, which brought many academics to Scotland who knew little or nothing of its educational traditions; the breaking down of older catchment areas for students and the vast increase in non-Scottish students, as well as the striking rise in student numbers, have done much to weaken old provincial connections and identities; and so on.

Yet all that was gladly suffered, even welcomed, in a period of high expansion. But times have changed again — and the experience of the 1980s, with enforced government cut-backs, much more direct government intervention, the increasing application of central policies without regard to local or regional conditions (e.g. financing by 'cost centres' which is destructive of faculty-centred policies in Scotland), have all had their impact. In the later 1980s the Scottish universities rejected the proposal that they should be devolved into a new management structure as part of a new Scottish educational system incorporating all schools, colleges and universities, all higher and further education. In the early 1990s, or so it seems, the eight Scottish universities are much more ready to run for shelter to the Scottish Office, and out of range of Whitehall and Westminster — and are ready to revive all kinds of arguments, valid or specious, for being treated distinctively because they are Scottish. Strangest of all, every now and again there appears the suggestion that some federated structure, some new formulation of a National University, should be seriously considered again. Are we about to come full circle?

———

The organisers of the Aberdeen conference, and editors of this volume, wish to record their thanks to all those who by their participation made the 1990 conference so valuable, and in particular to Sir Kenneth Alexander, Chancellor of the University of Aberdeen, for presiding over its final session. Attendance by scholars from many universities, in Britain and abroad, was made more attractive by the happy linking of our conference with one held immediately afterwards at the University of Glasgow, on the theme of 'The University in Society'. We wish also to place on record our thanks to the University Court of the University of Aberdeen for its continuing support of the Quincentenary History Project, of which this conference was one outcome. We thank too the generosity of the Aberdeen University Studies Committee, and the Trustees of the Carnegie Trust for the Universities of Scotland, whose grants-in-aid made publication of this volume possible. And we wish likewise to thank Messrs John Donald, whose valued support for Scottish history has been shown in so many previous publications, and now again in this one.

Part I
The Nation and Higher Education:
What is the Scottish Tradition?

1

The College-University: its Development in Aberdeen and Beyond

John M. Fletcher

At the Siena conference of 1988 to discuss the history of academic colleges, an attempt was made to list the various types of colleges established in universities before the close of the seventeenth century. The college-university was then noted as one distinctive type.[1] It was apparent, however, that no serious attempt had been made to consider the reasons for the emergence of this institution or to discuss the difficulties it experienced and the legacy it bequeathed. The first college-university, described by Rashdall as a 'new form of university',[2] was established at Sigüenza in 1489. Foundations at Aberdeen (1495) and at Alcalá (1499)[3] followed shortly afterwards, establishing, particularly in Spain, the acceptability of this type of institution. For the British Isles, the most important college-university was erected as Trinity College, Dublin, in 1592.[4] The reasons for the sudden appearance of several examples of this special type of university in the last decades of the fifteenth century will concern us later. It is difficult to trace any direct link between the three earliest foundations. William Elphinstone, when he planned the establishment of King's College in Old Aberdeen, can hardly have had any knowledge of the changes that had taken place at a relatively obscure college in Sigüenza. For Alcalá the stated model was not Sigüenza but the College of Saint Bartholomew at Salamanca.[5]

The organisation of a college-university, as its name suggests, involved in a variety of ways some amalgamation of the functions of the college and the university. It was not always clear exactly what was intended here. As late as 1821 the position of Trinity College was ambiguous; George IV on his visit to Dublin agreed to receive the university but not the college! A judicious alteration to the wording of the invitation on this occasion resolved the difficulty, but it was still occupying the minds of legal experts advising the Royal Commission on Trinity College in 1907.[6] The bond between college and university was cemented by the role allocated to the head of the college; he was given some important statutory position in the administration of the university. At Alcalá the early statutes record unequivocally that one person should be both head of the college and rector of the university.[7] At Aberdeen, the offices of principal of King's College and rector of the university were separated but the principal, by the terms of the founder's charters, always held one of the three keys of the university chest;[8] no financial decision, therefore, could be implemented without his knowledge and consent. It is possible that the role of the head of the college was perceived differently according to whether the founder envisaged that the future members of his university would include those living outside college jurisdiction.

The college-university was also different from other contemporary institutions in that it attempted to include in one complex all the various buildings required for the activities of a university. Fortunately the survival of several of these early complexes enables us to examine more clearly the intentions of the founders. From such evidence and from an inventory of residential accommodation made in 1542, it would seem that King's College, Aberdeen, provided a chapel, a library, a refectory with kitchen and storerooms, a lecture hall, and rooms for some twenty-four masters and students.[9] Since the hall, chapel or refectory could be used for university meetings and formal ceremonies, all the essential needs of staff and students could be supplied within this one college. However, such an arrangement would assume that numbers attending the university remained small and unchanging, and that the existing buildings and accommodation would continue to satisfy their requirements.

That three college-universities appeared over such a short space of time and in both Spain and Scotland would lead us to believe that some common factors were influencing founders at this date. It could be argued, from the example of Aberdeen, that the college-university represented the best use of limited resources in an economically backward area. The founder was compelled to provide the necessary university buildings and accommodation in the absence of private support from wealthy patrons or from families with money enough to pay for their sons' residence. Control over the endowments of a small university could be better arranged when the head of a college had complete oversight of all its buildings and residential accommodation. Whatever were the motives of Elphinstone, they could not necessarily be attributed to other founders. The rich cardinal-archbishop of Toledo, primate of Spain, was certainly not restricted by limited resources when he established his college at Alcalá. It was a much larger institution than King's College, with support for thirty-three collegiales, twelve capellani, thirteen cameriste and an undetermined number of portionists.[10] As will be noted below, Ximenes' later measures to endow further his new university were not the actions of a man constrained by poverty.

Perhaps more important in influencing founders at this date was a growing concern for the maintenance of law, order and discipline within the university community. As the early history of the universities of Paris, Oxford and Bologna had shown, tensions between privileged masters or students and aggrieved townsmen frequently ended in violence. Rival elements amongst masters and students themselves also often resorted to open street warfare; one of the earliest Oxford statutes attempted to bring peace to the quarrelling Irish and members of the northern Nation.[11] The expansion of universities in the fourteenth and fifteenth centuries spread this problem and an awareness of it. The magistrates of Brussels and Barcelona were so afraid of violence from undisciplined students that they strongly opposed attempts by state governments to establish universities in their cities.[12] This problem stemmed partly from an inability of early university authorities to control masters and students. When their members lived in rooms rented from townsmen, universities could do little to monitor the behaviour of students or prevent those accused from quitting the university speedily with their possessions; any aggrieved party was left without adequate remedy or compensation. The need to survey student behaviour and to apprehend criminal elements became more serious when universities were accused in the fifteenth century of harbouring heretics, especially followers of Wyclif and Hus. In Spain efforts to cleanse the kingdom of Jews and Moslems, a policy supported also by the founder of the University of Alcalá, encouraged concern for the stricter control of student activities. 'New Christians' were banned from attendance at the University of Sigüenza in 1497.[13] It is understandable that benefactors at the close of the fifteenth century wished to support a system whereby all or most students and masters lived in colleges under the supervision of a principal. Not only could such students be closely observed, but the threat of expulsion from their accommodation and seizure of any property could be real deterrents against misbehaviour.

The need to harbour resources and control students was a very real requirement, but less tangible influences on founders of the college-university may have been the desire both to strengthen college life and to enhance developments already seen earlier in universities. College founders in the middle ages held the view that the collegiate life was superior to that of the individual. Probably derived from an early respect for the common life of the religious, this belief was reinforced by an awareness of the practical advantages — interaction with other students and perhaps masters, the possibility of financial and moral support, access to a common library, experience of administration — that collegiate life could bring. The college-university, by requiring all members of a university to adopt the collegiate life, could be seen as reversing that damaging tendency towards individualism and selfishness that many prominent academics saw amongst their contemporaries.[14] Also, the institution of this new type of university could be seen as a logical extension of what had gone before. Whereas the earliest universities had been little more than gatherings of masters and students utilising what rooms and shelter they could find, by the close of the middle ages students were expecting more facilities. New foundations of the late fourteenth and early fifteenth centuries were often equipped from their beginnings with purpose-built lecture rooms, libraries and chapels. Such ranges of buildings survive today, as for example at Cracow where the Collegium Maius took its present form largely in the fifteenth century. Earlier foundations, Salamanca, for instance, now also acquired such groups of buildings. There was a movement away from seeing the university as a collection of students towards regarding it as a collection of buildings. Several universities, especially those in the Holy Roman Empire, that needed to attract qualified teaching staff, provided special colleges to accommodate their lecturers. It would seem a logical extension of these developments to expect the founder to provide *all* the buildings required by masters and students on one site. This would mean adding to the now usual chapel, library, and lecture rooms accommodation for teachers and students and the necessary refectory, kitchen and ancillary buildings to support this. The college-university perhaps arose from both a development of earlier precedents and as a response to difficulties that these foundations were experiencing.

Yet it may be argued that the college-university was itself already out-of-date at the time of its inauguration. Changes in the pattern of student and staff recruitment to the late medieval and renaissance universities made the concepts that lay behind the establishment of such college-universities no longer generally acceptable. Historians have correctly drawn attention to the changes in the curriculum that accompanied the reception of the New Learning by the European universities. The attack on scholastic logic and scholastic theology, the encouragement of the study of classical Latin and Greek grammar and the literature of Rome and Greece, the emergence of Hebrew as a university subject, efforts to 'purify' the study of law and medicine, certainly greatly changed the appearance of the curriculum of all universities. Such changes did little to affect the structure of these institutions. The universities could offer the new or remodelled subjects without altering their faculty, administrative or teaching structures. The same lecture rooms and the same buildings could accommodate and cater for students of these different subjects. The survival of so much of medieval terminology, of medieval academic organisation and of so many medieval buildings shows how the older universities could adopt the renaissance curriculum without a radical change in their form and appearance. They could not, however, adapt to major social changes at this date without abandoning some of their important and cherished characteristics. It is in this area, we may suggest, where the serious pressures for radical change originated; these pressures especially affected the college-university.

Firstly, we must consider the changing role of married students and lecturers. This has attracted little attention from historians of the medieval universities, perhaps intimidated by the harsh comments on women found in college statutes and by the much quoted judgment on a married student of Vienna 'uxorem duxit versus in dementiam'.[15] In fact, many universities assumed that there would be married students, masters and doctors amongst their members and, especially in the fifteenth century, made provision for the protection of their wives and families. No full investigation of the position of such married men within the universities has been made, but it is interesting to note that it was the role of the scholar or wife as a trader protected by university privileges that attracted the attention of the local civic authorities. Scattered references to this concern in the fifteenth century indicate that the number of married men within the universities was sufficient to provoke these authorities to take action. At

Oxford, for example, in 1459 an agreement between the university and the town defined the types of privileged persons allowed to remain within the jurisdiction of the university. It was expressly stated that scholars having 'a wyf and household within the precinct of the Universite' and engaging in trade were to pay the same charges as other burgesses of the town.[16] Again, at Freiburg at the close of the fifteenth century, the presence of married students, masters and doctors was continually souring relations between town and university.[17] If students did not intend to pursue a career in the church there was no reason why they should remain celibate. Civil lawyers and physicians in particular could find lucrative employment in lay society. Moreover, with the end of compulsory celibacy in countries that accepted the protestant Reformation, the necessity for theologians to refrain from marriage if they wished to follow a career in the church was here ended. The universities of the sixteenth century, especially in the protestant area of northern Europe, had to recognise that some of their members, especially their older masters and doctors, would be married with wives and probably children and servants to support.

The university colleges of northern Europe had to make an important reassessment of their position as this situation became more common. Already an occasional individual and unmarried member of a college had attempted to retain his fellowship and yet live outside the premises: a master of the Sorbonne in 1481 had his own house and complained that he could not sleep in the college because his books were kept at his home.[18] Even when the original numbers for which colleges were founded were reduced, the standard of comfort left much to be desired, and it is understandable that the more prosperous of university masters preferred to acquire their own privacy and accommodation. If such masters and doctors were married with families, it would be impossible to house them in colleges with very limited accommodation and rules for common meals in hall. The acceptance of such a situation implied the end of collegiate life as the medieval universities had known it; especially for the teaching staff. Some colleges, such as those at Oxford and Cambridge, survived with an uneasy compromise, allowing their heads to marry while the fellows had to remain celibate. Most had to abandon gradually any requirement that teaching staff should share a collegiate life. The universities sometimes accepted the need to cater for the children of such staff; Freiburg already in 1480 allowed the legitimate sons of its regent masters and doctors to matriculate without charge.[19]

If these changes threatened the existence of such colleges, they posed an equally serious threat to the survival of the college-universities. It would seem that Elphinstone, himself a trained lawyer with considerable experience of continental universities, was aware of this problem. He required his legal and medical teaching staff to live not in his college but in separate houses in Old Aberdeen. Probably the possibility that his university would have to recruit married men with families to fill some at least of these posts had already occurred to him. He also allowed his grammarian to live outside the college; many humanist teachers were married and preferred to work outside institutions with a clerical tradition.[20] Presumably students of civil law and physicians, the most likely to be married, received their instruction in these separate houses and so did not disturb the routine of the younger members of the college. Even when Trinity College, Dublin, was founded by a protestant monarchy, the medieval insistence on celibacy for its fellows was maintained. Clearly, both King's College and Trinity College would be in some difficulties when others, apart from lawyers and physicians, demanded the right to marry and yet retain their fellowships.

In fact, neither institution seems to have been able to cope satisfactorily with this situation. At the date of the Nova Fundatio for Aberdeen in 1583 there seemed no possibility of allowing any of the twelve bursars to marry and retain his scholarship. The position of the principal and the four regents is not clear. The statutes speak of the wives and daughters of the masters, so presumably these were to be allowed to marry. However, the same statutes require all members on the foundation except the grammarian to live in the college, but prohibit all women from entering! Are we to imagine that it was expected that the wives of the masters would live apart from their husbands and outside the college? The position is very unclear and it is possible that all provisions of the Nova Fundatio were not followed at King's College.[21] It does seem, however, that any attempt to require celibacy from the teaching staff had been by this date abandoned. At Trinity College, the formal prohibition of marriage remained binding on fellows until 1840. However, many fellows simply ignored this; in 1811, when action was taken to impose the regulation strictly, sixteen out of the twenty-five fellows were married.[22] It is apparent that the problem of accommodating married fellows was never satisfactorily resolved by either of these northern college-universities until more recent attitudes rendered any attempts to impose celibacy on teaching staff obsolete.

The second factor which seriously challenged the character of the college-universities was simply their need to expand. The difficulty here was how to maintain a growing university population all or mostly resident in one set of buildings. At Sigüenza, the college-university seems to have been very small and limited in its outlook; it provided for only a rector and twelve collegiales, following the pattern set by Christ and his disciples. One lecturer in theology and one in philosophy were established; the collegiales were forbidden to study canon law, although after 1505 they could begin such a course after six years' preparatory work.[23] Expansion at Sigüenza seems neither to have been anticipated nor greatly desired. The position was much different at Alcalá established by the ambitious and powerful Ximenes. Here, the instant success of the university and its reputation brought a sudden influx of students: 'plurimi . . . ad praefatum nostrum collegium et universitatem . . . confluunt', as the 1513 statutes declare.[24] Supported by its generous and wealthy founder, the university proceeded to establish no fewer than eighteen new colleges, twelve to accommodate 154 students, six to accept a further 72.[25] However, the authority of the head of the original college, instituted by the early statutes, was maintained by allowing him the right to remove the principals of these new colleges at will: 'ad nutum rectoris a mobile'.[26] In this way the university was assisted in its efforts to maintain a totally residential membership under the authority of the rector.

At Aberdeen we have seen that a number of students and teaching-staff was expected to live outside the college from the early days of its foundation. By the terms of the Nova Fundatio, as we have noted, all members of the foundation except the grammarian were required to reside in college. This unequivocable demand was made more understandable by the abolition of the posts of canonist, civilian and medical lecturer by the same Nova Fundatio, for these were the teachers allowed to live outside the college by the original university statutes.[27] No doubt the pressures on the college-university to expand its intake had been dampened by the depressed state of Scotland during the sixteenth century and then much reduced by the foundation of Marischal College in New Aberdeen in 1593. Even so, the requirement of residence could not be maintained, as the records of the 1619 visitation show, probably because the numbers entering the university exceeded the rooms available in the college; thirty-eight students entered in 1604 so that some sixty or seventy undergraduates required accommodation in each year of the early seventeenth century.[28] Certainly, later in the century, some students were allowed to live outside the college, to which they returned for their evening meal and for a period of study before leaving when the gates were closed.[29] Nevertheless, attempts were made again in 1724 and 1753 to enforce residence in college and the taking of meals at the common table.[30] The constant repetition of these requirements is in itself an indication that residence could not be enforced. Indeed, it is difficult to see how, without further building, expensive beyond its financial resources, the college-university could maintain such a requirement.

The need to enforce residence at Trinity College, especially in the first two centuries of its existence, was much more evident. The college had been founded to discourage the Irish from travelling to the continent for their education. It was expected to promote the protestant cause in a country that had so far proved largely resistant to its evangelism. Accordingly it was recognised that the best method of influencing the young was to place them under strict control in residential accommodation. Here their behaviour, morals and religious observances could be monitored as well as their academic progress supervised. Early humanist educators in Italy and elsewhere had stressed the importance of boarding, and the Jesuits were also to emphasise the role of residential education. The college-university in Dublin was expected not only to bring higher education to Ireland but also to convert the sons of Catholic families that it hoped to attract. In this way a strong and influential protestant party could be formed. Accordingly, the provision of residential accommodation was seen as an essential part of this ambitious scheme. Trinity College, therefore, made strenuous efforts to maintain its residential character. Conditions in Ireland during the sixteenth and seventeenth centuries did not favour the expansion of higher learning, nor did the turbulent and violent relations between the Catholic and protestant elements encourage an increase in Catholic participation in the expansion of a protestant college. Pressure on space at Trinity College was not a serious problem while such a situation existed in Ireland. Following the victory of William at the Battle of the Boyne in 1690, and the establishment of a virtually unchallenged English rule, an increasingly prosperous aristocracy and bourgeoisie sent its sons in growing numbers to the college. Between 1765 and 1790 the annual intake of students rose from around one hundred to about double that number,[31] and the college was unable to provide accommodation for this very considerable increase. By 1775 only 225 from a total of 598 could be found rooms in college buildings.[32] A greater number of entrants produced also an increase in the teaching staff employed. Nor could these new professors be accommodated in college: by 1830 there were thirteen professors who did not hold fellowships.[33] Inevitably this situation produced divisions within both the student and the teaching community. Despite its energetic building programme, Trinity College was unable to maintain a policy of complete residence for its staff and students as soon as more peaceful and prosperous times persuaded more young men to seek entrance.

The college-universities of Old Aberdeen and Dublin were, therefore, both forced to abandon one of their essential characteristics, the insistence on residence by most staff and students, in face of pressure of numbers and hostility to this concept especially by married members. Space does not allow a closer examination of the later history of college-universities in Catholic areas of Europe, but several important differences may here be emphasised. Firstly, the survival of religious houses in university towns there provided a means of recruiting both students and lecturers to the universities without the necessity of providing residential accommodation. Such members would be expected to reside in the houses of their appropriate order; nor was there a problem of married entrants here. Secondly, and more importantly, the spread of the Jesuit order in Catholic Europe brought a new stimulus to older universities but also encouraged the foundation of new institutions, several of which later acquired the status of universities. Often the Jesuits were able to realise most of the ambitions of the college-university: their buildings were frequently large and well-endowed, as a perambulation of the site of the Clementinum in Prague today still shows. The lecturers, being members of the order, were required to be resident and celibate; they encouraged students to be resident; finally, they were usually able to offer a complete programme of study in arts subjects, in theology and, less successfully, in canon law.[34] The success of the Jesuit order in attracting and in teaching students is perhaps a belated justification for the concept of the college-university. It must also be remembered that for students wishing to follow their studies at university by a career in the church, celibacy was still required in Catholic areas. Pressure on accommodation from married students was, accordingly, not so great a problem in these parts of Europe. Nevertheless, however successful the Jesuit revival of the college-university, social and political changes in the late eighteenth century in Catholic areas were working against the continuance of such institutions. The demand for an education free of clerical control and designed to produce graduates to serve a secular state was an essential feature of the Enlightenment. Like their predecessors, the college-universities of the Jesuits could not for long resist such pressures.

From this introduction to some aspects of the comparative study of the college-universities, it will be apparent that there are many further features of the development of these interesting institutions that deserve attention. Although college-universities emerged at an inopportune time, especially in northern Europe, problems associated with their peculiar constitutions remained to occupy the attention of their administrators for many centuries. It was not until 1836 that King's College, Aberdeen, reported that for several years past there had been no demand for a public table, and only in 1826 that it was noted that no students lived in the college.[35] For some three hundred years here the college authorities, it seems, had struggled to maintain one of the essential principles of the college-university.

At the close of the nineteenth century the universities of Europe reacted in various ways to the demands of women's organisations for equal treatment. Admission was first conceded, then the right to attend lectures and take examinations, and finally permission to take degrees and play a full part in university affairs. However, at Trinity College, the university buildings belonged to the college and were situated in its grounds. The university fought a strenuous and sometimes humorous campaign to keep out women, raising such profound objections as the impossibility of constructing a ladies toilet in the college. It was not until 1968 that women were elected to college fellowships and only in 1972 allowed to reside in college rooms.[36] Was this perhaps the last desperate effort of the college-university to maintain its unique character?

NOTES

1. See J. M. Fletcher, 'The History of Academic Colleges: Problems and Prospects', in D. Maffei, H. de Ridder-Symoens (eds), *I collegi universitari in Europa tra il xiv e il xviii secolo* (Milan, 1991).

2. H. Rashdall, *The Universities of Europe in the Middle Ages* (new ed., Oxford, 1936), ii, 105.

3. *Ibid.*, ii, 318–320 (the revised foundation date is taken from L. J. Macfarlane, *William Elphinstone and the Kingdom of Scotland 1431–1514: the Struggle for Order* [Aberdeen, 1985], 105–106).

4. The latest of many histories of Trinity College is that by R. B. McDowell and D. A. Webb, *Trinity College Dublin 1592–1952. An Academic History* (Cambridge, 1982).

5. Rashdall, *Universities*, ii, 106.

6. The problems concerning Trinity College are noted in C. Maxwell, *A History of Trinity College Dublin 1591–1892* (Dublin, 1946), 6 n.6.

7. 'Unus sit caput et rector totius collegii et universitatis': *Constitutiones insignis collegii sancti Ildephonsi* (Alcalá, 1716), 2.

8. Macfarlane, *Elphinstone*, 358.

9. *Ibid.*, 326–39.

10. The early documents are printed in *Constitutiones . . . Ildephonsi*.

11. S. Gibson, *Statuta Antiqua Universitatis Oxoniensis* (Oxford, 1931), 84.

12. See the discussion in J. M. Fletcher, 'Welcome stranger or resented intruder? A reconstruction of the foundation of the University of Aberdeen in the context of European university development in the later middle ages', *Aberdeen University Review*, 180 (1988), 311.

13. Rashdall, *Universities*, ii, 105 n.3.

14. See, for example, the attack on Oxford bachelors of law who wished to be known as masters 'propter lucrum et superbiam' in 1435: H. E. Salter, *Registrum Cancellarii Oxoniensis 1434–1469* (Oxford 1932), ii, 356.

15. Rashdall, *Universities*, ii, 242 n.4.

16. H. Anstey, *Munimenta Academica* (London, 1868), i, 347.

17. See the repeated disputes in the first volume of the unpublished Senatus Protocollum in the Freiburg University Archives.

18. 'Difficile enim esset ei penoctare in collegio et habere libros suos in domo quam habet in vico': R. Marichal, *Le Livre des Prieurs de Sorbonne (1431–1485)* (Paris, 1987), 245.

19. Freiburg Protocollum Senatus, i, f.78v.

20. Marfarlane, *Elphinstone*, 339, 378.

21. The Nova Fundatio is discussed in R. S. Rait, *The Universities of Aberdeen* (Aberdeen, 1895), 108–117, and in D. Stevenson, *King's College, Aberdeen, 1560–1641: from Protestant Reformation to Covenanting Revolution* (Aberdeen, 1990).

22. McDowell and Webb, *Trinity College*, 107.

23. I. Montiel Garcia, *Historia de la Universidad de Sigüenza* (Maracaibal, 1963), ii, 12, 20, 59, 81.

24. *Constitutiones . . . Ildephonsi*, 104.

25. The arrangements are noted in *Constitutiones . . . Ildephonsi*.

26. *Ibid.*, 106.

27. Rait, *Universities of Aberdeen*, 114.

28. *Ibid.*, 126, 120.

29. *Ibid.*, 156.

30. *Ibid.*, 200.

31. McDowell and Webb, *Trinity College*, 86.

32. *Ibid.*, 115.

33. *Ibid.*, 110.

34. See, for example, the interesting study of the Jesuits at Fulda, Würzburg, Ingolstadt and Dillingen in E. Schubert, 'Zur Typologie gegenreformatorischer Universitätsgründungen', in H. Rössler and G. Franz (eds), *Universität und Gelehrtenstand 1400–1800* (Limburg, 1970), 85–105.

35. Rait, *Universities of Aberdeen*, 223–24.

36. McDowell and Webb, *Trinity College*, 353.

2

A National System of University Education in Seventeenth-Century Scotland?

Christine Shepherd

The General Assembly of the Church of Scotland appointed a commission to visit the universities from 1639 to 1643. That commission enacted that in all the philosophy colleges of the universities there should be a uniform course of doctrine, government and discipline, and then went on to propose this curriculum:

1st year:	Greek and a compend of logic
2nd year:	Logic (Aristotle) and elements of arithmetic
3rd year:	Further logic (Aristotle) and ethics; compend of metaphysics; geometry
4th year:	Physics (Aristotle) and Aristotle's *De anima*[1]

This recommendation was typical of many attempts throughout the seventeenth century to impose some sort of uniformity on the Scottish universities. But how successful were these attempts? Can one talk about a national system of university education in seventeenth-century Scotland?

The commissions were appointed by the crown, by parliament, by the General Assembly of the Church, by the universities themselves and, in the case of Edinburgh, by the town council. They have left us a wealth of reports and recommendations, and documentation of their activities to be found in four volumes of parliamentary papers published in 1837, entitled *Evidence oral and documentary taken and received by the Commissioners appointed by His Majesty George IV July 23 1826 . . . for visiting the Universities of Scotland.* In addition, minutes of seventeenth-century Faculty and Senate meetings exist for some of the universities, along with other university records, and for Edinburgh, which was under the jurisdiction of the town council, many references to matters relating to the university are to be found in the council records.

In addressing the question of whether or not there was a national system of university education, it is worth asking *why* there were so many commissions in the seventeenth century. The answer lies in the close concern about the teaching in the universities shared by both the state and the Church: certainly, the concept of academic freedom was not one to which either state or Church

26

would have subscribed in seventeenth-century Scotland. Thus the way in which staff appointments were affected by the changing politico-religious situation in Scotland is indicative of the way in which Church and state tried to impose a uniformity on the universities. Although it is obviously a gross over-simplification to divide seventeenth-century Scottish political history into clear-cut periods of presbyterian and Episcopalian government, as far as the politico-religious upheavals affected the universities we can distinguish three definite crisis points which corresponded to changes in the form of government.

The first began in 1638–39 when the universities were purged of Episcopalian officers who did not support the Scottish national protest against Charles I's ecclesiastical innovations and, because of their political and religious allegiances, refused to subscribe to the National Covenant. At Edinburgh two regents were deposed. Most of the Aberdeen doctors lost their positions, including the principal of King's College; indeed, the principal of Glasgow University, Robert Baillie, tells us in his letters that a commission was specifically appointed in 1638 to remove disaffected regents from Aberdeen.[2] Glasgow and St Andrews seems to have fared better, though the visitation occasioned a considerable amount of dread in Glasgow;[3] and we learn from Baillie that the masters of St Andrews had originally resisted the Covenant, but soon gave way and signed.[4] The signing of the Covenant only marked the beginning of a period of great political unrest, and ten years later there was another mass expulsion, at the end of a period during which various acts were promulgated requiring the regents to take oaths of allegiance.[5]

In 1660 Charles II came to the throne, reintroduced an Episcopalian form of church government, and with it the second of our crisis points. This time many presbyterians installed by the Covenanters and their successors were expelled from the universities, and Episcopalians — in some cases the same Episcopalians who had been dismissed in the earlier purges — were put in their places. Again, from the 1660s until 1689 we find legislation stating that no university appointment could be held unless an oath of allegiance was sworn.[6] And in this period Edinburgh town council appointed four baillies to investigate the town's college, to ensure loyalty to the government, on pain of closure of the university.[7]

The third crisis point was in 1689 when William of Orange came to the throne and presbyterianism once more gained the ascendancy. A resolution was passed in 1690 to the effect that parliamentary commissioners were to 'take exact tryall of the Masters . . . Regents etc, if any of them be eronious in doctrine, and as to popish, arminiane and sociniane principles, which is to be searched from their dictats, or to receave information from other persons who have been conversant with them'; also to search their dictates for evidence of insufficiency and to ensure their loyalty to the present government.[8] This seems to have been the occasion for a general witch-hunt. Records of the proceedings at Edinburgh show that anyone who had a grudge against one of the regents regarded the occasion as a good opportunity to bring this out into the open.[9] At St Andrews too, numerous complaints were made by the town against the colleges; the townspeople doubtless welcomed the opportunity to exact revenge for disruptive behaviour by the students in favour of James II, which was not prevented and sometimes actually supported by the regents.[10] Around this time David Gregory left Edinburgh to become Savilian professor of astronomy at Oxford — a departure possibly not entirely unconnected with the fact that Gregory's family were Episcopalians, while Gregory himself was suspected of holding atheistic views (views not at all in accordance with presbyterianism). At St Andrews there was a great upheaval: of the eight regents belonging to its two colleges only one retained his position after the visitation. Glasgow, too, saw the departure of several of its teachers. Aberdeen alone seems to have been relatively unaffected by the 1689 Revolution, for all the officers at both King's and Marischal eventually took the oath — yet one cannot infer from this an act of conversion to presbyterianism in two universities which had for so long been bastions of Episcopalianism. Ten years later, in 1699, we learn that a sub-committee was appointed by the General Assembly to visit Old and New Aberdeen and report on persons found erroneous, scandalous, negligent, insufficient or disaffected to government.[11] It is worth noting the connection made here between error in religion and philosophy and unreliability in politics, an interrelationship which pervaded the attitudes of Church and state to the universities in the seventeenth century.

These three watersheds are the most obvious instances of the effect of Scotland's political upheavals on university staff, but we have evidence that politics and religion were a constant factor in the appointment of staff throughout the seventeenth century, even when times were relatively peaceful. In 1629 there was a debate in Edinburgh between Laudians and presbyterians over the appointment of a professor of theology there, in which the latter prevailed;[12] and in 1633, also at Edinburgh, the best candidate for the professorship of humanity was passed over because he was 'odious to the episcopal faction'.[13] Both church and state felt the need to keep a tight control over who was teaching at the universities, as well as over what was being taught, and this could, of course, be done without imposing a national system. However, the university commissioners on many occasions during the seventeenth century did recommend uniformity. The particular recommendations of the 1639 commission which are quoted at the head of this essay appear to have been ignored by the universities; in 1643 a new commission, which was appointed by the General Assembly, complained that none of the recommendations of the previous visitation had been carried out.[14] By 1646 there was a further note of impatience shown in the commission's resolution 'that every university provide some good overtures anent speedy prosecution of the intended "Cursus philosophicus"'.[15] Resistance on the part of the universities was probably deliberate, an attempt to preserve their autonomy in the face of government interference. The curriculum actually being taught was not so very dissimilar from that proposed by the commission, so there was unlikely to be any great barrier to carrying out the commission's recommendations on that score. In fact, we can gain an inkling of the reasons for the universities' delay in complying in the joint statement issued in 1647 by a meeting of their representatives in Edinburgh, 'that it was found expedient to communicate to the General Assembly no more of our University affairs, but such as concerned religion'.[16]

Yet the universities decided to produce their own joint courses, each university handling those parts earlier allotted to them by the commission. The representatives of each university were to produce at their next meeting a note of what was taught in every class. As a result, we have records of the courses in all the universities except Edinburgh, and hence a good indication of what was being taught in the middle of the century — information which is especially useful, since few student notebooks and graduation theses survive for this period.[17]

Despite the similarity between their curricula, this project by the universities themselves seems to have had no better success than the one proposed by the General Assembly commissioners. Glasgow may actually have got as far as appointing someone to compose its part of the joint course:

> Regarding the portion of the philosophy course assigned to our college . . . we willingly undertake the task allotted to us, and we shall try, God willing, to give some proof of our diligence at the earliest possible date.[18]

But we have no evidence that the scheme advanced any further than this. Indeed, notwithstanding earlier fears of church interference, Robert Baillie was asked in 1649 to petition the Assembly to lend the weight of its authority in urging the universities to complete their work, which resulted in the production of a list of *Rules agreed upon by the Commissioners of the Universities according to which the common course of philosophy shall be drawn*.[19] These regulations are fairly explicit, but still do not appear to have led to any concrete results. For the next forty years the reports of various commissions had little to say about the curriculum, apart from repeated injunctions to the universities to produce a uniform course.

In 1687 at a visitation of the university the masters of St Andrews proposed a specific method of teaching,[20] going into considerable detail. Their comments show that the curriculum was still Aristotelian in outline, but that the regents had ceased to comment on the texts of Aristotle. The only authority mentioned by name is Descartes; and there was evidently an increased emphasis on metaphysics and correspondingly less concentration on logic, possibly a result of this movement from Aristotle to Descartes.

Attempts to impose an education policy on the universities were revived with the recommendations of the parliamentary commission appointed at the time of the Revolutionary Settlement in 1690. Its proposals, for a common course to be taught in all the Scottish colleges, were:[21]

1st year: Greek to be taught with a fixed regent;

2nd year: Logic should be taught without mixture of what concerns metaphysics, and therewithal the common terms, notions and axioms should be taught;

3rd year: Ethics general and special, practice of oratory, and also the general physics should be taught;

4th year: There should be taught special physics and pneumatology.

If we allow for the fact that specific works of Aristotle were no longer mentioned, this is basically the course recommended by the commissioners of 1642. As in the 1640s, there was considerable reaction on the part of the universities to the commissioners' proposals. This time it is well documented.

Edinburgh and Marischal College in New Aberdeen both agreed to the recommendations of the commissioners. Glasgow, King's College in Old Aberdeen and the two St Andrews colleges, all had some reservations, mainly on the grounds that metaphysics had been omitted. Despite these objections, however, the colleges, apart from St Salvator's at St Andrews, were in favour of a uniform course, and this time the plan proceeded further than it had in the 1640s. Glasgow was allotted general and special ethics, St Andrews logic and metaphysics, Edinburgh pneumatology, and Aberdeen general and special physics. The 1690 commission decreed that, if the regents refused to join in the scheme, they were to be deprived of office. The faculties were to give in an outline of what points and articles they were to treat of; the several colleges were to keep a correspondence amongst themselves during the writing of their several parts of their work, and to send parcels of their writing to each college 'that the same may be revised, and that each of the said colleges be assistant to the others for the better carrying on of the said work'. A meeting was appointed a year ahead — July 1690 — by which time all the courses were to be ready. The universities consulted together and drew up certain general rules for the composition of their courses, mostly concerned with method. But it is noteworthy that the regents appeared eager to avoid any charges that their philosophy courses showed elements of atheism or scepticism; also, despite evidence in the surviving dictates which suggests the contrary, peripatetic philosophy still seemed to be held in very high esteem.

It appears that all the courses were actually produced and circulated, though not all within the required year. There is a large collection in Edinburgh University Library of the comments of the various universities on each other's courses,[22] and some outlines of the courses themselves have survived. However, they were probably never actually taught. From 1697 onwards resolutions, increasingly exasperated in tone, were agreed by the commissioners, enjoining the various regents and principals to produce their completed courses. By November 1699 still no progress had been made, and the principals were asked to go through the courses, to make remarks and to meet in May 1700. Thereafter, however, the commission seems to have given up trying to get the universities to adopt a uniform course.

While the chief concern of the various commissions was with the curriculum, they also sought to determine how courses should be taught. Their main recommendation was that the practice of dictating notes should cease, something already stated in 1642, and again in 1695 when it was urged 'that in tyme comeing the students shall not spend ther tyme in wryting ther courses of philosophie in their class, but in place thereof, that there be ane printed course thought upon'.[23] The responses to this overture make interesting reading. Edinburgh, St Leonard's, and King's agreed with the commission without making any comment. Marischal noted that a uniform course had already been adopted by them — and, indeed, the lecture notes of this period do suggest that some sort of uniform course was in existence at the two Aberdeen colleges. Glasgow agreed with the commission, but remarked on the disadvantage of a printed course, that 'it will be a temptation both to parents and students of coming too late and going away too soon'.[24] In spite of most of the colleges apparently accepting that the practice of dictating notes should end, it would appear that dictates only stopped when the regenting gave way to the professorial system in the eighteenth century. This ambivalence typifies the general position of the universities in their relation to Church and state.

In the 1640s the courses being taught in the various colleges were very similar to each other and to the courses recommended to them by the commissioners; yet the universities still failed to carry out either the commissioners' or their own plans for uniformity. In the 1690s the proposed course was not quite so close to what was being taught in the colleges, as the reaction of the various colleges shows. However, the basic outline was the same, and most of the colleges were in principle in favour of a uniform course; at the same time the colleges were agreed in their objections to the commissioners' proposals, all disliking more or less the same points, i.e. the omission of metaphysics and the separation of the two parts of physics. The masters, after all, even collaborated on a joint statement concerning the composition of a uniform course — a collaboration which would seem to suggest a considerable degree of accord about those authorities which were to be disregarded and why; they agreed with the commission's proposal for a uniform course, even submitting that the 'best way will be by causeing compose a compleat systeme of philosophy as speedily as may be to be taught in all the Universities at once; for we cannot think it adviseable that any course already printed can be fitt'.[25] Notwithstanding the apparent willingness of the universities to agree with each other and with the commissioners about a common course, the universities were also concerned to withstand any entrenchments on their several foundations. This fear of state interference with their chartered rights was obviously justified in view of the exceedingly detailed instructions for the running of universities which appeared in the commission reports.

The universities' reaction to such government intervention can be seen in their replies to section 17 of the Acts and Overtures of 1695. This section stated that 'Untill ther be ane printed course of Philosophie composed, the regents shall be obleidged yearly to produce . . . to the Principall or Dean of Faculty . . . the dictats that he is to teach his students the year following, and that these dictats . . . shall be subject . . . to the amendments and correction of the Principall and Faculty of the Colledge'.[26] Glasgow, the colleges in Old and New Aberdeen, and Edinburgh accepted this provision without demur (though whether from real conviction, or as a matter of policy is open to debate). Edinburgh commented that it was not easily practicable. St Andrews, however, as on other points, was strongly opposed to the motion, and interpreted it as interfering with academic freedom. The masters in St Leonard's were particularly outspoken:

> it will be found altogether impracticable (1) Because it cannot be supposed that any Regent, at his first entry, shall have his notes that he is about to dictat fully perfected and compleated; nay, perhaps most parte newly entring upon that station dureing their whole first course may scarcely have so much time, from one conveniendum as to prepare what he is to dictat another; (2) There is no man that diligently searches after truth in Philosophie, but will, as oft as he goes over a course in teaching, find occasion either to alter or add something, especially at such a time when there are new opinions in philosophie vented every day, which ought . . . at least to be taken notice of; and if fals or heterodox, refuted as occasion serves; (3) Because in this University, there being but one Dean of the Faculty of Philosophie for both Colleges, whose (duty) by the statutes of the University is to examine thinges of that nature, and approve or disapprove the same, it would be ane insuperable task for him every year to read over seriously 6 courses, before we beginne to teach.[27]

The failure of the 1640s attempts at uniformity lay in the universities' fear of losing their autonomy; and the same explanation holds good for the failure of the 1690s commission. In the 1690s, however, the universities could not afford to be too outspoken in defence of their right to govern their own affairs and determine their own courses, since sentiments of this kind might all too easily be construed as showing disaffection to the government and result in dismissals of staff such as had taken place in 1689 and 1690. Their resistance tended to show itself in more roundabout ways, such as sheer apathy. Meetings of the universities had frequently to be cancelled, because insufficient delegates were present; St Andrews, notably, seems very rarely to have been represented at the meetings. And, of course, these prevarications bore fruit, since the scheme was never implemented. The universities' joint letter to the commission seems to have had two aims: firstly, to convince the commissioners of the desirability of a course of their own composition, for in this way they would be able to retain some of their academic freedom; secondly, in order to achieve this, they had to obtain the good will of the commission by proclaiming their orthodoxy and freedom from all dangerous and heretical views. In both these aims they presumably succeeded, since they were allowed to compose their own courses, even although the commissioners remained doubtful about the content of the notes which were being dictated in the meantime, before the standard course should be ready.

To what extent, then, is it justifiable to talk about a national system of university education in seventeenth-century Scotland? Certainly the arts curriculum followed in all the Scottish universities was remarkably similar. The universities all maintained regenting rather than a professorial system for most of the century. All teaching was done by dictates, and examinations seem to have been conducted on similar lines in the different colleges. To this extent the system *was* clearly national. However, despite this, there was by no means an unquestioning acquiescence in the recommendations of the various commissions concerning the curriculum or methods of teaching. Either through active resistance, or more frequently by the safer and ultimately more effective means of inaction, the universities retained in many areas the right to determine their own affairs.

NOTES

1. *Evidence Oral and Documentary* (London, 1837), ii, 257; iii, 205.
2. *The Letters and Journals of Robert Baillie* (Glasgow, 1841), i, 491–492.
3. *Ibid.*, 171.
4. *Ibid.*, 62ff.
5. *Evidence Oral and Documentary*, iii, 208–09; Aberdeen University Library, Special Collections, MS M91; Cosmo Innes (ed), *Munimenta Alme Universitatis Glasguensis* (Glasgow, 1854), i, 333–34.
6. Glasgow University Archives: MS no. 26637; *Munimenta*, i, 413–14.
7. Alexander Morgan (ed.), *Charters, Statutes and Acts of the Town Council and the Senatus, 1583–1858 (University of Edinburgh)* (Edinburgh, 1937), 135.
8. *Evidence Oral and Documentary*, i, App., 36–37.
9. Robert K. Hannay, 'The visitation of the College of Edinburgh in 1690', *Book of the Old Edinburgh Club*, 8 (1915), 79–100.
10. Robert K. Hannay, 'The visitation of St Andrews University in 1690', *Scottish Historical Review*, xiii (1915–16), 1–15.
11. Cosmo Innes (ed.), *Fasti Aberdonenses* (Aberdeen, 1854), 383.
12. Thomas Craufurd, *History of the University of Edinburgh from 1580 to 1646* (Edinburgh, 1808), 114–15.
13. *Ibid.*, 124–25.
14. *Evidence*, iii, 208.
15. Quoted by Andrew Dalzel in *History of the University of Edinburgh* (Edinburgh, 1862), ii, 144.
16. *Fasti Aberdonenses*, p liii.
17. Glasgow University Archives, MS no. 26790; Craufurd, *History*, 151–153.
18. *Munimenta*, 315.
19. Glasgow University Archives: MS no. 26790.
20. Edinburgh University Library, Archives, MS Dc 1.4.
21. *Evidence*, ii, 269–270.
22. Edinburgh University Library, Archives, MS Dc 1.4.
23. *Evidence*, ii, 271.
24. *Ibid.*
25. *Munimenta*, ii, 530–531.
26. *Evidence*, ii, 272.
27. *Ibid.*, iii, 221.

3

Nineteenth-Century Higher Education: the Scottish-American Connection

Winifred Bryan Horner

In 1750, when England had two universities, and Scotland five smaller college-universities, the American colonies were supporting nine colleges offering post-school education: Harvard, William and Mary, New Jersey, King's, Philadelphia, Rhode Island, Queens, and Dartmouth. The early colonists had determined to provide themselves and their successors with good educational opportunities: 'One of the . . . things we longed for, and looked after, was to advance *Learning* and perpetuate it to Posterity'.[1] Later, it was remarked that 'the two cardinal principles of English Puritanism which most profoundly affected the social development of New England and the United States were not religious tenets, but educational ideals: a learned clergy, and a lettered people'.[2]

Many of these early colonial colleges were little more than log cabins, their rise to great institutions only dreams in the minds of their founders:

> Often when a college had a building, it had no students. If it had students, frequently it had no building. If it had either, then perhaps it had no money, perhaps no professors; if professors, then no president, if a president, then no professors.[3]

There were great difficulties in the new country. In Virginia the crown allocated 9,000 acres in 1619 for the foundation of a college, but an Indian massacre in 1622 eliminated most of the institution's supporters. In 1693, the crown granted a college charter to the state for the 'saving of souls', but the attorney-general in England reacted with the comment 'Souls! Damn your souls! Raise tobacco!'[4]

While the American universities were struggling for their existence in the early days, the Scottish universities were well established, generally with some public endowments, and already had a long history. The university of St Andrews was founded in 1413; Glasgow was established by papal bull in 1451; and St Mary's College in Old Aberdeen, later known as King's, was founded in 1495 to 'promote civilization among the Highland clergy'. A rival college — a strictly protestant institution — was established in Aberdeen in 1593, by the fifth Earl Marischal, by which time the 'town's college' in Edinburgh had been in existence for a decade, having been founded in 1583. Based on a relatively strong structure of parish and burgh schools, which were expected to teach Latin, a little Greek, and some basic mathematics, the Scottish universities could count on at least modest preliminary instruction for their students. In the American colonies, on the other hand, until the revolution in 1776, there was no statutory provision for public elementary education. Wealthier colonists provided tutors for their children, often Scottish tutors, but for the most part instruction in reading, writing, and arithmetic was the responsibility of hard-worked parents with little time or energy to spare for such pursuits.

With the widespread revival of religion in eighteenth-century America and the Great Awakening, congregations and churches split into a number of factions, and this in turn stimulated the erection of more colleges. The Congregationalists founded Dartmouth, and the Baptists and the Dutch Reformed followed suit with their own establishments. However, extended education in the colonies was still limited to the few, and it was generally considered to be unnecessary either for material success or for religious salvation. In 1775, it was estimated that only one out of every thousand colonists had been to a college, and most of those did not complete a full course. In the year of the revolution there were only 3000 living college graduates in the United States, and many of these became political leaders. It has been suggested that, although some middle-class and lower-class families sent their sons to college, the 'overwhelming majority of their sons stayed home, farmed, went West, or became — without benefit of a college education — Benjamin Franklin or Patrick Henry.'[5]

In the later eighteenth century, then, the American universities were still struggling. One historian of higher education recounts this harrowing tale of the early years:

> On a cold drizzly day in January 1795, a two-story empty brick building that called itself the University of North Carolina was opened to the public. An unsightly landscape of tree stumps, rough lumber, scarred clay, and a bitter wind greeted the governor, who had wanted to be on hand for this important event. He was also met by the faculty which consisted of one professor doubling as president. A month later the first applicant for admission knocked at the door. In the same year, far to the north the founders of a college that would be called Bowdoin were offering the entirety of a township in Maine to any contractor who would build them a four-story building. They could find no takers.[6]

The history of the University of Miami, now one of the prestigious state universities of Ohio, offers us the story of the Reverend John W. Brown, and his efforts to raise money for the fledgling college. The president of the United States, James Madison, offered no assistance, but in Delaware Brown raised $22, the president of Princeton gave him $5 and John Adams, in his retirement, gave him two books and $10. Altogether his efforts brought a wagonload of books and $700 for the new college. Life was hazardous for the traveller in those days, and soon after his return, Brown slipped and drowned in the Little Miami River.[7]

Natural disaster was a constant threat to continued existence. The log buildings of Nassau Hall at Princeton burned down, as did the first building erected at Dickinson College. At Ohio the only college structure was hit by lightning and was barely saved from total destruction by torrential rains. But the spirit persisted. In 1842, eight French priests, barely able to speak English, walked into northern Indiana and founded the college that would become Notre Dame. In spite of hardships, fires, and dissension, Americans never abandoned their dream of higher education. The nine colleges of the 1760s had become two hundred and fifty a hundred years later: of these no fewer than one hundred and eighty-two still survive.

The Scottish universities, meanwhile, free from the religious restrictions of the universities in England and Ireland, attracted students from America and the Continent as well as from England. Their attraction was all the greater for their readiness to innovate: agriculture was first introduced as a university subject there, Newtonian theories were taught, and the academic study of English literature was established. Edinburgh's well-known medical school attracted many students from America and the Continent. At Aberdeen, the Scottish school of common sense philosophy was established, which was to have lasting influence on the ideas behind the Declaration of Independence and the constitution of the United States. In Edinburgh Adam Smith and Hugh Blair introduced the concept of *belles lettres*, and it was Blair's and George Campbell's published lectures that were used by American college teachers for almost a hundred years. Warren Guthrie cites evidence that, before 1830, Blair's lectures were used in twenty of forty-three American colleges whose catalogues he examined, and remained in use at Yale and Williams until 1850, while Notre Dame still used them as late as 1880. Guthrie found twenty-six copies on the open shelves at Harvard in 1953.[8]

After the Act of Union in 1707 Scotland, freed of trade restrictions, prospered, and in the age of Enlightenment, her universities prospered as well. During the eighteenth century Oxford and Cambridge on the other hand were a preserve for the 'idle and rich'. They were expensive and elitist and offered little that was new for the well-prepared student.[9] The Scottish universities provided an education for the serious student from England and drew students from the Continent and America as well. And, as we have seen, the educational philosophy of the Scottish universities permeated the early thinking in American politics and education.

Like the Americans, the Scots had always placed a high priority on education. And their universities were open to all-comers — although the Scottish universities had a major role in the training of the presbyterian ministry, their religious restrictions on students in the eighteenth century were minimal. In their eighteenth-century academies and in the five colleges the Scots paraded their belief in a practical education — for farmers and merchants as well as ministers, teachers, doctors and lawyers. Americans generally shared in their conceptualization of the functions of schools and universities, and shared with the Scots too the notion that education should have two significant social attributes: the various social classes should benefit by being taught together; and there should be the opportunity for upward social mobility for the talented youth of the lower social orders through a cheap, publicly-supported educational structure. It is not surprising that the early founders of American universities looked to Scotland for both inspiration and leadership. Yet most historians of American education have failed to recognize this heavy Scottish influence. Frederick Rudolph remarks that 'with rare exception the American college for many years was significantly shaped by the English universities' and it is only recently that Rudolph's assumption[10] that Queen's College, Oxford, was the model for the Colleges of William and Mary in Virginia has been challenged — an assumption which entirely ignored obvious Scottish influences in its foundation, in particular the guiding hand of John Wotherspoon.

No fewer than four of the signatories of the Declaration of Independence were native-born Scots, and it has been recently pointed out that there is a striking similarity between the ideas of David Hume and those which underlay the formation of the United States.[11] One of these signatories, Witherspoon, had studied at Aberdeen, as had another, James Madison, who had also been a student of Witherspoon's in America. Witherspoon's Scottishness and his reverence for much that was Scottish was well-known, one of his colleagues during the 1777 Congress remarking of him:

> He can't bear anything which reflects on Scotland. The Dr says that Scotland has mainfested the greatest spirit for liberty as a nation, in that their history is full of their calling Kings to account and dethroning them when arbitrary or tyrannical.[12]

But Scottish influence was not to be dependent on emigrant Scots alone. In the eighteenth century many of the Americans who went to Scotland to study in its highly-respected universities returned to become statesmen and to occupy leading positions in American political and cultural life.

Indeed, by far the most direct influence exerted by the Scots on the new nation was in education. Two examples must suffice. Similarities between Harvard College and the University of Edinburgh have recently been pointed out, but it is in Williamsburg, at the college of William and Mary, the second university to be founded in the new world, that the strength of Scottish influence is particularly obvious. William and Mary was founded by James Blair, born in Aberdeenshire and educated at Marischal College. Under his influence in Virginia there were to be established, in due course, the kinds of specialised professorships which Marischal adopted in preference to the older regenting system — such as still operated at Harvard at that time.[13] It is notable, perhaps, that Blair appointed another graduate of Marischal, William Sharp, to the chair of mathematics in Williamsburg. Yet the full extent of Scottish influence in eighteenth-century American collegiate foundations, in and through Scots who taught in them and administered them, through returning Americans who had studied in Scotland, and through the pervading impact of Scottish educational ideas and practices, has still to be fully assessed.

In the next century, however, Scottish and American universities were to take rather different paths. Whereas Scottish universities were starved of endowment, it was otherwise in the United States. Great fortunes were amassed by 'robber barons' who salved their consciences and perpetuated their names by founding private colleges. Thus Vassar, Smith, Johns Hopkins, Stanford, Chicago and Wellesley were all founded by single donors, the respective states offering some support by granting land to them. However, in many instances the new foundations were sectarian and therefore cut off from such help, a fact which in its turn went to emphasise their private nature. In contrast the Scottish universities were considered to be public institutions.

The Land Grant College Act of 1862 brought developments which further distanced the American colleges from older influences. As early as 1848, Congressman Justin Morrill of Vermont had suggested that American colleges might well 'lop off a portion of the studies established centuries ago as the mark of European scholarship and replace the vacancy — if it is a vacancy — by those of a less antique and more practical value';[14] and introduced a bill in 1857 which included provisions for technical and scientific education, especially agricultural education which would be practically useful in saving the resources of the land from erosion and soil depletion. The College Act of 1862 was intended to institute in each state a college which would teach studies related to agriculture and engineering, but 'without excluding other scientific or classical studies'.[15] The act provided needed support for the establishment of state universities — some of these growing out of small denominational colleges, some combining with existing private institutions, others directly founded in response to the act itself.

The opportunity which now existed for states to found their own universities was not lost: out of this act came the great state universities of Michigan, Illinois, Ohio, Indiana, California, Minnesota, each of which now numbers over 50,000 students, with some (like California) grown into systems of ten or twelve institutions. The same kind of impulse to develop opportunities for studying the sciences was to be found also in Scotland. Within the universities there was much advance made in science teaching; but the more emphatically practical training in science tended to develop elsewhere — in schools of art and design and in mechanics institutes, in those institutions which were, in due course, to become substantial technical colleges: only in the 1960s did the most important of these reach university status when Strathclyde University in Glasgow and Heriot-Watt University in Edinburgh were chartered. In Scotland, in the course of the nineteenth and earlier twentieth centuries technological training came to be separated from what may be described as 'academic science'. In nineteenth-century America, particularly as public-sector universities expanded to serve their own populations, a college degree was seen as essentially career-oriented and came to be equated with an assurance of material success. In nineteenth-century Scotland universities were reformed in order to raise standards of instruction and it was the universities' role in the training for the professions and for public service administration which came to be emphasised, leading to their resisting the introduction of more practical and technical studies.

During the twentieth century the Scottish and American university traditions have diverged still further. In the United States, while many universities have introduced large postgraduate schools, all have played their part in expanding undergraduate access — to the point where 70 per cent of high school leavers go on to some form of higher education, and mega-institutions such as Ohio State with its 70,000 students have been created. Nonetheless, the costs of a good university education in the USA are now an obstacle to all but the rich; the poor cannot easily obtain scholarships or even, in many cases, an adequate school preparation for university. Scotland, by contrast, has retained a much smaller university provision, even with the existing eight universities, but none approaches in size the larger American institutions: and the British universities, including those in Scotland, have been much slower than their counterparts across the Atlantic to develop elaborate postgraduate schools. Yet in Britain, while Scottish universities are distinguished by wider accessibility than others, only 21 per cent of Scottish school leavers reach higher education, and that despite the availability of substantial public funding in fee-payments and towards the costs of subsistence. In the current reconsideration of higher education policies, taking place in both Britain and America, there is surely much to be learned — on each side — from the experiences of the other.

NOTES

1. *New England First Fruits* (London, 1643), 12.
2. Samuel Eliot Morison, *The Founding of Harvard College* (Cambridge, 1935), 45.
3. Frederick Rudolph, *The American College and University: A History* (New York, 1962), 47.
4. Albea Godbold, *The Church College of the Old South* (Durham, 1944), 11–15.
5. Frederick Rudolph, *The American College*, 21–22.
6. *Ibid.*, 44.
7. *Ibid.*, 44–45.
8. Warren Guthrie. 'The development of rhetorical theory in America, 1635–1850', *Speech Monographs*. 13 (1946), 14–22.
9. Winifred Bryan Horner, 'Writing Instruction in Great Britain' in James J. Murphy (ed.), *A Short History of Writing Instruction* (Davis, CA, 1990).
10. Rudolph, *The American College*, 24.
11. Archie Turnbull, 'Scotland and America, 1730–90', in D. Daiches, P. and J. Jones (eds), *A Hotbed of Genius: The Scottish Enlightenment, 1730–90* (Edinburgh, 1986), 137–52.
12. Quoted in Turnbull, 144, from V. L. Collins, *President Witherspoon* (London, 1755), ii, bk. III, ch. 8.
13. Douglas Sloan, *The Scottish Enlightenment and the American College Ideal* (Columbia, NY, 1971), 20–21.
14. Rudolph, *The American College*, 249.
15. *Ibid.*, 252.

4

The Idea of a National University in Scotland, c 1820–c 1870

Donald J. Withrington

Among the more distinctive marks of the Scottish inheritance in higher education in the nineteenth century were two underlying assumptions: that the Scottish colleges were part of a coherently-structured, all-through educational system, and that that system (schools and universities alike) had been established for the public benefit. In effect, the universities were both public and national. With no substantial endowment to support the system coming out of the patrimony of the pre-Reformation church, however, the Scottish parliament had had to act: thereafter schooling was to be paid for, in part at least, out of a land-based taxation placed on owners and occupiers in each parish, so that local school provision became a direct responsibility of the whole local community; and the universities were brought under the oversight of monarch and parliament, including the provision of some financial backing for stipends and for the erection and repair of buildings.

The poverty of the country also brought important changes in the planned educational structure, which it had been intended would comprise a four-tier, end-on system of local elementary schools, district grammar schools, liberal arts colleges placed in each county or diocese, and the universities. There was little or no money to fund scholarships for boarding-out students in the grammar schools or intermediate colleges, and there soon developed what came to be a very notable feature of Scottish education — a direct and close relationship between the local parochial school or burgh school (in both it was expected that Latin would be taught, and some Greek and mathematics too if possible) and the local university. By the end of the sixteenth century Edinburgh and Marischal College and University in New Aberdeen had been added to St Andrews, Glasgow and King's College and University in Old Aberdeen to provide a widespread network of colleges, ready to receive students from their hinterlands. For all the efforts made locally to appoint parochial schoolmasters who could teach Latin well, in the course of the seventeenth century it became clear that the five universities could not be guaranteed a full and complete grammar schooling in their entrant students, who arrived with very variable knowledge of the classical languages and mathematics.[1] Since the university teachers depended substantially for their incomes on student fees, and since they were keen to maintain the principle of offering advanced studies to all who might benefit from them, the colleges in Scotland reached down to make the transition from school to university as painless as possible — and so they all developed junior or introductory classes, in elementary Greek and mathematics, and were soon to incorporate these into the degree curriculum itself.

Thus entrance requirements were lowered, and other barriers to access to university studies were brought under scrutiny, particularly during the eighteenth century; the changes were aimed at making university studies possible for poorer students from the more remote and ill-schooled areas of the country who had not gained bursaries or had not the support of a wealthy patron. Hence, the length of the college sessions was reduced in order to make attendance cheaper, and the requirements to board in college and to eat at the common table were gradually dropped for the same reason — this last incidentally giving the university teachers an added opportunity to add to their meagre stipends by boarding the better-off students in their 'manses'. While bursars and any others who needed to graduate or to follow the full graduating course of 'gowned' study had to attend the stated curriculum, by the middle of the eighteenth century the rules for attendance on classes were being significantly relaxed: those who wished to attend only a few classes (in the order they chose and not according to the order of study laid down for the gowned students) were permitted to do so — the normal matriculation requirements did not apply to these 'occasional' students, who paid their class fees and received their 'tickets' for attendance as appropriate. In a period when newer occupations did not specify attendance on the whole arts curriculum, and when many potential university students were drifting off (with their fees) to take courses in 'modern' and more utilitarian subjects in private classes and academies, the Scottish universities survived by adapting to the new customer-demands, in particular the smaller colleges. Led by Marischal College, the two Aberdeen universities recast their arts curricula, for their many bursars as well as for occasional students, in order to draw in larger numbers but also to make attendance on the full graduating course more attractive. While the universities of Glasgow and Edinburgh, with their populous catchment areas and already bringing in many more English, Irish and overseas students, did not have the same stimulus to reconstruct the stated curriculum, they opened their doors wide to very large numbers of occasional students to whom such matters as entrance requirements, order of study of classes and examination regulations did not apply. It was usual for the universities to restrict, rather than increase, the hours of attendance on classes in order to allow their students the chance to attend the many private classes in other subjects (the attractive modern studies such as modern languages, book-keeping or music) which were often held in university classrooms rented out for the purpose or in nearby private accommodation.[2]

During the eighteenth century, then, the Scottish colleges tended to develop strategies to meet their own particular circumstances. In the two Aberdeen universities, as in St Andrews, the proportion of gowned students following the full curriculum remained high; in Edinburgh and Glasgow those who took the graduating course were swamped by the numbers of occasional students. Each college tended to go its own way — in adapting, or not adapting, the formal course of study and the regulations which governed it; in maintaining or weakening the old examining system for degree students; in providing or not providing public tutorial teaching in support of lectures, or leaving that to private enterprise for those who could afford to pay for it, and so on. Such divergence in practice was aided by the fact that parliamentary or governmental supervision of the universities in the eighteenth century was lax or non-existent, apart from a flurry of interest in the period of Jacobite rebellion; superintendance by the national Church became insignificant, and oversight by elected or appointed rectors in the colleges was at best nominal and formal. As a result, and almost unencumbered, the day-to-day management of the universities, and decisions about college appointments, college finances, as well as over academic matters, were left in the hands of the professors in their Senates or Faculties. Without effective supervision, corruption could and did reign; private interest could easily override the national interest, and often did.[3]

And yet, when it was suitable and convenient, the same professors could resurrect the national ideal and the concept of their colleges as part of a living national system. There was, in any case, the opportunity for the five universities to meet regularly once a year, for each sent representatives in May to the meetings of the General Assembly of the Church in Edinburgh; and there they could discuss issues of common concern. Occasionally, indeed, these representatives might be formally delegated by their Senates to act and vote in specified ways when some pre-announced topic was to be discussed. When there was a threat to them all, inter-college suspicions gave way to concerted action — and, very frequently in such instances, there would be heavily-underlined references to the national educational heritage, to the universities' public responsibilities and to the Treaty of Union of 1707 which secured — as was hoped for all time — the very existence as well as the rights and privileges of the five national institutions. Such arguments came to the fore when the universities joined together to petition parliament for the augmentation of professorial stipends in the 1780s, for government grants for building repairs or for new buildings, and in the strident claims made in the 1790s that Scottish students should be absolved from militia service.[4]

The national heritage in higher education came prominently to the fore again in the early nineteenth century, but this time from outside the universities themselves. As part of that cautious movement for political and administrative reform which began then, when attacks were mounted on the incidence of unwarranted sinecures, of nepotism and of general corruption in public offices, the case of the universities in Britain was not left aside. And those in Scotland who took up the cause of university reform began to question whether ancient chartered rights were being subverted, and to be critical of current practices in the colleges, on the ground that the national and public interest was being subordinated to selfish professorial advantage. But attention was not only, or indeed mainly, focussed on administrative misdemeanours, for both the character and the quality of teaching and studying were called into direct question.[5]

The reformers argued for the restoration of public accountability through royal or parliamentary superintendance as the best means of improving standards across all the country's universities — by providing some national regulation to ensure similar levels of prior learning before students were admitted, by reinstating a more uniform (but reformed) pattern of degree curricula and regulations, and by laying down guide-lines (based on current best practice) to bring a much-needed improvement in teaching styles and examination procedures throughout all the colleges. Generally, the reformers doubted whether pressures for piece-meal reforms, university by university with the backing of the local press, could be effective against the entrenched powers of the Senates; and from the beginning the idea was consistently floated that government and parliament would have to be persuaded to act in the national interest by setting up an enquiry into the whole system. Moreover, this intervention by government was all the more necessary because one vital improvement, the introduction of some form of entrance examination, would depend on improvements being made in national schooling to provide for adequate teaching in the classical languages and mathematics — and the parochial school system in Scotland had since 1803 been even more closely regulated by the state than it had been before.

There was much public debate in Scotland about the need for university reform by the early 1820s, and that was not only evident in liberal or radical newspapers but in journals and newspapers of every political hue; what is more, there was a general consensus that the initial step should be a royal commission of enquiry into all the colleges as part of the national educational establishment. There was no surprise, and indeed many welcoming comments, when Robert Peel, as Home Secretary, and William Rae, the Lord Advocate, obtained in 1826 the king's consent for an 'inquiry into the state of the Universities of Scotland'. There were certainly a number of local difficulties that cried out to be resolved — the battle between the Edinburgh Senatus and the town council there over the right to initiate changes in the medical curriculum; the well-publicised corruption in and the debilitating poverty of the colleges in St Andrews and Old Aberdeen; the decrepit state of the buildings of Marischal College in New Aberdeen and the opportunity there might be to unite the two Aberdeen colleges into 'one good university'; the enervating struggles in Glasgow between the 'Faculty' professors and their colleagues on Senatus; and there were, variously in the colleges, questions about the functions and effectiveness of the elected or appointed rectors, and about the forms of their election and appointment. But it is clear that the main reasons for setting up the commission were national rather than local. There was, above all, an immediate and a clamant need to do something about medical teaching in Scotland, for there was a very real threat that Scottish qualifications would not be acceptable for practice in England and the Empire; there would be in 1828 an opportunity to revise the regulations for the appointment of parochial schoolteachers, if an enquiry discovered that this was required before certain university reforms could be implemented; until the university charters were closely scrutinised government would be left unsure just what powers were lawfully in the hands of the professors and whether the monarch (and through him royal commissions) could claim overriding authority to supervise and direct the business of the colleges — a vital prior step in bringing in reforms; and, in general, there was too much hurtful notoriety about the supposed dubious financial dealings of the Senates and about the undoubted nepotism that occurred in making university appointments. Meanwhile, the swell of public demands that government should intervene in the national interest could no longer be readily dismissed, just as something had to be done to rescue Scotland's high reputation as a well-educated country at a time when outside observers (as well as those from within) were proclaiming its unmistakeable decline, not least in its university training.[6]

The commission set up in 1826 reported in 1830. Its main task, it stated, had been to restore the 'usefulness and prosperity' of 'national institutions of long-standing' which had strayed from the general principles under which they had been established. Time and time again, the report refers to the distinctive character of the Scottish universities in providing 'a general plan of education by which persons of all ranks may be benefited', in particular 'the means of regular or philophical education'. Such was the power of market forces, however, that there was too often little regulation of college studies, yet 'in Scotland it has always been thought that a systematic Course of Study should be afforded at the Universities'. The commissioners emphasised the national heritage, as they attempted to reintroduce greater coherence and a shared conformity of practice in reinstating a revered national educational establishment. The universities were public institutions, and a properly structured and 'rounded' education would not be possible 'without the aid and encouragement of public establishments'; indeed, without regulation for the public benefit, 'without the institutions and settled usages of an Establishment, the objects of national education could not be adequately secured'.[7]

The 1830 recommendations were intended to draw together again the four Scottish universities (for there was to be a union of the two Aberdeen colleges) as parallel agencies within a nationally-organised system, without interfering more than was necessary in their chartered rights. The commissioners believed they should act to maintain the 'sacred and almost pious duty' of offering to the nation 'the best possible course of study and the best system of instruction' (note the use of the singular here) to 'all those who can by possibility avail themselves' of such studies 'on the most moderate plan of expense'. The proposals included the setting of 'a uniform rate of fees to be paid in all the Universities', as well as near-uniform regulations in all colleges to govern entrance or matriculation standards, the holding of examinations both during and at the end of the graduating course, and recommendations about the preferred style of teaching which might be adopted. Again, all the universities were to have thrust upon them a new structure for their government, with the imposition of rectorial courts which would have wide powers over financial and other administrative matters, in order to ensure the public accountability of these national institutions.

Reactions to the commissioners' report, when it was published in late 1831, were almost entirely approving; ignored or judged acceptable in the Tory press, with a more enthusiastic welcome in the Liberal press.[8] There appeared to be little or nothing that was surprising in the recommendations, for these reflected much of the previous criticism and also the information which had been reported from the interviewing of witnesses. It is, indeed, very hard to discern anything in the report of 1830 which had not been canvassed before 1826 or was not offered to the commissioners in evidence during their sittings. And the published comments on the report seem generally to have accepted the main recommendations for changes in academic matters (in course structure, in curricula, in regulations for more and better examining — only the perceived unreadiness of the schools to meet the demands of the intended entrance examination was noted as a problem). Where there was greater concern, particularly in the Tory journals and press, was over the very considerable powers to be given to the new rectorial courts and the supposed invasion of professorial rights (rights claimed by usage rather than by law), and locally in the north of Scotland over the intended suppression of Marischal College and the siting of the new united university in Old Aberdeen.

There were many calls in the period after the report was published for government to act upon it, notably by the Earl of Aberdeen who had been one of the most active members of the commission. In the end the first move came from the Liberal MP for Aberdeen[9] who, in 1835 and after having seen a new principal appointed to Marischal College and after having obtained a large Treasury grant towards its rebuilding, felt secure enough to introduce a parliamentary bill for the reform and union of the Aberdeen universities: this was based on the 1830 report but included two significant novelties — the new united University of Aberdeen would be sited in New Aberdeen and not at King's College, and the proposed rectorial court would have no representative from the Church of Scotland. There was an immediate, furious reaction from the north of the country, and when Bannerman withdrew his bill in favour of a much more general bill, to be introduced by the Prime Minister, Lord Melbourne, for the reform of all the Scottish universities, the fury of the Church evangelicals (already sure that Melbourne intended to give advantage in all things to the dissenting sects in Scotland) was turned on that.[10] Hundreds of carefully-organised petitions rained down on parliament, and Melbourne was forced to withdraw, for it would have been impossible in the circumstances to get the bill through a House of Lords dominated by allies of the Established Church. The cry of 'the Church in danger' had won.

Melbourne's bill was not lost because of patriotic opposition to its intention to introduce the academic changes foreshadowed in the 1830 report, but because of the threat it might pose to the Church connection with the universities (and to the energetic lobby who acted on behalf of threatened King's College).[11] In fact, the government only retreated so far, for it proceeded at once to set up new commissions for Aberdeen, St Andrews and Glasgow in an effort to keep the reforming pot boiling and to persuade these colleges to adopt some at least of the proposals from 1830. It is not coincidence that the government ordered the publication of four, fat volumes of evidence to the commission of 1826–30 after its defeat: after 1837 there was certainly no lack of hard information about the debilitated state of the Scottish universities.

When individual reforming voices are heard again, almost as a matter of course they accept the recommendations of the 1830 report as the framework for advance for nation-wide restoration of the Scottish reputation in education. And in the later 1840s and 1850s, with the rise of a new nationalist fervour which made much of the distinctiveness of the Scottish educational tradition in pressing government to legislate to improve and extend parochial schooling,[12] there was additional support for university reformers who also wished government to intervene to revitalise the heritage in higher education.

Marischal College produced a string of the more remarkable of these university reformers, led by the acknowledged leader of the reform movement in Scotland, John Stuart Blackie. As early as 1845 Blackie was described as 'that devoted and most prominent advocate' of university reform,[13] and in 1846 would confirm the basis of his belief that reform must be national to be properly effective and hence must be initiated by government:

> the grand fact [is] that Scotland does indeed possess now, and has for ages possessed, a system of National Education . . . . . the Scottish universities are national institutions, existing for great national purposes and supported for the whole benefit of the nation . . . Justice therefore requires that they should be adapted to the present state of society.[14]

Blackie argued for government funding for new professorships in modern subjects, for the provision of tutors or assistants to the hard-pressed teachers of classics, mathematics and the experimental sciences, for better stipends in order to attract better-qualified professors (who should be appointed by the crown and not by cabals in university senates), and for grants for better teaching accommodation and equipment. Blackie agreed with the 1830 commissioners that there should be 'some sort of efficient Rectorial Court in each University' but he went further, suggesting 'also a supreme Board of Education in Edinburgh which shall have the power of acting as a court of arbitration in all academical matters that require general regulation'. The idea of a central board which might oversee the provision of national schooling in Scotland was already being mooted (perhaps something along the lines of the new Poor Law Board), but in Ireland there were developments in university education which offered a valuable precedent for those like Blackie who wanted government regulation and funding for the Scottish colleges. The Conservatives, under Peel, were in the throes of constructing a new government-funded and government-controlled university system there — the new Queen's University, a London-type examining body with three constituent teaching colleges in Belfast, Cork and Galway, with the crown having powers of nomination to chairs, to the college councils, and to the University Court which would administer the Treasury grant as well as secure academic standards through its control of examinations.

Yet Blackie kept alive some lingering hope that the Scottish universities might 'raise themselves', through 'a very little virtue, a few grains of decision, and some small attempt at cooperation', especially in coming to an agreement to introduce 'an entrance examination, uniform as much as may be over the whole of Scotland'. In 1848 it seemed as if such hopes were likely to be doomed:

> How are such things to be done? Certainly not by means of any mere Senatus Academici: in Scotland such bodies, even when they work together . . . are powerless enough. Certainly not by means of blue books, for we have enough already . . . The Scottish people, and the Scottish people only, can achieve university reform.[15]

And with this, so it seems, Blackie set himself on the long road to nurture the development of a public movement on behalf of Scottish university reform. He was already well launched into a programme of writing, in journals and in pamphlets and in the newspapers, by which to cajole his readers to join his crusade — and for a decade and more was hardly to relax his efforts. It is highly likely that one direct result of his initiatives was the formation of the Association for the Extension of the Scottish Universities, shortly after Blackie transferred from the chair of Humanity in Marischal College to the Greek chair in Edinburgh, as a pressure group to stimulate government to act.[16] Blackie frequently referred to the need to generate public support — 'the universities should put themselves in a favourable position before the public', he wrote in 1851, and insisted that (while it might need legislation to achieve them) it was vital to set up 'Boards of Examiners in connection with the Universities . . . to make all academical degrees satisfactory to the learned professions and to the public'.[17] And, in reality, only government could act with assurance on the public behalf.

Another Marischal College graduate, well-known to Blackie, was also active in pressing government to give itself more deliberate control over public institutions. In 1848, in a highly critical review of the state of 'English university education', Alexander Bain widened the argument to include all British universities:

> We cannot close without arguing the absolute necessity of a systematic government control of the Universities . . . it is obvious on every principle of good government,

of expediency, or of common sense, that such unspeakably important institutions should not be suffered to do what they like and neglect as many duties as they please. The state pays them, charters them, and gives them honourable standing, but makes no enquiry what they are about . . . But the nation ought to know how its money is used . . . Royal Commissions are the instruments usually employed by government in the rare instances of its interference with the chartered colleges. The experience which the Scottish Universities have of this proves everything we have just advanced . . . They have discriminated between the valuable and the noxious parts of the universities and have enabled government to give additional aid where it was much wanted . . . Now if occasional inspection be of so much use, how much more desirable a permanent superintendance . . . to be a vehicle of information to the public about their doings . . . to give opinion on the various systems and curricula and report on the acquirements of the students . . . . A government board would do almost unmixed good by a regular circuit of inspection, and by including in the one report a true picture of all the universities of the empire . . . There is no surer means of improving the entire circle of institutions than by keeping them aware of one another's proceedings. In the present state of things, Cambridge might have been stationed on the inhospitable Caucasus, and Oxford protected by the black-feet Indians on the banks of the Missouri, for all that they have learned from the experiences of the other universities of their fatherland.[18]

It is the characteristic Scottishness of Bain's attitudes and assumptions which make his commentary so revealing.

Yet another Marischal College graduate, a student reformer in the days of Joseph Hume's rectorial courts in Marischal in the mid-1820s and still active in the 1850s, Dr Alexander Kilgour, wanted government intervention to stimulate needed reforms but he had more doubts about too centralised a controlling machinery. With tongue in cheek, to some extent at least, he wrote in 1850:

Better than a non-working or inauguration-day, speech-making Rector would be the disposition at once of a Minister of Public Education — a Minister of State having power to give imperative directions in all that concerns the Scottish Universities, those officials not implicitly obeying him being ejected at his nod . . . The Universities will then be great Government schools, ruled and directed paid off or taken up, as the Minister of the time may see fit. He may, if inoculated with the grand leading idea of the day, centralise them, with a view to cheapness and economy to the State . . . or he may, perhaps, after American fashion, localise one in every county town and make them as plentiful as blackberries.

With more seriousness, he then went on:

That something like their Government rule is approaching is, I think, evident. We have not, as yet, one Cabinet Minister with absolute power over all the Universities, but we see two Universities of recent creation [i.e. London, and Queen's in Ireland] constituted as no University ever was before, for they are legislated for and governed by the nominees of the Prime Minister of the day, and with a veto in his hands . . .

What Kilgour wanted was legislation to lay down national guide-lines, for their more open government and financial rectitude, but leaving the reformed colleges with some freedom to respond to their own particular circumstances within an assured national framework:

> Would we not, as in England, likely get private foundations for Fellowships and Tutorships, for more Professorships and Bursaries, for Libraries and Museums, if our Universities were more national in their character, by being larger and more liberal and freer corporations . . . If I had not an objection to the constitution of London University and the Queen's University in Ireland on the score of their being too much under the control of Government, and too much on the centralization principle, I would consider it an objection that, being excessively under Government pay as well as management, they will not . . . produce that private beneficence . . . so beautifully illustrated in many of the old endowments in our Universities and Colleges.[19]

All three — Blackie, Bain and Kilgour — were dedicated Liberals in politics and vehemently opposed to the continuation of close corporations such as those still controlling the universities: these certainly had to go and some national structure of government and regulation had to take their place — but the extent and comprehensiveness of the powers which would then be vested at the centre were less easy to define. There was the possibility of greater agreement if central controls were to be limited to particular points of administration, and this was evident enough in the two reforms which, during the 1850s, figured in all the debates and writings: firstly, the need to introduce a common entrance examination; secondly, the need to raise standards in the degree courses. In 1856, for instance, Blackie privately applauded John Campbell Shairp for the way he had addressed the second of these in a pamphlet on university reform. Shairp wrote:

> It is much to be desired that, if possible, the four universities should combine for the purpose of granting literary degrees and only for this purpose; and that *one* board of examiners be appointed from among the professors and graduates . . . who shall preside over the yearly examinations and grant all Scottish degrees . . . It is clear that if all our universities separately grant degrees the worth of the degree will be measured by the size and importance of the university which grants it, and the degree of one may be lightly esteemed compared with that of another university — a result not to be desired.[20]

He went on to assert that, even with a single examining board, each university would be able to retain its own character, and while 'one would be more distinguished in Classics, another in Mathematics, another in Philosophy, there would arise in their common studies a more recognised standard and a more uniform practice'. Blackie was actually much more doubtful than was Shairp about the likely effectiveness of such limited cooperation and was much readier to remove controls from local hands in order to activate the full panoply of needful reforms: thus in 1858, in a letter to Mure of Caldwell about the scheme for reforming Cambridge University, he was sure that 'the great need there, as with us, is a strong central authority to overbear local opposition'.[21]

It is in relation to such arguments, about the most appropriate form and character of the central agency which would energise the universities into worthwhile and lasting reform, that the concept of a federal National University, with the existing institutions as constituent colleges, comes to the fore again and again. James Lorimer, for one, early made plain his partiality for such a solution.[22] Alexander Kilgour, while still finding things to doubt in the prospect of one degree-granting university for the whole of Scotland, was willing to see the incorporation of the two Aberdeen colleges and those of St Andrews into a new federal-type Edinburgh University, if that would remove obstacles to reform and at the same time keep both Aberdeen colleges in existence (which, he feared, a union in Aberdeen would not).[23] In the heated debates about the prospects for union of the Aberdeen universities in the mid-1850s, at a time when another commission was on the spot to recommend which particular form of union should be carried through, the Liberal *Aberdeen Herald* suggested a federal or multi-campus, new University of Aberdeen which would comprise King's and Marischal and another new college in Inverness, while hinting that some extended arrangement of the same kind might even be considered for the whole country.[24] Anxiety that King's College might be suppressed in a scheme of local union also convinced a spokesman for its graduates to come out, in evidence to the 1857–58 commission, in favour of a federal structure for all the Scottish universities: 'If there is to be a union of Universities, in order that degrees may not be granted without necessary qualifications, and that the standard may be sufficiently high, this object would not be secured without uniting all the Universities of Scotland'.[25] Blackie himself was to tell the same commissioners that he 'would have the whole colleges of Scotland put under one great university for Scotland', if only to put a stop to those crippling rivalries which currently barred all hope of achieving reform — in Edinburgh, he said, 'we cannot put our entrance examination into a satisfactory position, because they will not move in Glasgow'.[26] And another prominent reformer, Lord Elcho, was to write in London newspapers in late 1857 that reform would be best achieved, or would only be achieved, through the erection of a National University for Scotland: the *Aberdeen Herald* picked this up and reprinted it for its readers, adding that 'to Lord Elcho's proposal for a single university in Scotland, there is no sound objection'.[27]

Thus when parliament met to receive and to debate the government's Universities (Scotland) Bill in 1858, the issues had been very well and very publicly ventilated in the country. The bill carefully left aside complex matters of detail in order to avoid acrimonious exchanges over this or that local anxiety (as in the actual conditions for the union of the Aberdeen universities, even whether one or other college would be closed, or how far the former powers of the Edinburgh Town Council would be weakened in any new management arrangements in that city). The real decisions were left to a body of temporary commissioners, and it was to them that the reformers would have to look for the realization of their hopes and expectations. In fact, the act by way of its commissioners did much to implement the administrative proposals of the

1830 report and of many subsequent demands for radical restructuring of the management of universities, and added to the introduction of University Courts the novelty of General Councils of graduates. In its academic reforms the act was much less adventurous and proved more deaf to the reformers' demands: no uniform entrance examination was instituted, and there was no central board of examiners for degrees; the main changes were in a modest extension of the arts curriculum, a more varied pattern of possible degree courses, and the introduction of Honours courses. As is well known, those who framed the bill on behalf of the government, were surprised by a last minute intervention by Gladstone who was able to add to the bill a requirement that the commissioners should enquire into and report on 'how far it may be practicable and expedient that a new university be founded, to be a National University for Scotland . . . one central, examining and graduating body' to which the existing universities would be affiliated as colleges.[28] At the time, Gladstone's motives for his action in submitting the new clause seemed mysterious, beyond some vague notion that it was to give Scotland something parallel to the university structure in Ireland. Later, while the matter was still before the commissioners and reactions were being gathered from the universities, on 17 December 1863, Gladstone wrote to David Thorburn (who was promoting a new society to petition government for a much more generous endowment of the Scottish universities) about what he had had in mind:

> I confess it to be my decided opinion that the most practical and most practicable measure which could be adopted towards elevating the Scotch degrees would be the constitution among the four universities of a superior and distinct examining body on which the Degrees should depend, whether this body were clothed with the name of a National University or not. In the abstract it should, but it does not seem necessary, and might be dispensed with if the measure were thereby made more acceptable to the present governing bodies which are naturally reluctant to surrender their ancient rank and title. On the elevation of Degrees, influence and even endowment would be likely to follow by what I should think is the easiest as well as the most natural and legitimate process.[29]

It was thus the function of a federal or national university as an examining body which had provoked Gladstone to intervene, in an attempt to ensure that the standard of degrees would be sufficiently raised to gain Scottish higher education that reputation for quality which it lacked and which might even attract endowment to it.

Gladstone in his letter had sensed the opposition which his proposal would receive from the 'present governing bodies' of the colleges, even the new governing bodies indeed. It seems that, in any case, the commissioners were very half-hearted about the proposal (and were led in this by the chairman, John Inglis): they did not circulate any enquiry about it until November 1862, by which time it was unlikely that the new-look managements would be happy to vote themselves into limbo or out of meaningful power. In due course the commissioners commented that they were 'unable to report that it is either practicable or expedient that a new University should be founded to be a

National University for Scotland' and dropped the proposal. By then the very conservative *Aberdeen Journal* had let its readers know why it expected Gladstone's suggestion to fail:

> St Andrews, fallen from its high estate, will not willingly relinquish its position as the oldest University in this kingdom; Aberdeen cherishes the memory of Bishop Elphinstone; Glasgow will be the most refractory of all — for the metropolis of the West is proud, . . . that great mercantile community honours its distinguished academical institution and will never consent that any of its privileges should be lessened or taken away.[30]

The *Journal* was correct, and the idea of a National University was doomed. In any case, the government would have been foolish to run the risk of long and bitterly contentious legal battles with Senates and Courts and patrons and town councils, especially if it were possible to gain the substance of the reforms in other ways.

And so it proved. The commissioners of 1860–63 were able to issue ordinances to individual universities which imposed those changes in management and administration, in curricula and in degree structures, which were generally demanded and seemed most required, without directly infringing carefully-guarded, chartered rights. Sheldon Rothblatt is surely correct when he writes that in Scotland 'the system set up by the 1858 Act and continued in 1889 came as near to federalism as was compatible with the existence of independent universities'.[31] Scotland gained the substance of many of those advantages which federalism could offer without its universities having to suffer the ignominy of yielding up the outward signs of their independence and ancient privileges.

Yet the 1858 Act and its commissioners did not bring with them what Gladstone and so many others had seen as the prime agency for improving the quality and the reputation of Scottish university education, namely a central board to monitor or to award the degrees which would then be bestowed on their students by the universities which had taught them. And that leaves us with the question: why was it that the commissioners apparently ignored this matter, and why also they held off from any attempt to force a shared entrance examination on the universities (if only for bursars and those others who intended to follow the full graduating course)? Did they believe that, even within the universities, after all the public debating of the issues, there would be sufficient impetus to drive the colleges into cooperative action, and that these problems might be resolved without intervention — intervention which would alert the backwoodsmen and raise opposition against outside interference? Did they believe that other agencies were at work which might smooth the paths to these reforms? After all, there were signs that there was continuing improvement in the quality of teaching in the parochial and burgh schools, and the commissioners were not to know or to predict the crippling effects on the teaching of 'secondary' subjects from the Revised Code of the 1860s or from the payment system after the 1872 Education Act which proved to be even more injurious to the teaching of the 'higher subjects'. In the early 1860s all may have seemed to be set fair for universities to agree on a modest entrance examination for what should have been better qualified applicants. In the matter of the imposition of better standards for the award of degrees, there was also some hope that the professional bodies which, by and large, controlled 'postgraduate' studies would make more exacting demands on the prior training in arts, and that the expansion of open civil service examinations would also serve to force up standards, or to lead the universities into collaboration in order to meet new customer-demands. What is curious, and may be significant, is that when another royal commission on the Scottish universities took evidence in 1876–78, reforming demands for a central degree-examining board seemed to have virtually died off. On the other hand, there was still a vigorous demand for the introduction of an entrance examination to be equally applied in all the universities — 'I think this will never be done from within the Universities themselves', was the saddened conclusion of Sir Alexander Grant, principal of Edinburgh University[32] — and that was a reform which would finally be implemented by the 1889 Act.

In the evidence to the 1876–78 commission, another reform is frequently mentioned — action to take the appointment to chairs out of the hands of the individual universities, in order to remove what were called local prejudices and to provide a more open field to candidates of high quality. Here the proffered solutions were two: either the formation of a 'General Curatorial Board' which was composed of representatives from all four universities or the granting of all patronages of chairs to a 'Minister of Public Instruction' or to the crown in some other guise, on the grounds that this would ensure appointments being truly made in the national interest.[33] Needless to say, it appears that nothing came of either suggestion: here again, individual universities, and especially those which were guilty of introducing local prejudices, would not surrender patronage rights without a fight, no matter to whom they were to be transferred.

Whereas governments might act in a pretty cavalier fashion in forcing federal systems on their own foundations (as in Ireland) or on privately-endowed, uncharted and constitutionally-weak foundations which were being erected or would soon be erected in northern England and Wales, they had to be much more circumspect in their dealings with ancient, long-chartered and degree-granting college-universities such as those in Scotland. In fact, through the agency of the commissioners of 1860–63, the government at that time got away with what it could, without causing major constitutional and legal upsets. In what it did achieve through the 1858 Act, and a great deal was achieved for all the omissions from the more radical reformers' lists of recommendations drawn up in the 1850s, the government successfully underlined the strong national character of the Scottish universities, powerfully confirmed the public responsibility for them, stressed those features which by choice or enforced by ordinance they most obviously shared with each other, and supplied more formal and binding ties among them than they had known, enjoyed or suffered for centuries. If there was to be no National University after 1858, there was no doubting that there was a national system of universities in Scotland and a national ethos in higher education in which, perforce, all four shared. It had been one of the 1830 Commission's most cherished designs to bring the Scottish universities more firmly together again in a shared recognition of their national inheritance, and to reinvigorate that inheritance by adapting or reforming it to meet the changing circumstances of the nation which the universities were to serve: in and through the 1858 Act that design was substantially fulfilled.

NOTES

1. By the early 17th century we find complaints about the poor quality of teaching in Latin in both schools and universities: see D. J. Withrington, 'Education and society' in N. T. Phillipson, Rosalind Mitchison (eds), *Scotland in the Age of Improvement* (Edinburgh, 1970), 171–72.

2. *Ibid.*, 175–92.

3. The example of Aberdeen, both King's and Marischal, is well described in Paul B. Wood, *The Aberdeen Enlightenment: the Arts Curriculum in the Aberdeen Universities, 1717–1800* (forthcoming).

4. Occasional short articles and snippets of information which appear in the *Scots Magazine* in this period are invaluable.

5. For this and the following paragraph, reference may be made to: Michael Russel, *View of the System of Education at present pursued in the Schools and Universities of Scotland* (Edinburgh, 1813); [William Meston], *A Practical Essay on the Manner of Studying and Teaching in Scotland; or a Guide to Students at the University, to Parish Schoolmasters and Family Tutors* (Edinburgh, 1823); and a series of 'notices' of the Scottish universities in volumes xv–xviii (1824–25) of the *Scots Magazine*.

6. R. D. Anderson, *Education and Opportunity in Victorian Scotland: Schools and Universities* (Oxford, 1983), 37–39.

7. *Report to His Majesty by a Royal Commission of Enquiry into the State of the Universities of Scotland* (PP 1831), xii, 9–12.

8. The lively and radical *Aberdeen Chronicle* devoted three very long leaders to the printed report in the issues for 2 June, 9 June and 16 June 1832. See R. D. Anderson, *Education and Opportunity*, 52–53, for some later criticisms of the report written from a very Tory point of view.

9. Alexander Bannerman was an energetic and committed reformer, very antagonistic to 'the dirty, Tory corporation' of King's College throughout the 1830s and 1840s. His bill was astonishingly detailed, containing over 90 clauses, almost all of them designed to offend his opponents.

10. The Established Churchmen believed that Melbourne in 1835 had deliberately packed with seceders a commission to enquire into Religious Instruction in Scotland (accommodation available, attendance at churches and Sunday schools) in order to thwart their claims for state money for church extension.

11. This view contrasts strongly with the interpretation suggested by George E. Davie in his *The Democratic Intellect: Scotland and her Universities in the 19th Century* (Edinburgh, 1961), 34–41; for a more balanced account than Davie's, see R. D. Anderson, *Education and Opportunity*, 51–53.

12. J. D. Myers, 'Scottish nationalism and the antecedents of the 1872 Education Act' in *Scottish Educational Studies*, iv (1972), 73–92.

13. Alexander Anderson, *Five Letters to the Editor of the 'Aberdeen Banner' on Free Church University Education, with special reference to the North of Scotland and the Aberdeen Universities* (Aberdeen, 1845), Letter V.

14. *Education in Scotland* (Edinburgh, 1846), 3.

15. *University Reform: eight articles reprinted from the Scotsman newspaper, with a letter to Professor Pillans* (Edinburgh, 1848), 29–31, 39.

16. R. D. Anderson, *Education and Opportunity*, 57.

17. 'The Scottish Universities' in *Tait's Edinburgh Magazine*, 18 (1851), 70.

18. *Westminster and Foreign Review*, 49 (1848), 462–63.

19. *University Reform: Letters to the Rt Hon the Earl of Aberdeen on the Constitution and Government of the Scottish Universities* (Aberdeen, 1850), 13–14, 20.

20. *The Wants of the Scottish Universities and Some of the Remedies* (Edinburgh, 1856), 13, 41.

21. National Library of Scotland, Mure of Caldwell papers, MS 4955, June 1858.

22. *Universities of Scotland: past, present, possible* (Edinburgh, 1854), 54.

23. *University Reform: Letters*, 30–31.

24. 7 November 1857.

25. *Report of Her Majesty's Royal Commissioners appointed to inquire into the State of the Universities of Aberdeen* (PP 1857–58, xx), 25.

26. *Ibid.*, 110.

27. 9 January 1858.

28. *Hansard's Parliamentary Debates*, vol. cli (1857–58), cols 961–62, 5 July 1858.

29. David Thorburn, *The University Extension Movement* (Edinburgh, 1866), 33.

30. 31 December 1862.

31. Sheldon Rothblatt, 'Historical and comparative remarks on the federal principle in higher education' in *History of Education*, 16 (1987), 178.

32. *Report of the Royal Commissioners appointed to inquire into the Universities of Scotland* (PP 1878), Evidence, i, 10–11.

33. *Ibid.*, Evidence, i, 409; Evidence, ii, 31.

5

The Scottish Office and the Scottish Universities, c 1930–c 1960

I. G. C. Hutchison

I

There is an apparent paradox in relations between the Scottish universities and the Scottish Office during the middle third of this century. The establishment in 1885 of a separate governmental department for Scottish affairs, and the continuing expansion of its responsibilities thereafter, represented in part a response to growing signs of Scottish national feeling. Within the Scottish Office, the Scottish Education Department (SED) was a powerful force, particularly as the Scottish educational system (which it administered with closer attention and tighter control than that exercised by its English counterpart over English education) was widely perceived to be one of the most important components of a separate Scottish identity. Since the universities were held to be both the crowning piece of and an integral element in the structure of Scottish education, it would seem natural for close and friendly links to exist between the Scottish Office administrative headquarters in Edinburgh, St Andrews House, and the universities.

It is therefore surprising, at least at first glance, that the attitude of the universities after the inception of the University Grants Committee (UGC) was an adamant insistence that they preferred their affairs to be handled exclusively through the Committee, with minimal Scottish Office involvement. Three instances illustrate the consistency with which this opinion was held across the time-span of this paper. In 1937 Principal William Hamilton Fyfe of Aberdeen wrote to the Secretary of State for Scotland extolling the UGC ('the intelligence and independence of that body is beyond praise — and beyond the credibility of any transatlantic'), and counselling strongly against any Scottish equivalent being set up. The Balfour Committee of 1953, in the midst of its general desire to devolve the maximum amount of business to the Scottish Office, recommended that the universities should be left under the aegis of the UGC, as that arrangement 'works harmoniously and efficiently'. The Robbins Committee of the early 1960s was assured by the Scottish principals that there was no need for a separate agency (still less St Andrews House) to handle their concerns.[1]

The emphasis placed by the universities on as complete a divorce as possible from Scottish government no doubt has several causes. One was a belief that their international standing might suffer if they were no longer under UGC control. Again, the growing presence after 1918 of many English-educated academics may have reinforced this position. It is, however, possible that another factor may have been the experiences of the universities in their dealings with the Scottish Office in this period, as indicated by the following case-studies.

II

In the stringent public finance regime of the 1930s, the Scottish universities felt themselves to be starved of state funding to a dangerous degree and, moreover, some contended that the English universities received more generous support. The Scottish universities' grievance received a certain amount of public airing. Firstly in 1935 Sir Thomas Holland, principal of Edinburgh University, complained in a speech that while government grants worked out at £50 per student in England, they came to only £30 per Scottish student. A year later, much was made of this alleged disparity by the opposition candidates at a by-election in the Scottish Universities parliamentary constituency. The SED might have been expected to champion the cause of the Scottish universities. If the pinnacle of the Scottish education system was at risk, the potential injuries which might be inflicted on the schools (owing to the intimate connection between the two sectors) might perhaps have goaded the department to active involvement. Instead, the response of civil servants in the SED was negative.

At a meeting of the UGC shortly after Holland's outburst, a measured reaction was offered by the head of the SED, Sir George MacDonald, who sat on the UGC as the department's assessor. He urged that in the tables compiled by the Committee to show the grant distribution to each university, the list should not, as hitherto, be grouped by nation (England, Wales, Scotland) but should be listed alphabetically. He repeated this proposal in 1937 a little after the by-election, observing that the present layout:

> cannot but convey the impression that our distribution is somehow or other based upon 'national' principles. But 'international' jealousy is unfortunately a real thing, and it is dangerous to provide it with unnecessary opportunities for drawing foolish deductions. Already some over-ingenious patriots have discovered a Scottish grievance in our figures.[2]

An interesting light is cast by this suggestion on the estimation held by top civil servants of the intelligence of leading Scottish academics such as Principal Holland and the regius professor of Scots law at Glasgow University, A.D. Gibb, who as the Scottish nationalist candidate in the by-election had been to the fore in raising the question in the campaign. MacDonald presumably believed it was beyond the wit of these men to cope with extracting data from an alphabetical list.

The Secretary of State, who was anxious to have material to deflect these criticisms, received a memorandum, prepared by SED officials on the question, which offered a similarly superficial and hostile analysis. The paper argued that just because Scotland took nearly one quarter of all British university students, this did not create an incontestable right to an equivalent share of state funding: 'But Scotland cannot reasonably expect that her lavish provision of University education necessarily entitles her to draw *pro rata* from exchequer monies provided by a taxation system uniform over the United Kingdom.'[3] This seems a peculiar position for the SED to adopt: Scotland, precisely because its educational system was much more successful (by this yardstick) than England, could not therefore expect treatment equal to that given to its backward neighbour.

A more serious effort to improve the funding of the Scottish universities was, however, rather more discreetly under way at about the same time as these public controversies. In announcing its quinquennial allocation in 1936, the UGC stressed that it felt that the state-funded element in the total income of the Scottish universities was becoming rather too large. When the Scottish universities jointly approached the Committee seeking supplementation of their initial award, they were informed that no additional funds would be forthcoming from the Treasury while Scottish local authorities were less generous than those in England in contributing to universities. Whereas in England about 10 per cent of universities' income was derived from local government, the figure for Scotland was only 4.5 per cent. The Scottish Office intervened to suggest a solution which would ease the plight of the universities. Part of the reason for this support may have been more politically based than one arising from a concern about the provision of higher education. The middle 1930s saw a renewed upsurge in support for Scottish nationalism, but now, unlike in the 1920s when the main nationalist impetus was from left-wingers, it came from Conservative and Liberal supporters. The founding of the Scottish Party in 1932, composed as it was of establishment figures like the Duke of Montrose and Sir Alexander MacEwan, was significant. Some reasonable by-election performances, particularly Gibb's 31 per cent of the votes in the Scottish Universities' seat in 1936, may well have stimulated the Scottish ministers to seek to solve the universities' issue. The head of the SED drew the attention of all parties to a hitherto neglected sub-clause in the 1908 Scottish Education Act. This measure, part of which set up the Education (Scotland) Fund to finance educational provision in the country, made provision in clause 16(1)(b) for the Scottish universities to receive a share of the fund. However, the introduction of Treasury grants to universities shortly after the act came into force meant that the clause had never been applied, but it now offered an ideal solution. The allocation from the fund to the universities would otherwise have gone to local authorities, so it could be construed as local government support; moreover no individual authority would be giving more or less than any other, thus avoiding invidious comparisons and maintaining the concept of national, not regional, universities.

A committee was set up under Lord Alness and in 1938 it advised the Secretary of State as to how much support from the Education (Scotland) Fund should be given to the universities, together and individually. By comparing the workings and conclusions of the Alness Committee with a successor, the Cooper Committee set up in 1946, which reappraised the grant in the light of new circumstances, much can be deduced about the approach of the Scottish Office to the university sector. It appears that the Alness committee was effectively run by the SED official who served as its secretary, but the Cooper committee was very much controlled and led by the chairman himself, with the civil service secretary having a limited influence on its decisions. Analysis of these two committees' proceedings and recommendations highlights three features.

Firstly, the SED was extremely parsimonious in its approach to funding the universities. In their submission to Alness, the four university courts had asked for an award of £75,000. The sum initially mooted within St Andrews House was between £20,000 and £25,000, but this was revised upwards in the SED's submission of evidence to Alness to £36,000. The committee settled on £30,000, primarily because the UGC indicated pretty bluntly that this was the lowest amount which might persuade the Treasury to look more benevolently upon further approaches from Scotland.[4] After the war, all the principals, led by Hector Hetherington of Glasgow, appealed to the Secretary of State for a reassessment of the Education (Scotland) Fund allocation, on the grounds that the needs of universities had greatly expanded and that the Fund had grown much larger. The head of the SED, however, suggested to the UGC that in the light of the much increased sum administered by that committee to meet the wants of universities, the provision of any monies, far less an additional amount, from the Education (Scotland) Fund was no longer appropriate. He added that the department's financial adviser was of opinion that the enlarged UGC grants were 'more than sufficient' to satisfy the requirements of the Scottish universities. The UGC took quite the opposite line: *because* the state was now providing more funds, there was a greater need to maximise all other sources of revenue, so as to keep in check any tendencies to excessive reliance on public handouts.[5] In 1953 the SED again queried whether an award from their Education Fund need be continued, given the insignificant proportion of total university income that it constituted. Once more, the UGC negatived the proposal: it would create a hostile reaction in England and would run counter to the committee's desire to retain a diversity of funding sources. Indeed, it added, if the Fund contribution was minuscule, rather than eliminating it, there was 'a pretty strong case' for increasing it, in particular because local government support to the English universities had virtually doubled since the time of the Cooper committee in 1946.[6] In 1957 the SED returned to the issue, arguing that changes in the financing of Scottish education made impossible the retention of the Cooper grant. The UGC resisted, for it felt it unlikely that individual authorities would take upon themselves a financial burden on the scale provided by the Education (Scotland) Fund. The upshot was that a third committee, under Lord Sorn, was appointed; its report called for an increase of £25,000 to the universities from Scottish education funds.[7]

A second area of unease for the universities arose from the attitude taken by Scottish Office civil servants in dealing with the charge that Scottish local authorities were failing to match England in financing universities. In the 1930s the Alness committee seems to have accepted at face value the claims of Scottish niggardliness, and hit upon a sum intended to blunt the force of the criticisms. The Cooper committee in 1946, by contrast, defended stoutly the level of local government funding in Scotland, producing evidence and argument which indicated that, in reality, Scotland was outstripping England. For instance, Scotland came out on top if one looked, not at the share of total university income provided by local government, but at the contribution per head of population or per £ of rateable value in the respective countries. Moreover, if endowments were treated as a form of local contribution, Scotland's achievement was much enhanced. Lord Cooper's committee acidly concluded that the Alness committee had been too lenient in dealing with the UGC's strictures on Scottish local contributions,[8] but Alness, as we have seen, had reflected the St Andrews House view, and this doubtless alarmed the universities.

Thirdly, the scheme for distributing the Education (Scotland) Fund monies adopted by Alness also gave rise to concern. Once again, Cooper confessed that he had great difficulty in grasping the principles followed by the Alness committee. Finally he decided that the universities 'extracted what they could from the UGC and then came to Alness to balance their budget.'[9] This posed two problems for universities. Firstly, it seemed to some that profligate institutions were rewarded for their extravagant ways, while those that operated along more conservative budgeting lines found themselves starved when they most needed support. Aberdeen was the main casualty of the Alness distribution. The secretary of the committee pointed out that although the Aberdeen accounts for the previous year did record a deficit of £8,400, this was after a transfer from revenue to the building reserve of £10,000. Accordingly, only £4,000 went to Aberdeen out of the total of £43,000 allocated by Alness. Some two years later, when Aberdeen University found itself unable to continue with its ambitious building programme because it had exhausted its carefully husbanded reserves, and approached the Secretary of State for assistance, he replied that he was powerless to vary the decision of the Alness report. A second problem presented by the deficit-funding approach of Alness, inspired by civil servants, was that allocations bore little relation to the proportions of funding received from the UGC. While Aberdeen got under 10 per cent of the Alness grant, it was given some 15 per cent of the UGC's Scottish total. This erratic and uncoordinated system made forward planning extremely difficult for universities and, in Cooper's words, the Alness scheme was 'a thoroughly illogical and unscientific procedure which can never be made the basis of permanent policy for University Finance'.[10] The Cooper committee divided increased funding among the four universities in the same ratio as the UGC used, thereby ensuring consistency.

One reason for the hostile posture taken by the Scottish Office towards the financial claims of the universities was discussed frankly in an internal SED memorandum of 1937. This stressed the strong opposition expressed by local authorities to any diminution in the resources available to them from the Education (Scotland) Fund. Any reduction in state financing of education would have to be met by an increase in rates and that would be politically damaging; and just when the universities were making a bid for a share of the Fund, local education authority budgets were being stretched very tightly because they had to bear the cost of a range of new developments. Innovations in technical, physical and adult education were being introduced; nursery schools were being provided; and there were plans to raise the school leaving age.[11] The local government lobby was powerful and articulate, and its interests were always likely to prevail in the Scottish Office over those of the universities, especially because of its immense political leverage. The figure of £20,000 to £25,000 suggested by the SED as an appropriate grant to the universities by Alness represented an average rate increase of one sixth of a penny in the pound, a figure seen as the highest tolerable to local councils. In its evidence to the Cooper committee the Association of Town and County Councils re-stated local government's opposition to the Alness report and argued that recent additional financial burdens, particularly teachers' salary increases, would take almost all of the extra amount in the Education (Scotland) Fund, leaving virtually nothing for an increased grant to universities.[12]

Over and above the hostile weight of local government, the SED was unwilling for other reasons to open to scrutiny the topic of state funding of Scottish education. Predominant was the SED's awareness that the allocation to non-university education from the Treasury was over-generous. By the terms of the 'Goschen formula', which gave Scotland 11/80ths of total British expenditure, some £5.9 million should have been put into the Education (Scotland) Fund in 1935, but the actual figure was £6.35 million. Within the SED it was argued that to back the clamour for increased state support of the Scottish universities might well prompt the Treasury and English educationalists to demand, as a *quid pro quo*, the strict application of the Goschen formula. The Scottish Office was plainly not willing to take this risk, and hence had a strong motive for keeping any award it was forced to offer as low as possible.[13]

III

After the Second World War the development of higher technological education became a major concern of the British government, and the

Barlow and Tizard reports called for greater provision of these subjects at universities. Aberdeen University sought to associate itself with this trend by intimating to the UGC that it wished to establish departments of mechanical and electrical engineering wholly within its ambit. The university had offered degree programmes in engineering since the 1920s, but from the start the bulk of the courses had been held at Robert Gordon's College (RGC), with teaching staff and equipment provided by the College. The UGC unanimously rejected Aberdeen's scheme, because it preferred to concentrate on building up existing departments to a large size, rather than fostering a proliferation of small, inefficient and uneconomical units. The debate which ensued again highlights SED attitudes to the universities, and what is striking is the vehemence and persistence with which the SED acted throughout to persuade the UGC to veto any severance of the university from the college.

When Aberdeen first mooted its plan, the SED tried to persuade the college to resolve existing points of friction with the university in an effort to maintain the long-standing joint relationship. After it became clear that the university intended to persevere with its concept of an autonomous degree, the SED stepped up its counter-propaganda activities. In October 1951 it asked the UGC, which was known to be against the development, to encourage the university to seek a compromise with the college by 'indicat[ing], however obliquely, these doubts on the merits of the proposals.' An internal departmental memorandum commented that the real purpose of this appeal was 'to tie the UGC down to what Sir Arthur Trueman [chairman of the UGC] told me and at the same time to get them to move in the matter fairly quickly'.[14] The department also tried to ensure by more direct means that the UGC reached the conclusion the Scottish Office desired. Before coming to a decision, the full committee submitted Aberdeen's proposal to its technology sub-committee for expert appraisal. Two Scottish industrialists sat on this technology sub-committee: Sir Murray Stephen, the shipbuilder, and Sir Andrew McCance, chairman of Colvilles, one of the most influential businessmen in Scotland and an acknowledged expert on steel technology. At the crucial meeting in November 1951 of the sub-committee, when Aberdeen's case was considered, McCance took the lead by presenting in formidable style the argument against the university, concluding: 'In his view, the proposed duplication of facilities for teaching engineering at Aberdeen was unnecessary and wasteful, particularly as no criticism has been made of the way in which the College had discharged their [sic] responsibilities under the agreement.' Stephen then reinforced McCance's view: 'he saw no case for the proposed change.' It seems possible that the SED had colluded with McCance and Stephen to ensure that at this, and a subsequent, meeting of the sub-committee, the most vigorous refutation of Aberdeen's scheme was made.[15]

The SED felt confident after the November 1951 sub-committee meeting that it had won the battle for the ear of the UGC, but the full committee postponed its final verdict until a last appeal had been submitted by the university. At this hearing in February 1952 several factors were stressed:

demand for places at Aberdeen was high, with local candidates being turned away; industry in the region badly needed graduate engineers; expansion would relieve the huge pressure experienced at Glasgow; withdrawal of university students from RGC would release more space for the college to expand its own interests; moreover the opening of the new Chemistry Building at King's College eliminated the practical obstacle to a self-contained university degree scheme, for abundant space for teaching engineering students was now available at Marischal College. The UGC was favourably impressed with these points, as its secretary reported to the SED: 'I think it would be held that the case they had made was not one that could be lightly brushed aside'.[16] On receipt of this information, the civil servants at St Andrews House exploded in apoplectic tones. The official who liaised most directly with the UGC promptly fired off a rejoinder contending that Aberdeen had used 'specious arguments'. Then Sir John Mackay Thomson, head of the SED, weighed in with a memorandum charging the university with having committed some of the most heinous sins in the eyes of senior mandarins. Aberdeen's claims were 'ludicrous', showed a 'lamentable lack of knowledge', and so were 'scarcely relevant'. Perhaps most damning of all, at least from the standpoint of a bureaucrat, if not an academic, the university's arguments were 'purely hypothetical'.[17]

Aberdeen's plan was sent back to the technology sub-committee for reappraisal in June 1952. The previous negative decision was confirmed, and the sub-committee underlined its total rejection of the proposal by calling on the full UGC to make it plain to Aberdeen that if these recommendations were ignored in the 1952–57 quinquennium, 'it would be viewed with disfavour'.[18] The UGC concurred, and in some of the strongest language it ever used signalled to Aberdeen its total opposition, because 'the Committee was also agreed that it would be necessary to ensure that the University did not carry out this development after an adverse decision reached by the Committee after prolonged and exhaustive consideration'. The formula of phrasing was carefully chosen: steering between 'definitely forbid' and 'not convinced of the desirability', it settled for 'the Committee did not think that this development should be carried out'.[19] Aberdeen was therefore forced to suspend its vision of a separate engineering department until the next decade and the links with RGC were preserved. The SED had triumphed.

This unremitting hostility to the university's proposal on the part of the SED stemmed largely from a major difference between the responsibility for higher technical education north and south of the border. In England the Colleges of Advanced Technology were administered by local government education authorities, so that the Department of Education had little close or day-to-day involvement in their affairs. By contrast, the Scottish Central Institutions were directly and completely controlled by the SED. Thus St Andrews House had a particular concern to defend the standing of the colleges, as one official remarked to the UGC: 'I feel it is necessary to be watchful of the interests of these institutions'.[20] A rupture between Aberdeen University and Robert Gordon's College would clearly have diminished the prestige of the latter.

This protective stance was intensified by the SED's belief, trumpeted repeatedly in the late 1940s and early 1950s, that the central institutions were operating at a higher educational range than their English counterparts. The Tizard report of 1948 concluded that the well-established need to produce many more highly trained applied scientists could be met only by the universities, and so called for the entire funding of this expansion to be handled by the UGC. Lord Cherwell, the government's science adviser, told R. A. Butler, the minister charged with implementing this policy, that the role of the technical colleges was to be a low-level one: 'They train the NCOs of industry, not the officers'.[21] The SED kept up for a long period a strenuous resistance, asserting that whatever might be the situation in England, the Scottish Central Institutions were emphatically not of sub-university level. They 'have attained a higher status in the eyes of industry than most of the English colleges', and indeed taught more graduates of university standard than the Scottish universities themselves. At a meeting in 1951 attended by the SED, the Department of Education and the UGC to discuss the development of higher technological education, Sir John Mackay Thomson reiterated the claim of the six Central Institutions to be compared in the quality of their work in applied science not with the low-grade, locally-focused English colleges, but with the universities. The fact that the UGC gave grants to Heriot-Watt and the Royal College of Science and Technology reinforced this argument. The preferred approach urged on the Scottish Secretary of State by his senior civil servants was that the development of higher technological education would best be achieved not by following Tizard's proposals, but instead by ensuring ever closer cooperation between central institutions and universities.[22]

In this context the reaction of the SED to Aberdeen's projected divorce from Robert Gordon's becomes more intelligible. Moreover, a simultaneous squabble in Glasgow over the same issue, which was taking place between the University and the Royal College, served to stiffen the Scottish Office's determination to crush the Aberdeen initiative. Indeed there was an interesting link between the two conflicts. Sir Andrew McCance, who had so steadfastly opposed the Aberdeen proposal in the UGC sub-committee was one of the most active governors of the Royal College. It is likely that he was alert to the knock-on implications for the west of Scotland institution if Aberdeen University were to succeed in establishing the right to function independently, with a consequent downgrading of the local college, and SED officials may have drawn these factors to McCance's attention.

IV

The resistance displayed by the Scottish universities to any suggested dilution of their relationship to the British-wide UGC is perhaps less perverse than it might seem at first sight. Particularly relevant is the point that St Andrews House is not Whitehall writ small: in Edinburgh different departments occupy a more important position than in London. The success of the UGC in defending the interests of the universities came about partly because the committee fell under the protection of the most powerful department in Whitehall, the treasury. In the Scottish Office there was no equivalent to shield the university interest from the assaults of other departments with their own interests to promote. By further contrast, in Whitehall the Department of Education was small and relatively lightweight, but in Edinburgh the SED was a highly assertive and influential department; and the firm and detailed control exercised by the SED over its sub-university institutes of higher education must have given the universities pause for thought before agreeing to entrust themselves to any closer contact. During the tussle between Aberdeen University and Robert Gordon's College over the future of engineering, the secretary of the UGC had to reprimand SED officials for assuming that the committee had the power to instruct universities on matters of policy: 'You will appreciate that our hold over the Universities is somewhat limited . . . I am afraid that University autonomy would mean very little if it did not mean that Universities could sometimes do things the Government do not like!'[23] As the universities had contact with the central institutions, they would be very well aware of the extensive degree of supervision practised by the SED. This perception, together with the realisation that the Scottish Office was always more likely to respond to the demands of politically more powerful lobbies such as local authorities, were neatly linked by Principal Hamilton Fyfe when he voiced opposition to a Scottish UGC. The fact that Fyfe was widely regarded as a progressive both in education and politics (his brother was a prominent socialist journalist), makes his opinions the more striking. He told the Secretary of State in 1937 of his fears that such a Scottish body would be dominated by individuals 'whose interests were political and departmental' and would carry 'the looming danger of a committee composed of Labour politicians, eying the votes of the uninstructed, and Departmental officials armed to the teeth with axes, which in our opinion should not be ground upon academic bodies.' Compared to this nightmare, the gentlemanly UGC was infinitely preferable.[24]

NOTES

I wish to thank the Carnegie Trust for the Universities of Scotland and the British Academy for financial assistance towards the cost of research.

1. Scottish Record Office [SRO], ED 26/188, W. H. Fyfe to Sir G. Collins, 11 Feb. 1937; *Royal Commission on Scottish Affairs*, PP 1953–4, xix, 89; *Royal Commission on Higher Education*, Evidence, vol. D, PP 1963, qq.1136ff.

2. Public Record Office [PRO], UGC 1/2, UGC Minutes, 13 Nov. 1935; 18 June 1937, Appendix A.

3. SRO, ED 26/188, memorandum to Secretary of State from J. M. P[eck], 12 July 1935.

4. SRO, ED 26/391/25, evidence of J. Beresford to Alness Committee, 22 Nov. 1937.

5. PRO, UGC 7/84, J. M. Thomson to W. Moberley, 2 Jan. 1946; Moberley to Thomson, 6 Feb. 1946.

6. Ibid., W. Murnie to E. Hale, 29 Jul. 1953; Hale to Murnie, 31 July 1953.

7. Ibid., Murnie to Hale, 25 Apr. 1957; Hale to Murnie, 3 May 1957.

8. SRO, ED 26/637/19, minute of meeting of Cooper Committee, 27 Apr. 1946.

9. Ibid.

10. SRO, ED 26/637/13, memorandum by Cooper, 11 Apr. 1946.

11. SRO, ED 26/391, memorandum by J. M. Peck, 14 Jan. 1937.

12. SRO, ED 26/637/20-21, evidence of Association of Town and County Councils of Scotland, 23, 25 Apr. 1946.

13. SRO, ED 26/188, memorandum to Secretary of State from J. M. P[eck], 12 June 1935.

14. SRO, ED 26/1009, D. Milne to A. Trueman, 11 Oct. 1951; memorandum to Under-Secretary of State by H. H. D[onnelly], 9 Oct. 1951.

15. PRO, UGC 8/44, minute of UGC Technology Sub-committee, 13 Nov. 1951; SRO, SED 26/1009, memorandum by J. M. Thomson, 13 Mar. 1952.

16. SRO, ED 26/1009, E. Hale to H. H. Donnelly, 29 Feb. 1952.

17. Ibid., H. H. Donnelly to E. Hale, 3 Mar. 1952; memorandum by J. M. Thomson, 13 Mar. 1952.

18. PRO, UGC 8/53, minute of UGC Technology Sub-Committee, 10 June 1952.

19. PRO, UGC 1/3, minute of UGC, 26 June 1952.

20. SRO, ED 26/387, J. MacDonald to P. S. Ross, 30 Oct. 1948.

21. SRO, ED 26/1057, Cherwell to Butler, 1 Apr. 1952 (copy).

22. SRO, ED 26/387, memorandum to Secretary of State, 28 June 1951.

23. SRO, ED 26/1009, E. Hale to H. H. Donnelly, 5 Jan. 1952.

24. SRO, ED 26/188, W. H. Fyfe to Sir G. Collins, 11 Feb. 1937.

6

The Scottish University Tradition: Past and Future

R. D. Anderson

At the beginning of the 1990s, it seems a rational political calculation that the creation of a Scottish parliament whose powers include control of the universities will not be long delayed. Even within the present constitutional structure, the devolution of the universities, with a single planning and funding body for the whole of higher education, was recommended by the Scottish Tertiary Education Advisory Council (STEAC) in its report of 1985. This report, it is true, was rejected by the government, which later dissolved STEAC itself for good measure, and by the universities themselves. But since then opinion in the university world has been changing, one recent symptom being the conversion of the formerly anti-devolutionist Association of University Teachers.

If a Scottish parliament has to determine university policy, the nature of Scottish traditions will become a practical as well as an academic question. For it is is a well-known feature of Scottish educational discourse that it commonly includes an appeal to the past, or at least to an idealised version of it. In disputes over recent government legislation, it is striking how both sides have felt it necessary to claim the sanction of tradition, and to repudiate any 'anglicisation' of the Scottish system. Historians who have scrutinised this use of the past as myth have tended to observe that the myth's content has changed radically over the years, the one constant being that whatever distinguishes Scotland from England at any one time is regarded as traditional, even when the differences are quite recent. The undoubted legal and historical distinctiveness of the system has made education a plausible emotional focus for Scotland's assertion of its national identity. But if the past is to be a political battlefield, why should historians maintain a purely sceptical and negative attitude? As experts in the past, why should they not join in the game? To attempt to define the national tradition is in any case a valid intellectual exercise, and in this paper I want to suggest a few ways of doing this, to consider how the past might help to shape the future, and to point out the problems and the sometimes formidable obstacles in the way of any specifically Scottish educational strategy.

I shall deal comparatively briefly with two aspects of the universities — their 'democratic' character, and the extent to which they have had a distinctive curriculum reflecting national values. But first, and at greater length, I shall discuss their relationship with the state, and suggest that in this lies one reason for the widespread feelings of malaise about the treatment of the Scottish universities by a government committed to free-market ideology. Champions of this ideology have argued that the Scottish tradition is individualist rather than collectivist, and for them Adam Smith is a prize exhibit. There is no doubt that Smith criticised the permanent 'endowment' of universities, and thought that intellectual interests were best secured by professors being responsive to the market through dependence on fees; this corresponded (though only partly) to the actual state of the universities in the eighteenth century. But in the nineteenth century, it can be argued, this theory was specifically rejected in favour of a very widely held belief that universities should form a national system supported by the state.

This view was expressed in an influential form in the 1820s by Thomas Chalmers, who argued that education was a commodity for which demand did not arise spontaneously, since until it is freely available, consumers do not know that they want it. He considered that Smith was wrong to apply laissez-faire principles to education, and that, while it was right to charge fees, it was the state's duty, in universities as in parish schools, to pay for a permanent establishment of salaried teachers. Chalmers used a number of arguments, including the state's interest in the efficient training of the professions, and its duty to support the country's higher culture and learning; but at the root of his thinking was an analogy with religion and the need for a religious establishment. Chalmers' views had a deep influence on the clergy, the chief dispensers of educational ideology in the early nineteenth century, and constantly recur in contemporary debate.[1]

As a more or less random example, let us take William Brown, in his introductory lecture as professor of divinity at St Andrews in 1856. Its title was *The Scientific Character of the Scottish Universities*; their higher cultural mission was contrasted with 'the professional and mechanical view of them as mere teaching establishments', and with the utilitarian notion that they should be adapted to the practical needs of the age, 'the demand of the day being for business and working qualifications'. 'What method of support is most favourable to their scientific character,' asks Brown:

> that of permanent endowment, or that of mercantile voluntaryism, which would render them dependent on the marketable value of their teaching? It is undoubtedly on the basis of permanent endowment that all our great social institutions have heretofore rested, and by means of which they have been instrumental in training the national mind. Guaranteed in their permanence and independence, the life within them grows in its native soil, breathes its own native atmosphere, and ... has ... exercised a corresponding healthy and vigorous influence; hence the distinctive features of our national character, its intellectuality, its high moral tone, its thoughtfulness, its discreet soberness, its utter abhorrence of fanatical extravagance. It is in the repose and dignity of conscious power and independence that institutions, like individuals, cherish and manifest the highest and most commanding attributes.

Brown refers to the current effort to involve graduates in university affairs, which (then as now) 'has an eye to the social and pecuniary advantage which may thus ultimately accrue to the Universities through the influence and bounty of their grateful sons.' But, he concludes:

> let private and personal liberality be copious as it may, this does not supersede the social duty of making adequate public provision for social wants and social interests. . . . When a community ceases to recognise this truth, and is content to commit its institutions to the guardianship and support of personal voluntary enterprise, all guarantee for their soundness and permanency is gone. For the Universities, then, as national establishments, I ask adequate public support.[2]

It would be easy to compile an anthology of such statements, which contrast strikingly with the grudging and minimal view of the state's role in education which long prevailed in England. The Scottish view was expressed in Chalmers' day by the secular intelligentsia of the *Edinburgh Review*, in the 1850s by James Lorimer and John Stuart Blackie, champions of both university reform and the active state, in the 1870s by those who complained bitterly about the failure of the state to support secondary education, and right down to 1914 by James Donaldson, principal of St Andrews, who claimed for example in 1902 that, by contrast with England:

> from the first the Scottish Universities were under State control. The State was responsible for them and bound itself to maintain them in full efficiency. . . . The Scottish people held that all education concerned the common weal, and that the just and wise method of action in regard to them was to compel the various members of the State to contribute to their support in proportion to their means.

Like many others, Donaldson was deeply influenced by the German idea of the ethical state, and would have endorsed Matthew Arnold's view of the state as the organ of the national reason, the nation in its corporate and collective character.[3]

This Scottish view of the state, it may be argued, represents the secularisation of a religious ideal of unity which goes back to the seventeenth, if not the sixteenth century. Parish churches, schools, and the universities which trained ministers and schoolteachers were designed to impose orthodoxy and ecclesiastical authority, and to create in a fissiparous nation a single godly community under unified spiritual direction. Later, as William Brown's remarks suggest, this tradition took on new life as a way of preserving a national culture in the shadow of a more powerful neighbour. It helps to explain the acceptance in 1872 of a national, non-denominational school system, and the relative centralisation and uniformity of this system as it developed under the Scottish Education Department. In the twentieth century, welfare-state thinking has given the state a new role as the guarantor of equal opportunity and the impartial arbiter of the distribution of scarce social resources — though even for that argument earlier Scottish precedents could be found. More generally, attempts to define the Scottish tradition always come back — as in a recent report by a committee of distinguished educational and cultural figures — to the idea that education exists 'not only for individual advantage and advancement, but for the good of the community as a whole'.[4]

These notions of public authority, communal solidarity and collective improvement perhaps explain the lack of enthusiasm in Scotland for the present government's policy of allowing schools to opt out of local authority control. In universities, the attempt to inject market forces has taken the form of competitive bidding for funds, part of a broader policy of making university education demand-led by manipulating the balance between grants and fees. This encourages more diversity between universities; but it is diversity on a United Kingdom basis, in which, for example, Edinburgh and Glasgow might join a premier division of international, research-based universities, and draw apart from their neighbours. Some universities (or at least their principals) have embraced this idea of greater diversity with some enthusiasm. But pushed to its logical end, it would dissolve any common features which the Scottish universities retain, and it is certainly contrary to the traditional concept of a national system, in which universities are not seen as profit-seeking bodies, but as public institutions with defined obligations to society, including the preservation of equal opportunity. From this point of view, there is no intrinsic merit in competition; universities have the same basic mission, but exercise it in the context of their local and regional communities. The tension between this community role and current national policy came out particularly in the former University Grants Committee's treatment of the Scottish veterinary and dental schools; and readers of the collective volume on *Aberdeen University 1945–1981* will be struck by the way in which the university's arguments about its regional obligations were taken as obvious by everyone at Aberdeen, but met with complete incomprehension in London.[5]

It may seem a paradox to speak of a Scottish view of the state in the nineteenth century, when there was no longer a Scottish state; yet the political system did allow this tradition to be expressed in the process of university reform. The Scottish universities retained their subsidies, were always seen as state institutions, and were the subject of detailed parliamentary control in the Royal Commissions of 1826 and 1876, the acts of 1858 and 1889, and the executive commissions which followed those acts. Much of what these commissions did conflicts with the doctrines of university autonomy and academic freedom as they have developed over the last hundred years. They took for granted four axioms. First, the 1826 commission took over Chalmers' views in declaring that 'the principles applicable to trade' could not be extended to education, for 'without the institutions and settled usages of an Establishment, the objects of National education could not be adequately secured'.[6] Second, they assumed that it was the duty of public authority to lay down what universities should teach, how they should be organised, what should be their relation to schools, and so on. The Ordinances of the executive commissions severely constrained the autonomy of the universities in the years after 1858 and 1889, and they were not drawn up by academics, but by lawyers and politicians.

Thirdly, the commissions took it for granted that the Scottish universities should be as similar as possible; one aim of legislation was to correct divergences, forcing the universities to drop developments which were out of line with the common pattern. And fourthly, one aspect of this insistence on uniformity was the imposition of a common curriculum. There was much debate about what form this should take, but behind it lay the idea, widely accepted everywhere in the nineteenth century, that there was a definable standard of 'liberal' education which, once agreed on, should give all students a common intellectual grounding. This was linked with the rejection of the free market and the idea of the state as the guardian of cultural standards, for if parents and students had complete freedom of choice, the notion of a general education based on specified compulsory subjects would have no point.

This brings us to the second general point about the Scottish tradition: the university curriculum. And here, of course, one cannot avoid discussing George Davie's book *The Democratic Intellect* (1961). From the historian's point of view, there is much to criticise in Davie's detailed account of nineteenth-century developments, but his central point can scarcely be contested: that there was a specific Scottish ideal of general education, distinguished from others by its emphasis on philosophy. But Davie's claim that philosophy was at the heart of the curriculum ('compulsory philosophy', as he puts it, though in the fixed curriculum every subject was 'compulsory') can be misleading. It was the executive commission under the 1858 Act which did most to define the Scottish ideal of liberal education, drawing together more coherently the somewhat haphazard developments of the preceding hundred years, and giving them a new justification based on a tripartite classification of knowledge. Languages, philosophy and mathematics were all seen as essential to the ideal, working harmoniously to develop different aspects of the intellect. In the standard four-year curriculum imposed after 1858, languages accounted for five of the ten courses normally taken, mathematics and natural philosophy for three, and mental philosophy for only two. The commission failed to give natural science the position which it was already claiming, but it is important to note the central role of mathematics in general education in the nineteenth century. And many professors, not least in Aberdeen, saw the classics rather than philosophy as the heart of the Scottish tradition. Latin was the subject which linked universities and parish schools, while Greek remained a compulsory part of the uniform MA curriculum down to 1892.

A second reservation is that the 'democratic intellect' of Davie's title is the intellect of the nation's elite, not of the masses. Davie sees this elite as democratic partly because it was widely recruited, but partly also because, he claims, a philosophical training kept it in touch with its roots in a way which specialised education did not. Whether or not one accepts this slightly mystical idea, the Scottish tradition was only one version, though a distinctive one, of the nineteenth-century belief in liberal or humanist education as the appropriate formation for a country's professional and intellectual leaders. This is clear enough in Davie's latest book, *The Crisis of the Democratic Intellect* (1986), in which he aligns himself with the academic conservatives who inveighed against the rather modest university expansion of the 1920s.[7]

Here again, we are perhaps dealing with the secularisation of what had once been a religious ideal. For the clergy, no longer the country's cultural leaders, Davie would substitute a secular clerisy, trained in the traditions of Scottish philosophy, organically connected with Scottish society, and independent of metropolitan, Oxbridge values. This elite would provide Scotland with intellectual leadership, putting the head back on the Scottish body, and restoring the unity of the nation's culture. It is hardly surprising that this vision has inspired many nationalist intellectuals, and that Davie has become a cult figure for the group associated with the magazines *Cencrastus* and *Edinburgh Review*. The latest product of this school is the book *The Eclipse of Scottish Culture* by Craig Beveridge and Ronald Turnbull (1989), which argues that a continuous tradition of Scottish philosophy can still be identified in the twentieth century, and draws the logical conclusion from Davie that:

> the most important step towards the re-assertion of the Scottish intellectual tradition in our educational system would be the reinstatement of philosophy as a central study. This could be achieved by the establishment at the later secondary stage of a '*classe de philosophie*' which would serve to introduce pupils to the world of theory and ideas.[8]

This suggestion about secondary education is an interesting one — and accepts the fact that to restore compulsory philosophy in higher education today would be almost as quixotic an enterprise as restoring compulsory Greek.

The third historical aspect of Scottish universities is their democratic social role. The facts here are familiar enough: however much idealisation there may have been of the 'lad of parts', it remains true that in the eighteenth and nineteenth centuries Scotland had an unusually high ratio of university places to population, that access was comparatively easy in terms of finance and preliminary qualifications, and that what the universities offered was flexible and utilitarian. Until the 1890s there was no entrance examination, and students came at widely differing ages, often stayed for short periods without graduating, and could study on a part-time or intermittent basis. The negative side of this was the impersonal lecture-factory aspect of the universities, their absence of a developed community life. But Scottish opinion was rightly proud of what in the nineteenth century was called the 'popular character' of the universities, their openness to talent rather than privilege.

Even today, the proportion of the age-group participating in higher education, at 21%, is significantly higher than in England, where it is about 15%. But this Scottish achievement is less impressive by international standards, the western European norm being 30% or more. Moreover, social inequalities are still strong, as can be seen from the following table, showing the percentages in 1981–2 who left school with the qualification needed for entry to higher education, three Higher passes:

		Men	Women
Social class	I	61	58
	II	39	44
	III non-manual	26	34
	III manual	12	14
	IV	9	14
	V	5	5
All classes		19	22

The relation of these social classes to population means that in broad terms 'middle-class' children are four or five times more likely to reach higher education than 'working-class' ones.[9] The figures show that the real roots of inequality lie in the schools and in family background, and that democracy still has some way to go; but one can also derive some encouragement from them, for if 60% can qualify for higher education in one class, so they could in all others if motivation, cultural conditions and the quality of schooling could be improved.

In a historical perspective, the problem facing higher education at the end of the twentieth century is the transition from an elite to a mass system. In most continental countries, this has occurred through the retention of open entry to universities for all those completing secondary education. In the past, entry was automatically limited by the elite character of secondary schools and the limited range of occupations to which universities led; relaxation of these restraints caused massive expansion, creating many problems. Britain chose an alternative path, introducing selective entry to universities and preserving such elite (and expensive) features of the system as student residence, pastoral care and tutorial teaching. It could be argued that these were specifically English features, that the old Scottish system was potentially better adapted to an age of mass higher education, and that expansion was frustrated by the imposition of English patterns of selection in the 1950s and 1960s — but such an argument would have to ignore the many elitist aspects of the Scottish tradition itself.

What guidance, then, might a Scottish parliament derive from tradition in devising its higher education strategy? One possible answer is: very little. Traditions, by definition, are inherited from the past, and past experience may not be much use in a rapidly changing world. Although the Scots cherish the educational differences between themselves and the English, to outsiders these differences probably seem far less significant than the features which distinguish the British system as a whole. We live, after all, in an age of European and international harmonisation, in which professional, technical and managerial labour is highly mobile, and qualifications are becoming standardised. Fifty years ago, most Scottish graduates worked in professions with a Scottish cultural identity, or for firms with their managerial control in Scotland. This is no longer so, and for most employers a degree is a degree wherever it comes from. In the world of 1992 and after, can talk of a distinct Scottish elite be more than a sentimental or romantic fantasy? The days when a professor could influence a whole generation of students, sending them away to their schoolhouses and manses to spread the cultural gospel, have disappeared irrevocably; and even if the universities succeeded in turning out a Scottish-minded literary intelligentsia, what purchase would it have in a world where the decisions are taken by graduates in science, technology or business studies?

Moreover, however much nationalist theorists might like the Scottish universities to be stuffed with Scottish students, the students themselves, and their parents, may not agree. In the University of Wales, fewer than a third of the students are Welsh, and most Welsh school-leavers look to study outside the Principality. Here the proportion of Scottish students is still 65%, but there is no guarantee that this can be held, as the habit of going away from home, still comparatively new in Scotland, becomes more entrenched.

A further difficulty is this: to maintain the Scottish character of universities means not only keeping them different from English ones, but also keeping them more like each other, and restraining divergent enthusiasms. And this now means not only the eight universities — including the technological ones with their own traditions — but the whole of higher education. The rise of the colleges is one of the silent revolutions of recent years, for although the term 'binary' has generally been avoided, Scotland has followed the English path of diverting expansion into cheaper and less prestigious institutions. Official statistics for 'higher education' cover central institutions, local authority colleges, and the art and teacher-training colleges whose survival as 'monotechnic' institutions is another recent difference from England. They show that while universities still have a majority of full-time students (58%), if part-timers are included their share drops to 44%. Since most of the non-Scottish students in Scotland are in the universities, only 38% of Scottish school-leavers who go into higher education now go to universities. Or to put it another way, while 21 of 100 young Scots go on to higher education, only 9 of the 100 go to a university. And since government policy has held back university numbers, while both college places and the number of school leavers qualifying for entry have expanded, getting into a university is now more difficult than it was ten years ago.[10]

Moreover, it is the colleges, and the Open University, which have in many ways taken over the 'popular' side of the university tradition: they are more accessible to adults and non-traditional entrants, more likely to offer non-specialised degrees and part-time or modular study, more in touch with adult and continuing education. The universities are now making serious efforts in the same direction, but they have come late to the task, and it is still not easy, for example, to take a university degree on a part-time basis. At a time when demographic change is drying up the supply of traditional school-leaver entrants, there is a danger that the universities may be marginalised, and lose both popular and political support, if they seem to be cutting themselves off from their Scottish roots.

One urgent task, therefore, if the universities are 'repatriated' to Scottish control, is to determine their relation to the rest of higher education. A higher education strategy would be faced with difficult decisions about the distribution of functions within the system, the balance of teaching and research, and where expansion should be directed. Should universities expand pro rata, or retain a kind of elite role within the system? Is there any reason to deny the name 'university' to the leading colleges? What principles should underlie the division of subjects and the balance of general and vocational education? Should the universities seek to return to their popular character, or leave that form of public obligation to the colleges? How should academic autonomy be guaranteed? And, not least, there is the question of student finance, where Scottish tradition gives no clear guidance — universities in the past were relatively cheap, but lads of parts were expected to make sacrifices to attend them. Whatever the relative virtues of loans and grants, the current system does not give universities any incentives to widen their social base, while they can add substantially to their income by taking wealthy students from America or the Far East. If anything like the effort now put into overseas recruitment was devoted to the 85–95% of working-class school leavers who never see the inside of a university, the results might be dramatic. Here certainly there is an agenda for a Scottish parliament, which might well consider, for example, that the most cost-effective way of reducing inequalities of access was through maintenance allowances for pupils staying on at school beyond sixteen.

Finally, there is the question of the curriculum. Can it realistically retain any Scottish features? The arts degrees which are the focus of Davie's thesis are today only a small part of the spectrum of higher education. Yet in some ways general education becomes more rather than less relevant in an age of mass higher education. It is worth remembering that the Robbins Report, which was contemporary with Davie's *Democratic Intellect* and perhaps influenced by it, thought that expansion would require a move away from specialisation towards more general and interdisciplinary degrees. But this has not happened, at least in the universities, which have been protected by buoyant demand and by their privileged status in the binary system from having to reconsider the specialised Honours degree. Its prestige has indeed increased, and this has worked back to the schools through the progressive abandonment of subject breadth in university entry requirements. It has recently become fashionable, even south of the Border, to deplore over-specialisation in secondary schools, but this perception has not yet been extended to universities — just as many academics applaud the introduction of the national curriculum in schools, but would be horrified to see their own freedom constrained in the same way.

Although it is true that Scottish education remains less specialised than English, the merits of the Scottish system are sometimes oversold. One often reads that Scottish school students take five subjects in Highers spanning arts and science disciplines. And so they do — some of them. But while 36% of school leavers have at least one Higher, only 12% have five or more. Passes cluster around the basic subjects of English, mathematics and science, but numbers in other subjects like modern languages are much lower, and there remain significant gender differences in subject choice.[11] In the same way, Scots like to boast that their Ordinary degree gives a broad, general education; but it is now taken by only a minority in the arts faculties (about a third, compared with two-thirds at the time of Robbins), and those mostly because they have been excluded against their will from an Honours degree. The Ordinary degree has become something of a sham, as these weaker students are forced to take a wide spread of subjects, which may indeed include compulsory philosophy, while no such obligation is placed on the Honours students, whose four-year syllabus would allow more room for it. Indeed, one may question whether the universities make the best use of the opportunities presented by the four-year degree. Certainly, it allows wider study in earlier years, and Scottish universities have many joint as well as single-subject degrees. But there have been fewer experiments with true interdisciplinary degrees than in some of the new English universities, and it is doubtful whether Scottish graduates have any special intellectual identity as a result of their longer period of study.

In defence of the four-year degree, the universities have relied heavily on the argument that it is required by the one-year Higher course. But with the appointment of the Howie committee, Highers themselves are now in the melting pot, and it would be unfortunate if the universities' reaction to reform were dictated only by a defence of their own interests. There are powerful arguments against extending Highers to two years, notably the open-ended character of the present post-16 curriculum, and the encouragement to wider access given by a relatively low entry barrier. But on the other side of the argument is the possibility of strengthening the general education on which later specialisation should be based. After all, the 1858 tripartite scheme of languages, philosophy and science is not a bad model for a national curriculum for the last two years of secondary education, if suitably reinterpreted in terms of modern subjects. Both the International Baccalaureate and the various recent proposals for the reform of English A-levels provide models for this type of broad curriculum.

The fact that the reform of Highers is being considered quite apart from university policy illustrates the weakness of the present division of control. For many new possibilities would be opened up if the concept of a single point of transition between secondary and higher education gave way to a more integrated and flexible approach, in which students would come into higher education at the level appropriate to their previous qualifications, rather than, as at present, starting on the same level and diverging later into three or four-year courses. In a 'one-plus-three' arrangement, for example, students with two-year Highers or their English equivalent might enter a year ahead of those with one-year Highers (if that entry path was retained after reform), those with non-traditional qualifications, or those seeking to convert to new subjects. At the other end of the system, an undergraduate degree taken at a relatively early stage might be complemented by an optional but widely taken MA. Such possibilities, which have clear precedents in Scotland, and which are closer to both continental and American practice, are very difficult to envisage when the Scottish educational system cannot be planned as a whole. But if it could, Scottish universities might well take the initiative in devising a degree structure which was nationally distinctive and more progressive than the English pattern, and which might prove surprisingly attractive to students and employers.

To sum up: if tradition means anything — and 500 years of it ought surely to provide a sufficient basis for confident self-assertion — universities should now be seeking to act collectively to maintain their identity as a national system, to reinterpret their democratic role and their tradition of general education in a creative response to the needs of the next century, and to define their relationship with other institutions in an age of mass higher education. If any of these things are being considered, it is very imperfectly, and with little impact on public opinion. As a first step, the universities, preferably in conjunction with the rest of higher education, ought surely to set up a powerful representative forum to replace the defunct STEAC and to initiate the public debate which the emasculated Scottish committee of the Universities Funding Council has refused to engage in. Otherwise there is a danger of being overtaken by events. At present the political situation in Scotland is frozen in the pattern of 1979, but when the ice melts the stream may move very rapidly. My fear is that the universities will still be producing elegant arguments against devolution when it is becoming a reality, and may find changes forced on them by unsympathetic and impatient politicians, rather than themselves guiding the direction of the stream. For the best way to avoid heavy-handed intervention in the style of the nineteenth-century commissions is a whole-hearted and imaginative responsiveness to the needs of the community in which the universities have their historic roots.

NOTES

1. T. Chalmers, 'On the use and abuse of literary and ecclasiastical endowments' (1827), reprinted in *Church and College Establishments* (Edinburgh, 1848).

2. W. Brown, *The Scientific Character of the Scottish Universities, Viewed in Connection with Religious Belief and their Educational Use* (Edinburgh, 1856), 32, 38–41.

3. J. Donaldson, *Addresses Delivered in the University of St. Andrews from 1886 to 1910* (Edinburgh, 1911), 501. The other episodes are described in R. D. Anderson, *Education and Opportunity in Victorian Scotland: Schools and Universities* (Oxford, 1983).

4. Scottish Centre for Economic and Social Research, *Scottish Education: a Declaration of Principles* (Edinburgh, 1989), 15.

5. J. D. Hargreaves with A. Forbes (eds), *Aberdeen University 1945–1981: Regional Roles and National Needs* (Aberdeen, 1989).

6. *Report . . . by a Royal Commission of Inquiry into the State of the Universities of Scotland* (Parliamentary Papers, 1831, XII), General Report, 12.

7. See R. Anderson, 'Democracy and intellect', *Cencrastus*, no. 25 (1987), 3–4.

8. C. Beveridge and R. Turnbull, *The Eclipse of Scottish Culture: Inferiorism and the Intellectuals* (Edinburgh, 1989), 89–90.

9. *Future Strategy for Higher Education in Scotland: Report of the Scottish Tertiary Education Advisory Council on its Review of Higher Education in Scotland* (Cmnd. 9676, Edinburgh, 1985), 28. The higher school-leaving qualifications gained by women are a consistent feature of recent experience.

10. Scottish Education Department, *Statistical Bulletin No. 12/J2/1990: Scottish Higher Education Statistics*, Tables 1, 10B, 15 (figures for 1988–9).

11. For example, 23% of the women with Highers have a pass in a modern language, but only 10% of the men. Scottish Education Department, *Statistical Bulletin No. 11/E4/1990: School Leavers' Higher Grade Qualifications*, Tables 4A, 10B (figures for 1987–8).

Part II
Professional Training:
Opportunity and Social Mobility
in Scotland

7

Edinburgh and Philadelphia: the Scottish Model of Medical Education

Deborah Brunton

The pre-eminent position of the Edinburgh Medical Schools in eighteenth century medical education has long been recognised and celebrated. Although recent studies of medical training have tended to ignore the university medical schools and concentrate on the flourishing world of private teaching in London and the development of surgical training, it is still fair to say that the Edinburgh Medical School dominated medical education in the second half of the century. It held a position among the first rank of medical schools in Europe. Under such luminaries as Alexander Monro, William Cullen and Joseph Black, Edinburgh became an acknowledged centre of new ideas, where lecturers expounded new theories of disease. It was also one of the largest schools, with a faculty of seven professors and a huge student body. Courses in anatomy, chemistry and the practice of medicine regularly attracted audiences of two to three hundred listeners. Consequently, by the end of the century the British medical profession was dominated by Edinburgh-trained practitioners; they accounted for around half of all physicians, and a significant proportion of army and navy surgeons.[1]

These facts are well known. However, Edinburgh's influence outside the British Isles has received little scholarly attention. Historians have long noted the small numbers of foreign students at Edinburgh, mainly from the American colonies, and assumed that on their return to their native countries they spread Scottish medical ideas through their individual practice. They have not realised that new medical schools set up in mainland America reflected the Scottish training of their founders. The schools at Yale, Columbia, and particularly the University of Pennsylvania were consciously modelled on Edinburgh, and successfully transferred its distinctive ideas, teaching methods and organisation across the Atlantic.[2]

The initiative to found a medical school in Philadelphia came from two Edinburgh students; William Shippen and John Morgan. In many ways, Morgan and Shippen were typical of the American students who studied medicine in Europe. Both had already undergone a substantial medical training, serving apprenticeships with distinguished American practitioners; Morgan had actually practised for some years as an army surgeon before crossing the Atlantic. In Europe they sampled the best available teaching; both spent some time in London, enrolling at William Hunter's school and walking the wards of the large hospitals. Shippen spent one year in Edinburgh and Morgan attended for two years, taking several courses to prepare for the sequence of written and oral examinations for the MD degree.[3]

Initially Morgan and Shippen seem to have planned to found a private medical school, similar to that of William Hunter. After Shippen graduated in 1761 he returned to Philadelphia and began to teach anatomy, surgery and midwifery at his father's house. He also gave lectures using a fine set of anatomical drawings of the gravid uterus, housed in the Pennsylvania Hospital.

This initial scheme for medical teaching was never carried out. While Shippen was teaching, Morgan remained in Europe pursuing his studies. At some point, his ideas for medical education in America underwent a fundamental change. Instead of a private school, he began to plan a school modelled closely on that of Edinburgh. Like the Scottish school, it would be attached to a larger institution — the College of Philadelphia, a liberal arts school established in 1749, where Morgan himself had graduated. Without consulting Shippen, Morgan began to exercise his considerable talents to raise support for his schemes. By the time he sailed for home in 1765, he had the acknowledged support of Thomas Penn, the proprietor of Pennsylvania, and two members of the College's board of trustees. In addition, he carried letters of goodwill from two eminent London practitioners, John Fothergill and William Watson, and his two most famous teachers, William Hunter and William Cullen. Confronted with such authoritative support, the College trustees promptly accepted his proposals and appointed Morgan as professor of the theory and practice of physic.[4]

Although there are no records of the plans Morgan laid before the College, their substance is contained in a long speech given at the College commencement the following day, and subsequently published as *A Discourse upon the Institution of Medical Schools in America*. This document makes clear Morgan's debt to Edinburgh. The Scottish school had a dual role. Firstly, as one of the most distinguished centres of medical training in Europe, it was an obvious model for the actual teaching at Philadelphia. In describing the ideal form of medical education, Morgan suggested a curriculum of anatomy, botany, chemistry, theory of medicine, practice of medicine, materia medica and a course of clinical lectures: exactly the broad range of courses offered in Edinburgh. He hoped that the new school could eventually offer such a curriculum, 'conformable to that which is followed at the, so justly celebrated, school of physic at Edinburgh'.[5] He also suggested students should follow a plan of study beginning with anatomy, botany and chemistry, which provided a grounding in the structure and function of the body and its fluids, before tackling the more complex theory and practice of medicine — a programme not unlike that frequently adopted by Edinburgh students.

Morgan also exploited the success of the Edinburgh school as a means of winning support for his plans. On his return to Philadelphia, Morgan had no position and little prestige in the city. His explicit criticism of American standards of medical education — and therefore of the training and qualifications of nearly all Philadelphia's practitioners — aroused considerable hostility within the medical community.[6] In the *Discourse* Morgan appealed to the civic pride of its citizens, by presenting an attractive picture of the benefits brought to Edinburgh by its flourishing medical school. There, the original staff, 'with countenance and support from the patrons of the university, and by the great abilities, assiduity and experience of those gentlemen . . . the reputation of that place is raised to such a height, that to their immortal honor, it already rivals if not surpasses that of every other school of Physic in Europe.'[7] Given similar 'countenance and support', Morgan suggested, a school could bring similar pecuniary benefits; students residing in the city would spend considerable sums of money while studying.[8] In addition, the city would enjoy prestige and deference due to a centre of learning:

> The resort of strangers to any city for the cultivation of science must give it proportionably a pre-eminence over others. An education in any place begets that place an interest, and as it were naturalizes strangers to it. In return for a dispensation of knowledge, it collects a tribute of riches as well as of affection from all quarters.[9]

Perhaps the citizens of Philadelphia were beguiled by these rosy prospects. Certainly Morgan succeeded in implementing his ambitious proposals. The school's curriculum was set in place just as Morgan had hoped. From the outset, the school offered classes in all the subjects outlined in the *Discourse*, even though it had only three teachers. In addition to the theory and practice of medicine, which he was appointed to teach, Morgan gave short courses in chemistry and materia medica. Shippen continued to give his courses in anatomy and surgery while Thomas Bond, a prominent Philadelphia practitioner, gave clinical lectures at the Pennsylvania Hospital.[10] Morgan's teaching load was eased in 1768, when Adam Kuhn returned from studies in Europe — including periods with the great botanist Linnaeus as well as in Edinburgh — and was appointed professor of botany and materia medica. The small faculty was completed a year later with the election of Benjamin Rush to the chair of chemistry. Rush was groomed by Morgan for the post. Rush had been one of his first students, before travelling to Edinburgh, where he took Joseph Black's course twice. He returned confident of the appointment, bringing with him a set of demonstration apparatus.[11]

Edinburgh also provided the model for the structure and content of individual courses. In mid-century, the teachers there had pioneered a new system of teaching. Instead of giving Latin commentaries on medical authorities — either directly on classical texts or more modern syntheses, such of that of Boerhaave — lecturers gave a systematic and comprehensive exposition of their particular subjects. The courses were 'synthetic', moving from general principles to specific instances and problems, a form which had already been developed in Scottish philosophy courses. Thus chemistry courses began with a description of chemical principles, which were then used to describe and classify substances. In medical courses, the basic theory of physiology and pathology provided a frame of reference with which to classify and describe diseases, and to suggest forms of treatment.

Philadelphia's young faculty, perhaps, did not make a deliberate decision to follow this form of teaching; all had trained in Edinburgh, and when they took up their appointments, they relied heavily on the lecture notes they had taken at Edinburgh. Consequently their lectures adhered closely — and sometimes slavishly — to the form and content of the courses taught at Edinburgh. In his first years, Benjamin Rush seems to have simply read his lectures from notes taken in Joseph Black's classes. In later years, as he and his colleagues developed their courses, they gradually moved away from those of their Scottish counterparts, although they retained the synthetic form.[12]

In the *Discourse* Morgan had given no indication of the medical school's status within or its relations with the College of Philadelphia, but here too the new American school closely resembled that of Edinburgh. There, the medical faculty had a peculiar semi-autonomous existence, its professoriate enjoying a high degree of independence. Lecturers functioned almost as private teachers. Most received no salary from the university, but drew their income from class fees. The content and form of courses, and the standard of knowledge required to pass examinations was left to the professors' discretion.[13] Their students, too, had an unusual degree of freedom. They could take as many or as few classes as they wished, and the majority attended the school with no intentions of taking a degree. In mid century, those who wished to become candidates for the MD simply enrolled in as many courses as they felt necessary, then presented themselves for examination; thereafter, the university began to set degree requirements, specifying the number of courses and period of study.

Although this administrative structure was not specified by Morgan's *Discourse*, the Edinburgh system was replicated in Philadelphia with clear benefits to all parties. For the faculty — all of whom were young and did not have the financial security of an established medical practice, teaching brought in a welcome — and eventually a substantial — income. The connection to the College gave their teaching immediate intellectual respectability, and the right to grant degrees. In turn, the College benefited from the matriculation, library and graduation fees of the medical students, and rent paid by the professors for the use of College classrooms.

The Edinburgh style of medical education proved highly successful in America. There are no records of student numbers from Philadelphia for the eighteenth century, but the school graduated up to ten students a year through the 1770s and 1780s, which suggests a student population of anything up to a hundred. After the hiatus caused by the Revolutionary Wars — from which the medical faculty and its professoriate emerged more or less unscathed and attached to the new University of Pennsylvania — the school flourished. The number of graduations rose dramatically around the turn of the century, and in 1810 over four hundred students matriculated in the school.[14]

The success of the Scottish model of medical education was based on its broad appeal. Both the Edinburgh and the Philadelphia schools were able to exploit a similar marketplace for medical education. Edinburgh had always served a traditional audience of students who wished to take a medical degree and practice as physicians. But, as the medical profession greatly expanded in the second half of the century, the old patterns of education with the divisions between apprentice-trained and university-educated practitioners began to break down. From the earliest years, the Edinburgh school had offered a training which was not simply the preserve of the elite. Increasingly, apprentices finished their practical training by attending lectures. In America, these divisions of training and practice had never existed; the vast majority of medical men trained though an apprenticeship and acted as general practitioners. They worked alongside the few who were able to raise the substantial sums required to go abroad and take a degree, and who were informally recognised as an elite — although they took on the same range of cases.

The Edinburgh and Philadelphia medical schools attracted a remarkably similar pool of students. Relatively few students who attended the schools intended to graduate; in Edinburgh that was around ten per cent of those who matriculated.[15] Graduates probably made up about the same percentage in Philadelphia. Although they were a small potential audience, Morgan took great pains over the degree — in an attempt to fulfil his own plans to found a College of Physicians to regulate practice in America. He was concerned that the Philadelphia degree should stand comparison with those of the older institutions in Europe and, like those from Edinburgh, be 'a real mark of Honor, the reward only of distinguished learning and abilities'.[16] It was reflected in his concern that the school should, from the outset, provide teaching in a range of subjects. In 1767, only two years after the school's founding, and at a time when it boasted only three teachers, Morgan and the trustees framed a set of formal degree requirements. Recognising that the standard of teaching was not equal to European standards, the College offered the degree of Bachelor of Medicine, for which candidates had to attend all the school's courses, attend the Pennsylvania Hospital for a year, then undergo a series of written and oral examinations. Perhaps recognising that this formal education was no preparation for practice or, more likely, to mollify the resentment of the medical community at Morgan's seizing control of medical education, the College also required its students to serve a proper apprenticeship. For the MD, students had then to practise medicine for two years and return to present their theses.[17]

However, in the American school, as in its Scottish counterpart, students were under no obligation to take a degree; they were free to take as many courses as they wished. Consequently, most were apprentices, completing their training by attending a few classes — anatomy, chemistry and the practice of medicine being the most popular choices in Edinburgh. Judging by the numbers of extant sets of lecture notes, these courses also drew large audiences in Philadelphia.

The key to this broad appeal was not simply that apprentices had easy access to courses, but also in the structure and content of the lectures. All lecture courses had the strong theoretical underpinning which characterised earlier university teaching. Humoural and nervous theories of disease provided a basic framework to explain the appearance and progress of diseases, and to rationalise therapeutic approaches. However, the lectures also had a more practical theme; those in the practice of medicine set out comprehensively to describe the symptoms of illnesses, their prognosis and proper treatment. Their value is testified by the large number of carefully preserved and indexed sets of notes, which clearly served as textbooks or *aide memoires* during years of medical practice.[18]

Over time the close links between Edinburgh and Philadelphia gradually dissolved. In the nineteenth century, the Scottish school lost its intellectual leadership, and Americans increasingly chose to study in London or Paris, bringing back new ideas with an increasing emphasis on surgery. But these too were integrated within the flexible framework of the school — new chairs and new subjects were added to the curriculum, and new degree requirements set, but the basic features of the Scottish model remained; the broad curriculum, the students' freedom to take as many or as few courses as they wished (although at both Edinburgh and Philadelphia, an increasing proportion of students chose to take the MD degree) and the odd, semi-autonomous status of the medical school within the broader institution.

NOTES

1. J. B. Morrell, 'The University of Edinburgh in the late eighteenth century: its scientific eminence and academic structure', *Isis*, 62 (1971), 165; Joan Lane, 'The medical practitioners of provincial England in 1783', *Medical History*, 28 (1984) 366.

2. A longer and more detailed study of the creation of the Philadelphia school and its links to Edinburgh can be found in Deborah C Brunton, 'The transfer of medical education; teaching at the Edinburgh and Philadelphia Medical Schools' in Richard B. Sher and Jeffrey Smitten, (eds), *Scotland and America in the Age of the Enlightenment* (Edinburgh, 1990), 242–58.

3. Whitfield J. Bell, Jr, *John Morgan*, 46–99; Betsy Copping Corner, *William Shippen, Jr, Pioneer in American Medical Education* (Philadelphia, 1951), 11–34, 65–73, 90–93.

4. Joseph Carson, *A History of the Medical Department of the University of Pennsylvania* (Philadelphia, 1869), 40–43.

5. John Morgan, *A Discourse upon the Institution of Medical Schools in America* (Philadelphia, 1765), 36.

6. The published version of the *Discourse* included a long defence of his arguments for dividing medical practice between physicians, surgeons and apothecaries, as in Britain.

7. Morgan, *Discourse*, 29.

8. *Ibid.*, 29.

9. *Ibid.*, 52.

10. Carson, *History of the Medical Department*, 56.

11. *Ibid.*, 64–65, 72–75.

12. Brunton, 'Transfer of medical education', 247–49.

13. Morrell, 'The University of Edinburgh', 160–66.

14. Carson, *History of the Medical Department*, Appendix F, 218–219.

15. Lisa Rosner, *Medical Education in the Age of Improvement* (Edinburgh, 1991), 62–104.

16. Carson, *History of the Medical Department*, 61.

17. *Ibid.*, 60.

18. Christopher Lawrence, 'Ornate physicians and learned artisans: Edinburgh medical men 1726–1776' in W F Bynum and Roy Porter, *William Hunter and the Eighteenth-Century Medical World* (Cambridge, 1985), 171–73.

8

'Pulpit and Gown' — Edinburgh University and the Church, 1760–1830

Lawrence Williams

'How I pity you in Scotland, the only country in the world in which the wealthy and intelligent middle class submit to the domination of a spiritual tyranny.'[1] This was Richard Cobden's view of Scotland in 1836 as expressed in a letter to his friend George Combe. In Cobden's estimation, the Calvinist Reformation had penetrated all aspects of Scottish life and its influence remained potent in the era of the Anti-Corn Law League. This study will attempt to analyse how far Edinburgh University was subject to such a 'tyranny'.

John Knox's views on this subject were quite unequivocal and in 1572, the last year of his life, he reminded the General Assembly that they should:

> Above all things preserve the Kirk from the bondage of the Universities. Never subject the pulpit to their judgement, neither yet exempt them from your jurisdiction.[2]

Church control of the universities was seen to be justified and necessary because of the latter's vocational role as educators of the clergy and their secular partners, the parish schoolmasters.

This inter-dependence of Church and university was reinforced by the Act of Union of 1707. Scotland lost her parliament in that year but preserved intact the independence of her Church, universities and legal system. Together, these institutions had a symbolic as well as a practical role in maintaining Scotland's sense of national identity. Edinburgh might have lost its parliament but it preserved its 'capital' status in other ways. Apart from having Scotland's largest and most prestigious eighteenth-century university, Edinburgh was also the legal centre of Scotland and the place where the General Assembly met annually. Such meetings gave members of the university's divinity faculty the opportunity to play a prominent role in church debates. This also applied to the Edinburgh University principal who had the advantage of being an ex-officio member of the General Assembly — a privilege which Principal William Robertson was to use with particular effectiveness during the 1760s and 1770s.

The divinity faculty, therefore, had every reason to see itself as the university's senior faculty, and outward appearances certainly confirmed its own good opinion. Only the professor of divinity, along with the principal, had an official residence in the 'Old College' grounds. Subsequently, when the foundation stone of the 'New College' was laid in 1789, the academic procession was headed by the principal with the professor of divinity at his right hand and the professor of ecclesiastical history on his left.

The Church's real power over Edinburgh University, however, rarely matched these symbols and does not begin to compare with the power of the university's main paymaster — the Edinburgh town council. Indeed, from many standpoints, Edinburgh University constituted a largely secular environment for staff and students alike.

One striking feature of the university's eighteenth-century development was its failure to provide any facilities for the moral supervision of expanding numbers of students. The university took no responsibility for accommodating its students, who were expected to make their own arrangements and stay with relatives, with friends or in lodgings. This lack of residential colleges meant that students — often as young as fourteen — were left to their own devices outside class hours. Traditionally, the university had exercised a degree of moral and academic surveillance by attaching each year's intake of students to a single teacher who acted as 'regent' to them, supervising their studies and general progress throughout their undergraduate lives. The regent system came to an end in Edinburgh in 1708 when Principal Carstares carried out far-reaching academic reforms. In future, students would be taught by a range of specialist professors rather than by a single regent. These reforms undoubtedly laid the basis for improved academic instruction in Edinburgh, and in due course at the other Scottish universities, but this was at the expense of a system which facilitated moral paternalism.

Apart from being expected to organise their own leisure and accommodation, students also had to make their own arrangements for religious worship, given that Edinburgh — unlike the other universities in Scotland — had no chapel. When Robert Adam included a chapel in his plans for the new university buildings it was denounced by Professor Black as 'in imitation of the English and foreign colleges'[3]. Adam's chapel was removed from the plan and the 1826 University Commission was to comment upon its absence.

If chapels were seen as foreign institutions in Edinburgh, it remains to be examined how far native presbyterian influences otherwise made themselves felt at Edinburgh University. The principalship of William Robertson provided an ideal opportunity for these influences to bear fruit. Robertson was principal from 1762 until 1790, and until 1780 he was also the leader of the dominant 'Moderate' party within the Church of Scotland and moderator of the General Assembly between 1766 and 1780. However, Robertson used his position and political skills to promote harmony between church, university and town council rather than to assert the church's claims in particular. His sermons were ethical and undoctrinal, and his scholarly pursuits were historical rather than theological. As principal, he was concerned to enhance Edinburgh

University's reputation as a centre of teaching and scholarship and worked closely with the town council to this end.

There was a mutual recognition that the long-term interests of city and university were interdependent. Distinguished professors would attract students, and hence trade, to Edinburgh; civic pride also dictated that the city should have a university worthy of its 'capital' status. Hence, the criteria for making professorial appointments were secular rather than religious and there is no evidence that Robertson's 'Moderate' colleagues dissented from this viewpoint. According to Richard Sher:

> In no country were the principles of the Englightenment so deeply rooted in the universities or so openly and enthusiastically espoused by the leaders of the established church. No where else do clergymen and professors make up such a large proportion of the men of letters or produce so many works of polite literature.[4]

It is significant that Sher makes no reference to theology, which was the one field of study where Edinburgh University produced no work of major importance during this period. Robertson's most highly regarded work was a biography of the Emperor Charles V whilst his prominent Moderate ally, Hugh Blair, was a professor of rhetoric and not theology.

In many respects, Robertson and his fellow moderates within the university and the General Assembly of the Church of Scotland took a remarkably detached and critical view of the Reformation which had produced their church. They were inclined to see all religious creeds, including their own Westminster Confession, as flawed products of an age less enlightened than their own. This capacity for tolerating other faiths and seeing imperfections in their own was manifested in the history lectures delivered by Professor Alexander Tytler between 1798 and 1800.[5] In his survey of religious history, Tytler described the *Koran* as being 'full of fine conceptions'. When he reached the Reformation, Tytler understandably devoted a lot of attention to it but was strikingly critical of its leaders. For example, he contended that 'neither Calvin nor Luther assumed the character of divine inspiration, which it is as well they did not, for their vices and follies would have shown the falsity of the pretence'. Even John Knox did not emerge unscathed from Tytler's lectures: 'He was a man of great virtue, well meaning and eloquent, but his maxims were severe and his impetuous temper often led him wrong.' Turning to sixteenth-century catholicism, Tytler described Queen Mary of England as 'a cruel monster', but the monasteries were discussed with some affection and their destruction by Henry VIII was deplored: 'It was a pity more moderation was not used which might have preserved to us those ancient and beautiful gothic buildings and the treasures of learning which were destroyed with them.' There is no evidence that anyone in either church or university looked askance at Tytler's interpretations.

This broadmindedness was also manifested in the university's attitude towards both staff and students. In theory, all professors were required to sign the Confession of Faith of the Church of Scotland but this practice had fallen into disuse in Edinburgh. Between 1758 and 1826 only one professor there signed the Confession of Faith and this was in line with Robertson's policy of not putting unnecessary barriers in the way of recruiting the best minds available. The university, admittedly, drew the line at accepting David Hume for a chair, but in every other respect Hume, for all his scepticism, was 'accepted' and mixed freely in the circles of the Edinburgh Moderate intelligentsia.

The university's tolerant approach also paid dividends in terms of its student intake. Student admissions were boosted during the later part of the eighteenth century by significant numbers of nonconformist and Roman Catholic entrants from England and Ireland. These students were attracted by the university's academic reputation but also by its religious liberality, in marked contrast to Oxford and Cambridge with their Test Acts. Catholics were particularly appreciative of this liberal admissions policy during the Napoleonic War years,when continental colleges were closed to them.

Students were drawn to Edinburgh by the fame of its teaching and scholarship in the arts and medical faculties. In comparison divinity, for all its seniority, was less highly regarded. The reasons for this are not hard to find. In the first place, divinity students were usually part-time — often very part-time. Until 1826, they were only required to attend 'occasionally' over a six-year period. Such students might stay just long enough to matriculate before going home, although this would not suffice every year because of the need to complete certain prescribed exercises in order to qualify for a class certificate. However, the fact remains that a divinity student would not expect to encounter a rigorous examination until he applied for a vacant ministerial post and had to undergo trials before the appropriate presbytery.

In the earlier nineteenth century, presbyteries could certainly afford to be selective when considering such applications; then an average year would provide about thirty ministerial vacancies throughout Scotland in comparison to about five times as many qualified divinity students. Matriculated divinity students were often employed contemporaneously as school teachers, thereby having a modest but assured income during their period of training. Teaching also provided a longer-term career for many students unsuccessful in their pursuit of a church living. In this event, a student's secular education, notably in Latin, would have a far greater vocational relevance than anything taught by the divinity faculty.

Presbyteries were expected to investigate proficiency in classical languages when interviewing aspiring ministers. However, the secular subject held in highest regard by the church was moral philosophy. Most contemporary Scottish moral philosophers belonged to the 'common sense' school whose writings and teachings set out to combat Hume's scepticism by providing a rational basis for belief, and a code of ethics to live by. Understandably, therefore, moral philosophy — when it was in the hands of famous teachers such as Professor Dugald Stewart — was seen as an essential pre-requisite for theological studies. In 1801 the Edinburgh senatus authorised the divinity faculty to refuse admittance to any student who had not completed three full sessions embracing logic, moral philosophy and natural philosophy.[6] In 1803, all the Scottish universities were warned by Dr Archibald Davidson, the principal of Glasgow University, that any attempt to reduce their philosophy requirement from three years to two would be 'materially hurtful to the education of the clergy of the Church of Scotland'.[7]

This warning suggests a perceived threat to the status of philosophy. A further challenge came in 1830 when the lawyers and landowners, who formed the bulk of the university commission set up in 1826, argued for a more substantial role for classics in the arts curriculum. Significantly it was left to two clerical members of the commission, George Cook and Thomas Taylor, to defend the superiority of philosophy 'for the cultivation of the intellectual and reasoning powers'.[8]

Although moral philosophy was of prime importance, the Church also esteemed the study of natural philosophy. For instance, in 1791 thirteen prospective students were only allowed to enter the divinity faculty on condition that they remedied their lack of natural philosophy by attending its classes side by side with their divinity courses.[9]

There were also opportunities for prospective and actual divinity students to study a broader range of scientific subjects whilst at Edinburgh University. A reading of the parish surveys written by Church of Scotland ministers for the *Statistical Account* of the 1790s and the later *New Statistical Account* suggests that these scientific interests were long-lasting; some of the longer surveys devoted many pages to local geology or botany. In some cases, indeed, they occupy far more space in the parochial reports than do church-related matters.

In general, presbyteries in this period saw little conflict between science and religion, whilst scientists, for their part, often showed a full awareness of the divine relevance of their subject. Professor Robison maintained that his natural philosophy students 'should not only learn the laws of nature but should also perceive that these laws are beautiful marks of wisdom prompted by beneficence'.[10] Looked at in this light, geological evidence — including fossils — was a further indication of the complexity and fullness of God's creation, rather than a trigger for religious doubts. Certainly, there is no evidence that the Established Church was officially concerned about the explosion of geological interest in late eighteenth-century Edinburgh, associated with the long-running debate between the Huttonian and Wernerian schools of thought.

A broad secular education was also deemed to have a social importance for the prospective minister. The Church Moderates accepted the patronage system and, hence, the need for clergy and landowners to have a good mutual understanding. John Witherspoon, writing in the 1770s, maintained that 'a clergyman should be a man of liberal knowledge and fit for the conversation and society of men of rank and letters.'[11] Sir Walter Scott, writing a generation later in 1816, expressed similar sentiments. Scott believed that literary talent in a clergyman was 'always graceful, becoming and suited to his character, and in general by attracting attention and patronage they secure advancement'.[12]

The Church of Scotland's accommodating approach to the patronage system was in line with its overall desire to avoid controversy in matters of university government. At the same time, this consensus depended upon the Moderates retaining control of the General Assembly and, by the 1790s, there is every indication that this control was being challenged. The rising Evangelical party within the Church of Scotland was questioning a number of Moderate premises whilst, in a less specific sense, the Romantic movement was reacting against the Enlightenment's secularism and pursuit of reason. At the same time, with the passing of Robertson's generation, the Moderate party's leadership lacked the intellectual distinction and political skills of their predecessors. They had become more patently the servants of the Dundas Tory party in Scotland and shared its fear of change in the shadow of the French Revolution.

The growing rivalry between Moderates and Evangelicals by the end of the century opened up issues which had remained, more or less, dormant in William Robertson's time. There were two issues which concerned Edinburgh University in particular: the nature of instruction in divinity and the question of pluralities. The Moderates, for their part, cited the Scottish democratic tradition in support of the status quo. They argued that it was vitally important for the cost of studying divinity to be kept to a minimum if the poor 'lad o' pairts' was to enjoy his birthright of access to the ministry. Full-time attendances on divinity studies at university would prevent such a person earning his livelihood at the same time and, since the traditional livelihood of divinity students was parish school teaching, that in turn would be disrupted.

The debate over pluralities raised wider issues and was contested with great vigour. The Evangelicals maintained that if a professor occupied a university chair and a church living, one if not both of these duties must be neglected. The Moderates argued that such pluralities were a necessary means of supplementing professorial incomes, thereby avoiding the alternative step of raising student fees. It was felt to be especially important that divinity should be studied free of charge in order to give further encouragement to the 'lad of pairts'. This absence of fee income made it, therefore, particularly important for divinity professors to retain the option of holding a church living. The Moderates also maintained that the presence of divinity professors in local presbyteries and amongst local congregations was a channel through which the university could serve the wider community.

According to Stewart Brown, the recent biographer of Thomas Chalmers, 'with the pluralities agitation the Evangelical movement in the Church of Scotland came of age'.[13] Evangelicals and Moderates had their first major public trial of strength in the 'Leslie case' of 1805.[14] John Leslie was a candidate for the vacant mathematics chair at Edinburgh University in that year. His academic credentials were excellent but in earlier scientific writings he had defended Hume's theory of causation. Leslie argued that he was writing purely as a scientist and was not seeking to endorse Hume's religious scepticism, but opinions which would have been tolerated in Robertson's day were now seen as subversive by his successors.

However, in putting forward Thomas MacKnight, of Trinity College Chapel in Edinburgh, as a rival candidate to Leslie, it soon became apparent that the Moderates were seeking to do more than oppose Leslie's candidature. They clearly wished to have a showdown with the Evangelicals on the whole question of pluralities, and to this end insisted, as a condition of their support for MacKnight, that he retain his parish ministry in the event of securing the chair. Leslie was a curious ally for an Evangelical party, but at this juncture the principle had become more important than the man. At least, Leslie was unencumbered with church responsibilities and likely to remain so. Apart from evangelical support, Leslie had the backing of leading Edinburgh professors such as Dugald Stewart and John Playfair, Playfair arguing that the successful candidate should devote all his time to teaching and research without any parochial distractions and that Edinburgh University should seek to attract the best candidates from all over Scotland and not be forced to accept the local candidate of a local clique.

Leslie was successful and even the General Assembly, by a narrow majority, approved his appointment. This victory can be seen to mark something of a watershed in the rise of the Whigs and Evangelicals in Edinburgh at the expense of the Tories and Moderates. In supporting Leslie, however, the successful evangelicals were, ironically, adopting the standards of the old-style Moderates of Robertson's generation: appointing the best candidate to the chair according to intellectual criteria.

The Evangelicals had won a battle rather than the war. However, their confidence had been boosted, and their cause soon attained further moral and intellectual credibility under the leadership of the ex-Moderate Thomas Chalmers. Chalmers combined moral and intellectual forcefulness to a high degree and by 1815 he had become the recognised leader of the Evangelical party in the General Assembly and the most frequent and eloquent contributor to its debates. In addressing the twin issues of theological education and pluralism, Chalmers believed that the way forward was through the full-time commitment of all concerned. Glasgow and Edinburgh were rapidly expanding cities and huge problems of deprivation: material, moral and spiritual. Such cities needed full-time ministers with a strong sense of vocation towards their parishioners. Likewise, if the academic status of divinity training was to be raised, students must attend its classes on a full-time basis and be taught by professors who were themselves full-time and not distracted by parochial responsibilities. Until such changes were introduced, theological education would remain 'degraded in the general estimate of men of learning . . . What could they think of the dignity of that for which so meagre a preparation was deemed sufficient'?[15] The Church of England, argued Chalmers, for all its deficiencies, at least gave its clergy a theologically superior education.

Chalmers' critics, however, drew different lessons from the English comparison; arguing that Church of England clergy were 'born to genteel society and altogether unqualified from personal experience with the character of their parishioners'.[16] According to this argument, Chalmers' urban poor would be the losers if the lad of pairts, who had known poverty, was deterred from entering the church by the financial barrier of full-time divinity education. Furthermore, in attacking pluralities, Chalmers was seeking to destroy 'the last link in the chain which bound the church and the universities together'.[17]

Chalmers and his allies in the General Assembly secured a modest victory on the pluralities issue in 1817 when it was agreed that no professor could in future hold a parish living outside the boundary of the appropriate university town.[18] The inadequate financing of some chairs, however, still constituted an impediment to full progress on this issue. In 1825, the General Assembly estimated that the office of principal and the chairs of divinity, church history and oriental philosophy were not as yet sufficiently well funded to justify debarring their occupants from also holding church livings.[19]

Two years later, the Evangelical campaign was greatly encouraged by the appointment of Chalmers to the Edinburgh University chair of divinity. Chalmers had stressed at the outset that he would regard his appointment as full-time and expect to receive an adequate stipend supported by student fees. The Edinburgh town council, in electing Chalmers, accepted the principle of full-time theological education and this decision was endorsed for Scotland as a whole by the university commission in 1830, thus 'effectively ending the practice in the Scottish Establishment'.[20]

The 1826–30 commission also gave emphatic support to Chalmers' campaign for more rigorous academic standards in the teaching and assessment of students of divinity. The commission was established in 1826 and, significantly, in the same year, the General Assembly finally took the decision to require all divinity students to attend regularly for at least one full year. Encouraged by this, the commission themselves proposed a systematic full-time teaching programme of theology, Hebrew, ecclesiastical history and biblical criticism, leading to the degree of Bachelor of Divinity.

The vigour of Chalmers should not, however, blind us to the largely secular function of the university commission. This was reflected in its membership: three churchmen out of a total of twenty-two. Also, the commission's overall conclusions as to the role of the church in university education were not encouraging for the Established Church. The commissioners recognised the contribution of presbyteries and General Assembly to the divinity faculties' work, but added that:

> In other respects, the Universities in Scotland are not ecclesiastical institutions; not being more connected with the Church than with any other profession. They are intended for the general education of the country and in truth possess scarcely any ecclesiastical features except that they have a certain number of professors for the purpose of teaching theology in the same manner as other sciences are taught.[21]

Such a conclusion would not have been congenial to John Knox but one suspects that Principal William Robertson would have recognised and accepted this description.

NOTES

1. Charles Gibbon, *The Life of George Combe* (1878), 314.

2. *Dictionary of National Biography*, XI, 325.

3. Edinburgh University Library (EUL), GEN 875/111.174–5.

4. Richard Sher, *Church and University in the Scottish Enlightenment* (Edinburgh 1985), 151.

5. EUL, DC 8, 144 and DC 6, 115.

6. EUL, Senatus Minutes, 7 Dec. 1801.

7. Ibid., 31 March 1803.

8. *Royal Commission of Inquiry into the State of the Unversities of Scotland* (PP 1831, xii), 91.

9. Scottish Record Office [SRO], Edinburgh Burgher Presbytery Minutes, CH3/111/6, 12 May 1791.

10. J. B. Morrell, 'Professors Robison and Playfair and the *Theophobia Gallica*: natural philosophy, religion and politics in Edinburgh, 1789–1815', *Notes and Records of the Royal Society of London*, 26 (1977), 43.

11. *The Works of John Witherspoon* (Edinburgh, 1804–5), viii, 26.

12. H. J. C. Grierson (ed.), *The Letters of Sir Walter Scott 1815–17* (London, 1933), 467.

13. Stewart Brown, *Thomas Chalmers and the Godly Commonwealth in Scotland* (Oxford, 1982), 88.

14. J. B. Morrell, 'The Leslie affair: careers, kirk and politics in Edinburgh in 1805', *Scottish Historical Review*, liv (1975), 63–82.

15. *Edinburgh Magazine*, June 1821, 506.

16. *Ibid.*, 507.

17. SRO, Church of Scotland General Assembly Minutes, CH1/4/25, 25 May 1825.

18. Ibid., CH1/4/22, 28 May 1817.

19. Ibid., CH1/4/25, 25 May 1825.

20. Stewart Brown, *Thomas Chalmers and the Godly Commonwealth*, 179.

21. *Royal Commission into the Universities of Scotland: Report* (PP 1831, xii), 8.

9

Privilege, Patronage and the Professions: Aberdeen and its Universities, 1760–1860

A. Allan Maclaren

This paper sets out to examine within the context of a developing capitalist economy the relationship between the Aberdeen universities and what might be termed the four graduate professions: university professors, ministers of the church, lawyers, and medical practitioners. Industrialisation wrought many changes including the creation of a highly specialised division of labour, and a heightened entrepreneurial spirit. It led to an ever-increasing competition among capitalists, which in turn produced a combination of mutual dependence and conflict between capitalist and worker. Perhaps above all the period saw the emergence of market forces as primary determinants of prices and occupational income.

Whilst the nature of the four occupations is remarkably different, they do share common features. All enjoyed some measure of protection from full exposure to market forces. Thus, for example, although one might expect a minister's stipend to bear some relationship to the wealth of a parish, generally stipends were 'fixed' and not related to whether another colleague would be willing to undertake the work of the parish for a smaller salary. To a greater or lesser extent this lack of overt economic 'competition' applied to all of the other three occupations.

Such relative freedom from market forces might be expected to allow these occupations to adopt a more generous attitude of cooperation among their own kind, rather than the competition which prevailed between capitalists, and between capitalists and workers. Cooperation might take a number of forms but would certainly include some measure of internal discipline by means of institutional controls over practising members, professional ethics and behaviour. Ultimately it might be expected to include some measure of control over recruitment to the profession involving both moral and educational criteria.

In examining these four professions it is helpful to distinguish between types of scientific knowledge. Friedson[1] classifies professions into two broad groupings — scholarly (pure knowledge) and consulting (applied knowledge). Following this classification university professors and ministers of religion could be placed in the first grouping, and lawyers and medical practitioners would fall into the category of consulting professions. Although this type of classification has certain drawbacks in terms of overlap between professions and in the uncertain distinction between scholarly and applied knowledge, the division remains a useful one.

Scholarly Professions

In this period Aberdeen had two university institutions, King's College and Marischal College. Almost an identical range of chairs existed at each. If the professoriate at King's had a tendency to sneer at Marischal, which was in terms of buildings very run-down, by the beginning of the nineteenth century Marischal College held the reputation as being the more progressive. As far as numbers were concerned King's continued to attract students to its arts and divinity classes, but law was weak, and medicine had declined to the point of virtual non-existence. There is some evidence to suggest that the content of the education provided in the two colleges may have been significantly different.[2] Nevertheless whatever the possible qualitative differences between the institutions, the two professoriates can be treated as one concerning their professional behaviour.

It is remarkable how little change there was between 1760 and 1860. Anderson has shown how professors 'tended to see their chairs as freeholds' which possessed certain rights to income, rather than viewing themselves 'as professional men or as employees, either of the state or of the university'.[3] Appointments were regarded as a form of sinecure — a property which included, among other things, the right of choosing a successor. As professors were appointed for life little could be done to ensure that they carried out their duties satisfactorily. Alexander Bannerman, appointed to the chair of medicine in 1792, was to give one lecture in the next 22 years. His son inherited the chair and continued the same tradition.[4] Father and son practised as doctors and regarded the chair as 'family' property. Records of Senate meetings abound with similar cases. It was so unusual not to wish to exercise such rights that, when one professor resigned, a formal deed had to be drawn up passing the right to Senate to 'chuse a fit person.'[5] Occasionally a limited form of market control acted against such conventions in that a professor was entitled to the fees of enrolled students but if a class historically had long ceased to attract students there was no inducement to re-commence it.[6]

In 1824 the King's College Senate, under some pressure, recommended that those concerned with the provision of lectures in divinity, law, and medicine should perform their duties, but not one of those concerned bothered to comply.[7] The practice of nominating a successor was accomplished by appointing a substitute who would undertake the work of the chair for a small salary on the basis that he would eventually inherit the full appointment. Such arrangements resembled a form of apprenticeship similar in some respects to that of medicine and law. Senate supported this practice regarding it as a rational solution to the absence of a pension fund. Indeed it was the unresolved vacancies which led to prolonged and bitter disputes as each professor sought to gain a more lucrative chair by changing disciplines. One such dispute extended over ten years involving numerous law suits.[8] Such struggles tend to demonstrate just how little credence was given to ideas of appointment by professional merit.

On rare occasions professors were prepared to make a stand on a matter of principle regarding their appointments but this was both unusual and remarkable. One well-publicised case occurred in 1839 on the appointment of John Stuart Blackie to the chair of Latin in Marischal College.[9] Blackie refused to sign the Confession of Faith 'except in his public professional capacity'. The local presbytery declared that he could not fill the chair under these conditions and another person was appointed. Blackie appealed to the Court of Session and was reinstated. Such behaviour was untypical. Generally professors were reluctant to take risks regarding their appointments. When the Disruption of the Established Church took place in 1843 those professors most inclined to support the Evangelical cause did not secede for fear of losing their appointments.[10] Overall there is little evidence of the development of any professional ethic within the professoriate which 'did not feel a need to elaborate a special ethical code, or to adopt strategies for improving their social status which was already high'.[11] Nor can either Senate be seen as acting to regulate the behaviour of its members; its role might be seen as defending its constituents' property rights. Pressure for change came from outside the profession, taking the form of a series of parliamentary commissions. Indeed, not until the union of the colleges took place in 1859 was the basis laid for future reform of the profession.

An examination of the other scholarly profession — ministers of the Church — reveals close links between them and the university. It was from the ministry that divinity professors, and many of the arts professors, were recruited. Before being appointed to their chairs they served as parish ministers, and in a church with no bishops, professorships were the only permanent offices above parish level. For those ministers which academic ambitions the attractions of a university chair were obvious.

As a profession, ministers in this period suffered a crisis which was to lead them to differ in quite fundamental respects from their university counterparts. Although the Disruption of the Church of Scotland in 1843 had wide societal implications,[12] ostensibly it took place over the fundamental issue of patronage in the church, and the rights of patrons to 'intrude' their nominees upon the parishes. Opposition to patronage in the Church of Scotland had a long history and had led to previous secessions in the eighteenth century, but the schism on this occasion was far more serious and long-term in its consequences. As far as ministers were concerned it would be true to say that the Disruption marked a distinct watershed in their professional development.

Whilst in 1760 a minister would be presented by a patron's recommendation with the acquiesence of the presbytery, from the middle of the nineteenth century onwards clerical patronage declined in significance in the presbyterian denominations. Increasingly kirk sessions and congregations chose their own ministers to serve in the respective churches. These ministers would be educated at a university, tested, and formally licensed by a presbytery as suitable candidates for the ministry. As far as the presbyterian ministry was concerned, the trend towards a professionalism based on merit and ability was evident in a manner very different from the situation within the universities. Standards were enforced regarding entry to the profession in terms of qualifications, competence, and moral behaviour by a professional body (presbytery) which acted to maintain a theological and moral orthodoxy. No minister could be presented to, or leave a charge, without due certification from the presbytery. On the other hand strict controls, and popular selection according to merit, brought new tyrannies. Liberation from the bonds of patronage was not necessarily accompanied by freedom of expression. If the Disruption laid the basis for a new professionalism it also drew the clergy into a novel dependency-relationship with their middle-class sponsors.

The experience and attitudes of the two scholarly professions — university professors and ministers of the church — differed radically. The break from the bonds of eighteenth-century patronage so evident in the latter was absent in the former. University professors continued to regard the rights of patronage as a form of heritable property to be retained, as far as possible, within their own possession. If industrialisation and the development of a market economy made its impact on the clergy, university professors were left relatively unaffected and independent of such forces. Both professions were highly regarded within society and it followed that neither needed to consider advancement of their social status as a professional strategy. Increasingly, clergymen were to be drawn more tightly into the bourgeois social structure than were university professors who remained more or less independent of market forces and its needs. Indeed if the professoriate had any uniform role it was one of maintaining eighteenth-century privilege against the threat of nineteenth-century liberalism. Corresponding differences can be detected within the consulting professions.

Consulting Professions

We have observed already that academically-inclined ministers regarded the professoriate as an avenue of mobility and to some extent this was true also of lawyers and doctors. On the other hand neither of these professions saw a university chair as a sufficient source of income in itself. A chair was both a status symbol and a means of supplementing a salary obtained from providing professional services in the community. Professors of law and medicine normally had lower salaries than other professors, which emphasises the fact that their professorial roles were secondary.[13]

In other respects law and medicine differed from the scholarly professions. University attendance was not required in order to obtain practising qualifications although increasingly — certainly with regard to lawyers — attendance became the accepted norm. The consulting professions employed a system of apprenticeship broadly comparable to the custom of appointing 'substitute' professors, but in effect standing nearer to a craft-type apprenticeship. It was customary for individuals to be apprenticed to a practising lawyer or doctor for a specified fee, and rigorous conditions were laid down concerning duties and the maintenance of a strict code of moral behaviour.[14]

On the other hand it is clear that lawyers throughout the period progressed much further down the path of professionalism than their medical counterparts. Lawyers tended to be recruited from leading city families and the close-knit kin and business relationships of the eighteenth-century city probably ensured that any deviation from 'ethical' standards of professional behaviour was readily noted. Lawyers were also governed by a long-standing professional body — the Society of Advocates in Aberdeen, which drew members from throughout the North East. This institution exerted a considerable degree of control over the behaviour of its members. Membership was sought after but was not granted routinely and the Society resolutely excluded those who were regarded as unsuitable. Admission to membership was a recognition of respectability and must have created new avenues of professional opportunities, although non-membership did not prevent a lawyer from practising in court. In one protracted case, extending over ten years, an applicant repeatedly petitioned for membership and was on each occasion rejected on the basis of 'sundry objections' to his 'character'. Continual frustration led him to take his case to the Court of Session in Edinburgh where the Society, at considerable financial cost, successfully defended the action. The bitterness continued thereafter as the Society sought to end his court practice by disciplining members who acted alongside him 'before any of the Courts at Aberdeen in time coming'.[15]

The Society also instituted recommended fees for conveyancing and other services and validated those seeking to undertake apprenticeship. Apart from the substantial indenture fees involved, those admitted after 1800 were required to have undergone two sessions at one of the universities.[16] A close scrutiny of all those admitted to full membership of the Society confirms that this regulation was being enforced. Between 1760 and 1799 of the 42 admitted to membership, 18 had not attended university. However, in the period 1800–30 of the 152 admitted only five had not been at university; the last of these five was admitted in 1813. There was also a remarkable increase in the numbers graduating, as opposed to attending, in this same period.[17]

The Society was keen to improve standards and in 1786 they warmly welcomed a proposal to establish university classes in civil and Scots law and confirmed that all apprentices would be required to attend them. When such proposals failed to materialise the Society itself in 1819 founded lectureships in Scots law and conveyancing at Marischal College.[18] However it is evident that soon after the beginning of the nineteenth century a general university education became the expected norm for a practising solicitor in Aberdeen and the North East. The profession — through its governing body — held a university education in high regard and had established close links with the university.

Unlike the lawyers, doctors remained at an earlier stage of professional development. Medical knowledge itself retained a mystical, near-magical aspect in the popular mind. Indeed the craft remained ill-defined in terms of the distinction between surgical skills and medical knowledge. The situation was made worse by the fact that many eminent doctors acted as tradesmen, finding a lucrative supplement to their income by selling proprietary medicines to the public.[19]

The absence of any effective body governing the profession made control over such activities very difficult. For the same reason access to the profession was remarkably 'open'. Although a system of formal apprenticeship acted as the cornerstone of professional training, admission to the profession was possible in a number of other ways. Both Aberdeen universities operated a formal procedure of conferring medical degrees by recommendation rather than attendance. A degree candidate was required to submit a recommendation by another physician along with his degree fee. This was a similar pattern to that of St Andrews, but different from the universities of Edinburgh and Glasgow, both of which produced trained graduates.[20]

As far as the Aberdeen universities were concerned, such a convenient means of raising money meant that many degrees were conferred upon unknown candidates, often from England or from abroad. Scandalous errors occurred. In 1791 Marischal College was so appalled by the 'notorious and impudent quackery' of one of their graduates that they sought to 'degraduate' him but were advised that this was legally impossible.[21] Lesser scandals haunted both universities[22] and in 1817 a series of new regulations were enacted at King's College requiring the recommendations of two physicians and an account of the candidate's education. In 1825 Marischal College followed with regulations along the same lines. The net result was a drastic fall in the number of degrees conferred and regulations were again relaxed.[23]

Initial 'practical' experience leading to entry into the profession could be obtained by a number of means other than formal apprenticeship. Medical officers were in short supply during the Napoleonic Wars and as a consequence the government sought to recruit 'young men of ability' from both colleges by offering surgeons' commissions to arts students 'who could pass some slight examination'. Others went abroad to gain practical experience. One eminent doctor began his career when 'at seventeen he went to Greenland with a sailing whaler as surgeon'. The East India service attracted others. Patronage was a strong element in obtaining posts.[24] Unlike the legal profession, where the Society of Advocates acted to control entry, the medical profession lacked any governing body although the founding of a student Medical Society in 1789 laid the basis for the eventual emergence of such an institution.[25]

Such openness of recruitment must have increased economic competition for patients in an already 'overcrowded profession',[26] and was unlikely to further the promotion of a professional behavioural ethic. Although by the 1820s some attempts were being made by the universities to grapple with the problem of conferring degrees, it was not until the 1860s that anything approaching effective controls are evident within the newly-united university. By then the Aberdeen Medical Society had emerged also as an institution exerting control over entry into the profession. However, until the mid century, in almost all respects medical practitioners lagged behind their legal counterparts regarding professional training and development.

Concluding Considerations

The remarkable diversity between the four occupations makes generalisation difficult. The distinction between scholarly and consulting professions is not always clear and, within each category, significantly different characteristics can be observed. Thus if professors and ministers shared the scholarly aspects of their respective professions in terms of recruitment, and if both might be seen as 'graduate' professions, it is clear also that the differences between them are great. Professors sought to defend their rights of privilege and patronage within the universities and are generally remarkable for their lack of changed circumstance in these hundred years. Ministers underwent sweeping changes which were to alter the nature of their profession. Likewise in terms of institutional controls, the behaviour of the clergy was subject to strict regulation whilst university professors were under little or no effective bureaucratic control.

Regarding the consulting professions, indentured apprenticeships were practised by both lawyers and doctors; thereafter great differences are apparent. More than any of the other occupations, lawyers had progressed further along the path towards professionalism. Institutional controls were being exerted over members' ethical behaviour and by the early nineteenth century attendance at university was regarded as an essential feature of a lawyer's education. These features were accompanied by a growing stress on the vocational aspects of that university experience. Doctors were the least professional of the four occupations in terms of recruitment and, like university professors, lacked any effective institution which promoted the control of ethical standards. If the universities failed to provide medical education it is clear that doctors did recognise the need for formal university qualifications and, in a sense, the purchased MD degree, awarded on the recommendation of one's peers, was a clear recognition by doctors of the importance of a university professional education.

In their very different ways the clergy, lawyers, and doctors had all clearly established academic links with the Aberdeen universities. The nature of those links, and their comparative strength or weakness, was in no small part determined by the professoriates, whose interpretation of their own professional function in society was central to the development of the other professions.

NOTES

The author gratefully acknowledges the financial support of the Carnegie Trust for the Universities of Scotland in the undertaking of this research.

1. E. Friedson, *The Profession of Medicine* (London, 1970), 232.
2. Significant differences may have been present in education within the divinity faculties. Of the 27 ministers ordained in Aberdeen Church of Scotland and Free churches between 1830 and 1860, 16 had attended one or other of the two universities, viz. eight from King's and eight from Marischal. At the Disruption all but one of those educated at King's remained in the Establishment whilst all those educated at Marischal seceded: see A. A. Maclaren, *Religion and Social Class: the Disruption Years in Aberdeen* (London, 1974), 221–4.
3. R. D. Anderson 'Scottish university professors, 1800–1939: profile of an elite', *Scottish Economic and Social History*, 7 (1987), 27–54.
4. E. H. G Rodger, *Aberdeen Doctors at Home and Abroad* (Edinburgh, 1893), 70. See also R. S. Rait, *The Universities of Aberdeen. A History* (Edinburgh, 1885) 225.
5. Aberdeen University Library [AUL], King's College, Minute Book XII, 19 March 1782.
6. W. Kennedy, *Annals of Aberdeen* (London, 1818), ii, 119–20.
7. Rait, *Universities of Aberdeen*, 215–17.
8. AUL, King's College, Minute Book, XIV, 26 May 1817. The dispute was formally resolved but the acrimony continued.
9. This was the first challenge to the Test Act, which was amended in 1853 to exclude lay chairs. For a straightforward account of this complex case, see J. M. Bulloch, *A History of the University of Aberdeen* (London, 1895), 184–5.
10. The most notable example was that of Principal Daniel Dewar of Marischal College: MacLaren *Religion and Social Class*, 221.
11. Anderson, 'Scottish university professors', 28.
12. For a full discussion of these see Maclaren, *Religion and Social Class*, passim.
13. See Royal Commission, *Report on the State of the Universities of Aberdeen with a View to their Union* (Edinburgh, 1858), 114–5, 130–3.
14. For a description of the process of arranging an indenture see Rodger, *Aberdeen Doctors*, 57.
15. See *Sederunt Book of the Society of Advocates in Aberdeen* (dated 1776). The early parts of the volume are missing. The many entries concerning the case [Alexander Laing] extended from 7 December 1779 to 24 November 1789 and beyond.
16. Before entering indentures an applicant had to produce a certificate as to 'having studied Latin under some master of character for at least four years successively and two sessions at one of the universitys': item XV of the regulations of the Society in *Sederunt Book of the Society of Advocates in Aberdeen*. Apprenticeship fees varied but were around 20 guineas.
17. These figures are extracted from entries recorded in J. A. H. Henderson, *History of the Society of Advocates in Aberdeen* (Aberdeen 1912).
18. *Sederunt Book of the Society of Advocates in Aberdeen*, 4 October 1786, *Records of Marischal College and University* (Spalding Club, Aberdeen, 1889, 1898), i, 489; ii, 71.
19. Such behaviour although frowned upon was found to be very profitable even with the professoriate. William Chalmers, professor of medicine at King's College, practised as a doctor and traded as a chemist.

20. I. Loudon, *Medical Care and the General Practitioner, 1750–1850* (Oxford, 1986), 183.

21. P. J. Anderson, *Officers and Graduates of the University and King's College of Aberdeen* (New Spalding Club, Aberdeen, 1893), 130–75; *Fasti Academiae Mariscallanae Aberdonensis* (Aberdeen, 1898), 120–81. They were warned by the solicitor-general that it would be prudent to 'submit to silence' and to take warning from this case concerning their readiness in bestowing degrees (*ibid.*, 133–4).

22. From as far away as Suffolk complaints came in that apothecaries were buying Aberdeen medical degrees 'after a few years in their shops' (Loudon, *Medical Care* 144).

23. The total number of degrees conferred between 1826–39 amounted to only 29 (Rait, *Universities of Aberdeen*, 210, 212–3).

24. Aberdonians were specially favoured because of the presence of Sir James McGregor, son of an Aberdeen stocking-manufacturer, who rose to become Director of the British Army Medical Board; and because of powerful positions held by others within the East India Company: see Rodger, *Aberdeen Doctors*, 100, 104, 127, 138, 203.

25. In its early years the Society was hard-pressed to survive in the face of ridicule and disinterest. Eventually it did win support from certain university professors and doctors and much later emerged in a new governing role regarding the profession. The process is described by Rodger, *Aberdeen Doctors* but a reading of the first *Minute Book of the Aberdeen Medico-Chirurgical Society* (Aberdeen, 1789) shows just how tenuous was its existence.

26. The profession was widely held to be overcrowded: see D. Hamilton, *The Healers: a History of Medicine in Scotland* (Edinburgh, 1981), ch. 4 *passim*: Loudon, *Medical Care*, 208–23. Even the sick poor sought second opinions: see W. Henderson, *Observations on the Medical Attendance of the Poor in Their Own Homes* (Aberdeen, 1822), 17.

10

From Scottish Generalism to European Experimental Specialism: Developments in the Teaching of Physiology at Aberdeen, 1860–1920

Carolyn Pennington

Before the fusion of Marischal and King's Colleges in 1860 the subject of physiology, or institutes of medicine as it was then known, was taught at Marischal by George Ogilvie. He had graduated MA at Marischal College in 1838 and MD at Edinburgh University in 1842, and until 1860 was an untenured lecturer dependent on student fees. In anticipation of the eventual amalgamation of the two Aberdeen universities he petitioned the government in 1855, urging the claims of the Aberdeen medical school. The petition was signed by the dean, principal and professors of Marischal College and by the lord provost and the city's MP. An appendix to the document was signed by nineteen eminent medical men, including William Sharpey, professor of anatomy and physiology at University College, London; Hughes Bennett, professor of institutes of medicine at Glasgow; Allan Thompson, professor of anatomy at Glasgow; and William Carpenter, professor of medical jurisprudence at University College, London and author of a well known text book of physiology, thus adding much professional weight to the local pressure. All these gentlemen testified to the value of medical education at Marischal College, but added that the efficiency of the school would be promoted if some existing lectureships were converted to professorships. They singled out the subject of physiology because of its importance to science and also because it required more time 'and more withdrawal from the pursuit of Medical practice' than was the case with most medical sciences.[1]

In the event, in 1860, a chair of institutes of medicine was created along with three other new regius medical professorships when the two Aberdeen universities were amalgamated by the Universities (Scotland) Act of 1858. Ogilvie was its first incumbent. Similar chairs existed at Edinburgh and Glasgow, but elsewhere in Britain physiology tended to be taught as a part of the anatomy course. Scottish practice was thus more in line with that of Germany where a practical, experimental approach to the subject was proving to be highly successful, as the publication record of German universities and research institutes shows.

In Aberdeen an examination of the facilities available to Ogilvie and the sort of course that he taught indicates that his teaching owed little to continental developments and much to the traditional, natural-theological and anatomical approach which was common in Britain. When Ogilvie's colleagues supported his claim to the proposed new chair, they had spoken of his command of the rapidly advancing subject of physiology and pointed to his newly-published book, *The Master Builder's Plan*[2]. This sought to show the underlying plan of things in the animal kingdom, revealing the perfection of the Creator's scheme of life and the infallability of the Hidden Hand. It was a book very much in the natural-theological tradition and owed nothing to developments in modern continental physiology; rather it reflected the writings of Paley, published in the 1800s, and of the authors of the Bridgewater Treatises of the 1830s. *The Master Builder's Plan* was completely overshadowed in the following year by the publication of Darwin's *Origin of Species*. Ogilvie's approach was largely theoretical, as Professor Allan Thomson of Glasgow noted when commenting on some papers on reproduction that Ogilvie had sent him.[3] He criticised Ogilvie's treatment of the subjects 'as if the information with regard to them has some character of completeness', whereas research was likely to change currently-held views.

The teaching facilities available for physiology in the new Aberdeen Medical School, which was established along with classes in law in the Marischal College building, reveals that little practical work was involved in the course. After the fusion all the arts classes were moved to King's College in Old Aberdeen, and at Principal Campbell's request the rooms at Marischal College were assigned by the chairman of the University Commissioners, Lord Justice Clerk Inglis, in person. Inglis was on circuit in Aberdeen and visited Marischal College accompanied by a representative of the Board of Works (which, under the terms of the 1858 Act, was the government agency required to maintain the fabric of the university buildings, and which was prepared to carry out any immediate minor works that were needed). Some professors, anatomy for example, were assigned practical rooms, laboratory or museum space; Ogilvie was given the old Greek class room, and there was no mention of a practical room for him.[4]

The textbooks prescribed by Ogilvie also show the traditional nature of his approach: Kirkes' *Handbook of Physiology* and Carpenter's *Manual of Physiology*.[5] Carpenter's book is a descriptive morphological textbook, at one point stating that, while the physiologist studies the actions and phenomena peculiar to living beings and the fundamental properties of organised structures, at the heart of everything in science were certain 'ultimate facts' which could be explained only as the Will of the Creator. It represented rather a fatalistic approach and one which was not very helpful to attempts to increase knowledge of the basic functioning of the body. Ogilvie's texts in practical physiology were Kolliker's *Manual of Microscopic Anatomy* (trans. T. H. Huxley and Busk)[6] and Morel's *Compendium of Human Histology*, and certainly Kolliker's book was a thorough and up-to-date account of microscopical anatomy. Ogilvie himself was a keen microscopist, but his interest in practical physiology seems to have begun and ended there. He was president of the local, amateur Aberdeen Microscopical Society, and the physiology department duly acquired microscopes for the use of the students — one of them recalled years later the brightly-lit table in the physiology room with five or six microscopes, set up with appropriate histology slides, to illustrate the lecture of the day. He also recalled that there was no other sort of apparatus and rarely were there any specimens on display.[7] The fact that John Thomson, the minister of the nearby Greyfriars Kirk, could take the summer microscopy course in the early 1860s reveals the unspecialised nature of the teaching that was given.[8] Thirty years later it is hard to believe that a local minister would have been much help in a physiology class room.

Whatever the inadequacies of the rest of the course, students seem to have acquired a sound knowledge of microscopy. Alexander Ogston took Ogilvie's course and the Rev. John Thomson's microscopy course.[9] His most notable published work, the first description of the microscopic organism *Staphylococcus aureus* was, among other things, high-quality pioneering, basic microscope work. Ogston was by no means the only student of Ogilvie's to advance knowledge of organisms through microscopy; a contemporary of Ogston's in the Aberdeen Medical School was Patrick Manson. After leave in the UK in 1875, Manson returned to Amoy in China where he was medical officer to the local Imperial Maritime Customs, taking with him a new wife and a new compound microscope made by Nachet Fils of Paris with which to continue his work on elephantiasis. With the help of that microscope he was able to identify the filaria parasite in his patients' blood and later demonstrated its life cycle in the mosquito. Manson's work on other parasitic tropical diseases is well known, most notably his formulation of the mosquito-malaria hypothesis, later confirmed in the field by Ronald Ross.[10]

Despite such successes, Ogilvie himself was well aware that Aberdeen was not keeping up with modern developments. In 1876 he wrote to the dean, pointing out that a laboratory for practical classes, suitably equipped for microscopy teaching and for what he called 'observations of the vital functions, and the chemical examination of the tissues and secretions of the body' was essential for Aberdeen physiology if it was to keep up with other medical schools.[11]

T. H. Huxley was the most influential exponent of the general need for a more rational, practical medical course, and for a more practical approach to the teaching of physiology in particular. Between 1856 and 1870 he was university examiner in physiology and comparative anatomy, and also in zoology, in the University of London,[12] and by the early 1870s, as secretary of the Royal Society, he was one of the most important figures in scientific education. In 1870 he made clear his views on the teaching of physiology when he addressed students of medicine at University College, London: when he examined students, he complained, he found that they did not know physiology in the way that they knew anatomy, as a matter of 'autopsy, and observation, and strict discipline'; in many cases physiology had been taught 'as if it were a mere matter of books and hearsay',[13] whereas it should be taught with 'the same definiteness and precision as anatomy is taught'.[14] Huxley believed that the basic physical sciences should be taught to students before they embarked on a medical course and that botany and zoology did not belong in the course at all.

Huxley's views were shared in Aberdeen by John Struthers, the professor of anatomy, who had found that his Darwinian teaching of comparative anatomy, in his view an important part of the anatomy course, overlapped with the course of zoology and comparative anatomy given by the professor of natural history. Struthers firmly believed that the study of zoology was well as botany and chemistry should be confined to the first year of the four-year medical course and should not impinge on the teaching of subjects more relevant to medicine. In the run-up to the rectorial election of 1872, Struthers urged a students' committee to put forward T. H. Huxley as a candidate and pleaded with Huxley to agree to stand despite his ill health.[15] In the ensuing contest, medical student support was crucial to Huxley's election as rector and when he assumed office he was sympathetic to student demands for a more rational medical course. In a letter to John Webster, the rector's assessor, Huxley insisted upon 'practical Physiological teaching in place of the time at present wasted on Zoology and Botany',[16] but he was unable to have implemented any restriction of basic science teaching in the medical course during his rectorship. As a member of the royal commission appointed in 1876 to inquire into the Scottish universities, Huxley continued to advocate these and other changes: in Aberdeen practical physiology teaching would come only at Ogilvie's retirement, when it was obviously important that he was succeeded by a modern physiologist used to the experimental approach favoured by Huxley.

The individual who was responsible for bringing modern, continental physiology to Britain was William Sharpey, professor of anatomy and physiology at University College, London from 1836 to 1874, who taught many of those who became leaders of the field in London and Cambridge. Sharpey was an Edinburgh graduate who had studied in Germany and after his appointment to University College encouraged men like Michael Foster who became instructor in practical physiology at UC in 1867 and introduced practical teaching with simple experiments on muscle and nerve and the study of physiological chemistry. He later moved to Cambridge, where his practical course became famous and where he established the so-called Cambridge school of physiology.[17]

These metropolitan developments had a direct effect on physiology teaching in Scotland because the chair of institutes of medicine at Aberdeen, and the parallel chair at Glasgow, both became vacant in the 1870s and both were crown appointments. In 1875 William Sharpey discussed prospective candidates for the Glasgow chair of physiology with his old friend Allan

Thompson, then professor of anatomy at Glasgow. He referred in passing to a young Edinburgh graduate, saying, 'I have heard of Mr. Stirling most favourably — but beyond that I could form no opinion.'[18] Two years later, in 1877, when candidates for the Aberdeen chair were being canvassed, Sharpey tried to lobby in favour of William Stirling by approaching William Jenner, professor of clinical medicine at University College Hospital in London and physician-in-ordinary to Queen Victoria, some time professor of pathological anatomy and of medicine at University College, and probably the most prominent medical man of his day. Sharpey hoped that Jenner would speak to Richard Cross, Disraeli's Home Secretary, on the matter. Jenner apparently would only speak to Cross if he happened to meet him, as he had been snubbed on an earlier occasion. However, Sharpey was soon writing to say that he had met Stirling in London en route for Paris 'to look after teaching and working appliances suited to his new position' as professor of physiology at Aberdeen, an appointment which was a great satisfaction 'not only on his account but as some token that Government patronage in the Scottish Universities will be thoughtfully and judiciously bestowed'.[19]

William Stirling was only twenty-six when appointed to Aberdeen. He had won a gold medal for his MD thesis and was very much the product of the modern continental school of physiology, having studied in Leipzig, Berlin and Paris before returning to work for Rutherford in Edinburgh. He used to speak of du Bois Raymond of Berlin, the leading proponent of the 'physical approach' to physiological problems, as his 'patron saint' whose experimental instruments — the induction coil, key and myograph — were 'indispensable' and found in daily use by students in every physiology laboratory.[20] His second mentor was Carl Ludwig in Leipzig — by 1900 there were few physiologists of any note who had not studied with Ludwig.

Stirling was, therefore, a convinced disciple of German experimental physiology, but when he arrived in Aberdeen he found no facilities for teaching practical, experimental physiology. He asked that a lecture table with a gas and water supply be provided in his lecture room so that he could perform experiments for the students. He also required a practical class-room, and suggested the adaptation of the adjoining midwifery class-room. Principal Pirrie wrote to the Board of Works asking that these alterations be carried out for the new professor at Marischal College, 'a man of high qualifications' recently appointed by the crown who was unable at present to conduct his class efficiently.[21] The Board of Works agreed that the work was essential, but the Treasury was unable to sanction the expenditure, and Stirling seems to have gone ahead with the alterations expecting a Treasury grant to be forthcoming in the following year. He later complained to the Lords of the Treasury that it was unfair to expect a professor to pay for his own lecture room and class fittings, and noted that in the previous year he had paid out some £200 (about a third of his income) for apparatus. Physiology, he told the Treasury, was now an experimental subject and provision for this was essential.[22] Stirling sent the accounts for the work to the Board of Works who forwarded them to London where payment was finally authorised. But not until January 1881 was money made available to convert the midwifery class room into a properly filled physiology laboratory.[23]

In addition to introducing the teaching of practical experimental physiology to Aberdeen, Stirling also translated L. Landois's *Textbook of Human Physiology* from the German and added some chapters of his own.[24] This is a detailed two-volume textbook of physiology and histology: there is a brief resume of pathological variations of each physiological process and details of experiments to demonstrate these processes. One of the sections (s. 56) added by Stirling, for example, is a detailed account of the physical examination of the chest and heart — explaining inspection, palpation, percussion, and auscultation. This was no doubt of great help to students and the book became the standard recommended text for the course. Stirling does not appear to have done any research work at this time, or indeed after he moved to Manchester in 1885, when the Aberdeen student magazine noted: 'Mr. Gladstone's government has two great problems to solve. It has to settle the Irish difficulty and it has to appoint a suitable successor to Dr. Stirling'.[25] The solution to the latter problem was not difficult, for there was an obvious candidate.

John MacWilliam, a farmer's son from Invernesshire, an Aberdeen medical graduate (1880) who had learned his anatomy from Professor Struthers and physiology from Professor Stirling, was a demonstrator at University College, London. He was barely thirty when appointed and was to occupy the chair at Aberdeen for the next forty years. His MD thesis in 1882 was on cardiac and diaphragmatic muscle, which continued to be one of his life-long interests. He had worked in Edinburgh, and then with Ludwig in Leipzig, and Kronecker in Berne, before becoming demonstrator in physiology to Schafer the professor of physiology at University College London in 1882, where he remained till 1886. There he was associated with Halliburton and even taught Starling, the discoveror of hormones, in an advanced physiology class.[26]

His first substantial published work was on the heart of the eel, extending the work Gaskell was doing in Cambridge.[27] In Aberdeen he continued this work on many different species of mammalian hearts and showed that conclusions drawn from electrophysiological studies of invertebrates could also be applied to mammals.[28] His students noticed at once that the heart of this physiologist 'is with his apparatus in the Laboratory', and that his pet research 'is muscle in general and the obscurities of heart muscle and muscle-tremours in particular.' He had apparatus 'for catching the contractions of a frog's muscle under varying degrees of heat' and for investigating the knee jerk as well as an 'arrangement of tubes and cisterns' to measure the nature of heart contractions:

> There are tambours, registering cylinders, Grennet's batteries and induction machines; and to these how many eels, frogs, guinea-pigs, rabbits, cats, and dogs must yield up their secret! But vivisection? Yes, the professor has a licence and he is kind to his animals — kinder than the Vivisection Act requires him to be.[29]

MacWilliam was the first person to analyse the phenomenon of ventricular fibrillation and sudden death[30], and he is also credited with suggesting that the rhythmic beat of the heart could be restored after cardiac arrest by electrical stimulation,[31] something that did not become a practical proposition until the 1960s. He published his findings in the *Journal of Physiology*, the *British Medical Journal*, and before an International Medical Congress in Washington D.C. in September 1887 but, for reasons that remain unclear as his successor J. J. R. McLeod noted,[32] their significance to clinical practice was not appreciated at this time. Simple instrumental means of analysing phenomena like ventricular fibrillation and cardiac arrest at the bedside only became available some twenty to thirty years later.

With the extension of the medical course to five years in 1892, a practical course in physiology was made mandatory. More space was provided for the physiology department in extensive new premises in the extension to Marischal College that faces Broad Street. MacWilliam continued to work and publish on cardiovascular matters (including some work on blood pressure) and interest in his early work revived in the first decade of the new century. His work had been quoted in a chapter in Schaffer's two volume *Textbook of Physiology* (vol.ii, 1900) by Gaskell[33] and eventually came to the attention of James MacKenzie, the great pioneer of British cardiology, with whom he corresponded. Mackenzie had turned to experimental physiology to help him elucidate his clinical problems. By the 1920s MacWilliam's earlier researches had been summarised and extended in several papers and he was elected to the Royal Society. Today his work continues to be cited regularly in the medical literature, particularly with reference to modern, aggressive interventionist treatments of heart disease based on electrophysiological principles.

The careers of Aberdeen's three teachers of physiology — Ogilvie, Stirling and MacWilliam — illustrate how complete was the transformation of this subject between 1860 and 1920. In fifty years physiology in Aberdeen had moved from book-based teaching, financed largely out of student fees, to an enterprise well in the mainstream of European experimental science.

NOTES

1. Aberdeen University Library [AUL], Ogilvie-Forbes of Boyndlie Collection, MS 2740, box 16, bundle 'university', [G. Ogilvie Forbes], Aberdeen Medical School [Jan. 1855], 7.

2. G. Ogilvie, *The Master Builder's Plan* (London, 1858). On natural theology see E. Mayr, *The Growth of Biological Thought* (Cambridge, Mass., 1982), 103–5.

3. AUL, Ogilvie-Forbes of Boyndlie Collection, MS 2740, box 17, bundle ex drawer marked 'Critique', [Allen Thomson to Geo. Ogilvie Forbes], 21 Nov. 1859.

4. AUL, Secretary's Papers, CT box 50, envelope Princ. Campbell, [John Inglis], 'Memorandum as to the occupation of the Buildings, formerly belonging to Marischal College, during the Winter Session of 1860–61'.

5. W. S. Kirkes, *Handbook of Physiology* (London, 1848); W Carpenter, *Manual of*

Physiology (London, 1846), 15.

6. A. Kolliker, *Manual of Human Histology*, trans. T. H. Huxley and G. Busk (London, 1853); G. Morel, *Compendium of Human Histology* (New York, 1861).

7. J. G. McKendrick, 'The professor of physiology, 1860–1877', *Aurora Borealis Academica* (Aberdeen, 1899), 264.

8. AUL, Minutes of Medical Faculty, MS U 96/1, 13.

9. W. Ogston, *Alexander Ogston K.C.V.O.*, (Aberdeen, 1943), 54.

10. P. Manson-Bahr, *Patrick Manson* (London, 1962), 18–25.

11. AUL, Ogilvie-Forbes of Boyndlie Collection, MS 2740, box 16, undated letter to the dean.

12. C. Bibby, *T. H. Huxley, Scientist, Humanist, and Educator* (London, 1959), 218. Huxley was also influential in the U.S. He was consulted in 1875 by Gilman about faculty for the new Johns Hopkins Hospital and Medical School. He recommended H. Newell Martin who introduced modern physiology teaching: see W. B. Fye, *The Development of American Physiology* (Baltimore, 1987).

13. T. H. Huxley, 'On medical education', *Science and Education* (London, 1910), 309.

14. *Ibid.*, 310.

15. A. Keith, 'Anatomy in Scotland during the lifetime of Sir John Struthers (1823–99)', *Edinburgh Medical Journal*, 8 (1912), 21.

16. AUL, Autograph letters addressed to John Webster, MSS 888.

17. G. L. Geisson, *Michael Foster and the Cambridge School: the Scientific Enterprise in late Victorian Society*, (Princeton, 1978).

18. L. S. Jacyna, *A Tale of Three Cities, the Correspondence of William Sharpey and Allen Thompson* (London, 1989), 137.

19. *Ibid.*, 142–3.

20. W. Stirling, *Some Apostles of Physiology* (London, 1902), 109.

21. AUL, MS U 400, Marischal College, Classroom of the Professor of the Institutes of Medicine, 1877–78 [Correspondence].

22. Ibid.

23. Ibid.

24. L. Landois, *Textbook of Human Physiology and Microscopic Anatomy*, 2nd. edition, trans W. Stirling (London, 1886), 107–8.

25. *Alma Mater*, iii (1886), 138.

26. H. McLean, 'John Alexander MacWilliam', *Aberdeen University Review*, xxiv (1936–7), 127–131; and see W. B. Fye, 'Ventricular fibrillation and defibrillation; historical perspectives with emphasis on the contributions of John MacWilliam, Carl Wiggars, and William Kouwenhoven', *Circulation*, 71 (1985), 858–865.

27. J. A. MacWilliam, 'On reflex excitation of the cardiac nerve in fishes', *Proceedings of the Royal Society*, 38 (1885), 31–41, and J. A. MacWilliam, 'On the structure and rhythm of the heart in fishes, with special reference to the heart of the eel', *Journal of Physiology*, 6 (1885), 192–245.

28. J. A. MacWilliam, 'On the rhythm of the mammalian heart', *Journal of Physiology*, ix (1888), 167–198.

29. 'Hours with the Professors, VII, Physiology', *Alma Mater*, v (1887), 72.

30. J. A. MacWilliam, 'Fibrillar contraction of the heart', *Journal of Physiology*, viii (1887), 296–310 and 'Cardiac failure and sudden death', *British Medical Journal*, (5 Jan. 1889), 6–8.

31. J. A. MacWilliam, 'Electrical stimulation of the heart in man', *British Medical Journal*, (2 Feb. 1889), 348–350.

32. J. J. R. McLeod, 'John Alexander MacWilliam, MD, FRS', *Aberdeen University Review*, xv (1927), 224–6. McLeod was MacWilliam's successor and his most distinguished student. He shared the Nobel prize for medicine in 1923 with Banting and Best for their discovery of insulin.

33. W. H. Gaskell, 'The contraction of cardiac muscle', in E. A. Schafer, *Textbook of Physiology*, ii (London, 1900); and see J. MacKenzie, 'Observations on the inception of the rhythm of the heart by the ventricle', *British Medical Journal* (27 Feb. 1904), 534–5.

11

Scottish Influences in British Natural Philosophy: Rise and Decline, 1830–1910

David B. Wilson

Two things have long been obvious about physics in the Victorian–Edwardian period. First, the early decades were dominated by the ideas of two Scots, William Thomson (later Lord Kelvin) and James Clerk Maxwell. Kelvin's formulation and extension of the science of thermodynamics in the 1850s and Maxwell's creation of the electromagnetic theory of light in the 1860s combined to transform physical theory. What Darwin was to Victorian biology, Kelvin and Maxwell were to Victorian physics. The second obvious thing is the dominance of Cambridge University's Cavendish Laboratory in the later part of the period. Opened in 1874, the Cavendish led British studies in the new physics of electrons, radioactivity, and atomic structure from about 1895 onwards. The principal physicists here were J. J. Thomson, long-time director of the Cavendish, and his student and successor, Ernest Rutherford, neither of whom had any Scottish connections. Various institutional transformations were to accompany the changes in physical theory, as the Scottish dominance of natural philosophy gave way to that of England.

The careers of Kelvin, Maxwell, J. J. Thomson, and Rutherford reveal part of the story. Though born in Ireland, Kelvin (1824–1907) moved to Glasgow as a child when his father became professor of mathematics there. He began attending classes at Glasgow when he was ten years old and went on to Cambridge in 1841, being placed as second wrangler in Cambridge's mathematical tripos in 1845. He returned to Glasgow as professor of natural philosophy the next year, resigning a half century later in 1899. Maxwell (1831–1879) went to the Edinburgh Academy before attending Edinburgh University for three years and going on to Cambridge, to be second wrangler there in 1854. In the late 1850s, he was professor of natural philosophy at Marischal College, Aberdeen, losing his position to the professor of natural philosophy at King's College, David Thomson, when King's and Marischal were united in 1860 to form the University of Aberdeen. In the early 1860s, he was at King's College, London, and then spent several years without a post before becoming first Cavendish professor of experimental physics at Cambridge in 1871, remaining there until his death in 1879. Thomson (1856–1940) grew up in Manchester and attended Owen's College, Manchester, before entering Cambridge where he was second wrangler in 1880; remaining in Cambridge, he was appointed director of the Cavendish in 1884 and held the position until 1919. Rutherford (1871–1937) came from New Zealand to the Cavendish in 1895, under new regulations that allowed graduates of other universities to earn a Cambridge degree. In 1898, he accepted a professorship at McGill University in Montreal, returning to England in 1907 to head the physics laboratory at Manchester University. After succeeding Thomson, he remained at the Cavendish until his death in 1937.

These biographical outlines shed some light on the process by which Scottish physics was anglicised, enough for us to see that it was not simple and straightforward. Kelvin and Maxwell attended Cambridge in addition to Scottish universities, after all, and Maxwell was a professor at Cambridge. There were other Scottish and English universities besides those attended by Kelvin and Maxwell — Owen's College, Manchester, for one. In the event, however, the somewhat entangled process did depend primarily on developments at Glasgow, Edinburgh, and Cambridge, with the Victorian growth of other English universities playing a subsidiary part.

1830–1870

What exactly were the roles of Scotland and Cambridge in shaping the physics of Kelvin and Maxwell? Taking a natural philosophy class at a Scottish university was quite different from preparing for the mathematical tripos at Cambridge. The first was usually a one-year course in a four-year curriculum that was more-or-less equally devoted to several subjects. The second was a long and intense study of mathematics and mathematical physics, the thoroughness of the study being scrutinised by a several-day examination.[1] The Scottish natural philosophy course included the subjects of heat, electricity and magnetism; the tripos did not. Cambridge deemed theories in these subjects not sufficiently mathematical to be included in the tripos. The tripos was not primarily a training for physicists but a liberal education designed to produce logical thinkers. Hence, pure mathematics and mathematical physics were included, non-mathematical (and therefore experimental) areas of physics were not. The tripos thus comprised mechanics, hydrodynamics, geometrical optics, and, at the highest levels, gravitational theory and the wave theory of light. The natural philosophy class embraced these subjects, too, but the expected level of mathematics was not so high as at Cambridge. Though Scottish professors upheld the ideal of a high-level mathematical physics, they could not count on having students with a Cambridge-like preparation in mathematics. The experimental subjects of heat, electricity and magnetism fit easily into this mathematically less intense atmosphere. In conjunction with lectures, professors would perform demonstration experiments, something not heavily (or even usually) a part of tripos preparation.

More than the Cambridge tripos, the courses in Scotland nourished a tradition of philosophical reflection on the power and limits of human knowledge. From those bright lights of the Scottish Enlightenment, David Hume and Thomas Reid, at least through to William Hamilton, who was professor of logic at Edinburgh from 1836 to 1856, the Scots debated the methodology of scientific knowledge — the possibility of knowing the existence and properties of unobservable entities, the reliability of analogical thinking in the attempt. The tradition expressed so many different views that it would probably be mistaken to conclude that it constrained or guided natural philosophers in only one specific way. Rather, it is important to recognise that the debate itself infiltrated natural philosophy courses, with each professor presenting his own thoughts on the matter, and that such concerns were part of the natural philosophy classes at early-Victorian Glasgow and Edinburgh.

William Meikleham, professor of natural philosophy at Glasgow from 1803 to 1846, had won an undergraduate prize at Glasgow 'for the best explanation of Sir Isaac Newton's Rules of Philosophising'. When he addressed such issues in his own teaching, he denied that the causes of gravity, electricity, and magnetism were understood, but did not deny that knowledge of the unseen material world was possible. He used analogies in two ways to justify the universality of gravitation — as Newton had in his third rule of reasoning, and to discuss similarities between different areas of natural philosophy, especially electricity and magnetism. Moreover, he went beyond the questions of similarity and analogy to that of unity: 'It is daily becoming more probable that the wonderfully varied effects of electricity, fire, heat, magnetism, and gravitation, may be at some future period, assigned to one common origin'.

In his teaching of natural philosophy at Edinburgh from 1833 to 1860, Professor James David Forbes increased the mathematical level for part of his class but retained its broad Scottish scope. In both research and teaching, Forbes stressed the importance of paying attention to analogies and connections between the branches of natural philosophy in advancing scientific knowledge. Analogies between light and radiant heat were crucial to his own research, and in his class he included various connections and analogies between heat, light, electricity and magnetism. On the basis of his own research, he concluded that light and radiant heat were the same thing, and, following Michael Faraday, he said the same about chemical affinity and electrical action.

Subjects in the mathematical tripos lent themselves less well to such considerations. Cambridge undergraduates would learn about similarities between sound and light, and they might come across mechanical analogues to optical phenomena, but that was all. It was not that there were no Cambridge writers on these subjects. John Herschel and William Whewell dealt with methodological questions, considered the role of analogies, and addressed the subjects of heat, electricity and magnetism. But such writings were more intimately a part of Forbes' course at Edinburgh than of a potential wrangler's path to the tripos.

Cambridge thus offered an advanced mathematical comprehension of a few, separate branches of physics, but not a vision of analogous threads of natural philosophy with the potential of being woven into a unified whole. In this sense, whatever the precise Scottish and Cambridge influences on Kelvin and Maxwell may have been, their new physical theories were decidedly more Scottish than Cantabrigian.[2]

In the 1840s and 1850s, Kelvin not only was instrumental in creating thermodynamics but also developed an approach to conceptualising electricity and magnetism that profoundly influenced Maxwell. Recognising the significance of James Prescott Joule's experimental research, Kelvin published a pivotal paper on thermodynamics in 1851, establishing the two laws of thermodynamics, the conservation and dissipation of energy. As energy changed from one form to another, its total remained constant while its usability decreased. In 1842, Kelvin published a paper expounding the mathematical similarities between the phenomena of heat flow and electrostatic force. In 1847, recognising the significance of one of Faraday's experimental discoveries, he presented a 'mechanical representation' of electricity and magnetism which depended on the analogy between certain strains in an elastic solid and particular phenomena of electricity and magnetism. With light included, it offered a unified theory of light, electricity, and magnetism. The representation was somehow analogous to an unseen physical reality without necessarily providing a literal picture of it. And in 1856, he published a 'dynamical illustration' which utilised the idea of heat being the motion of material particles to reduce various physical phenomena to a system of material particles rotating within a fluid medium. This 'illustration' was potentially even more unifying than the 'representation' of 1847. Kelvin's 'model building' style of physics thus exploited similarities between branches of physics and created mechanical models that bore essential similarities to the reality that underlay and unified diverse physical phenomena. The eventual goal was the discovery of the hidden reality itself, but in the meantime models made progress possible.

Following Kelvin's approach, Maxwell commenced research on electricity and magnetism after taking his Cambridge degree in 1854, publishing his electromagnetic theory of light in the early 1860s. The theory was embedded in an elaborate mechanical model that had helped him arrive at his theory and which was intended analogically to represent the underlying unity of electricity, magnetism and light. It is undoubtedly the best-known model formulated within this distinctive Victorian brand of physics. Even more than Kelvin, Maxwell reflected on the strengths and weaknesses of mechanical models and emphasised the importance of presenting physical theories in different ways. He certainly presented his own theory in different ways; his *Treatise on Electricity and Magnetism* (1873), the grand summation of his reconceptualisation of electromagnetic theory, was quite different from his publications a decade earlier.

Around 1870, therefore, a Scot could indeed be proud. Thermodynamics was coming to enjoy considerable acceptance. Though too early to declare Maxwell's electromagnetic theory correct, the theory obviously possessed striking originality and Maxwell had demonstrated profound insight. The strengths of Maxwell's theory were certainly sufficient to help justify the characteristically British 'field' view of physics, which may be seen to have been originated by the Englishman Faraday but was then greatly extended, conceptually and mathematically, by the Scots, Kelvin and Maxwell.

Cambridge, it must be presumed, contributed to the overall endeavour. Although both Kelvin and Maxwell were accomplished mathematicians before entering Cambridge, they each spent four years studying mathematics there. Peter Harman, for example, has shown how Maxwell used particular mathematical advances in the development of his theories, and he links that to Maxwell's mathematical studies at Cambridge.[3] Harman also sees Whewell's philosophy as influencing Maxwell more than Hamilton's, contrary to what others have maintained.[4] Crosbie Smith and M. Norton Wise argue that early-Victorian Cambridge mathematicians were emphasising analogies that existed between different areas of pure mathematics, thereby influencing Kelvin's analogical physics.[5] Also, mathematical theories of fluids and solids developed by Cambridge wranglers could be incorporated by Kelvin and Maxwell into their mechanical models. Even granting such points, however, it remains the case that none of the wranglers from the period who had only a Cambridge education even attempted what Kelvin and Maxwell did. Of the wranglers from 1830 to 1854, only Kelvin and Maxwell pounced on the results of Joule and Faraday and worked them into comprehensive physical theories.[6] Naturally enough, Cambridge wranglers published on the *Cambridge* subjects that they had been studying so intently for so long. George Gabriel Stokes (1819–1903) is the best example here, the most powerful Cambridge-educated physicist of the day. Senior wrangler in 1841, he published pathbreaking papers on hydrodynamics, elastic solids and optics during the 1840s. Kelvin and Maxwell relied on his results, but it was they and not he who sought nature's underlying unity. In 1870 a strong case could be made for the existence of a causal connection between Kelvin's and Maxwell's Scottish education and their 'Scottish' physical theories.[7]

A Scot could also be proud in 1870 of the natural philosophy classes at Glasgow and Edinburgh. Kelvin had been professor at Glasgow since 1846 and in the 1850s was providing the most modern physics instruction offered anywhere in Britain.[8] P. G. Tait (1831–1901) was then just concluding his first decade at Edinburgh. Like his friend Maxwell, Tait had attended Edinburgh Academy and Edinburgh University before going to Cambridge, where he was senior wrangler in 1851. Like Kelvin and Maxwell, though less successfully than they, Tait had first turned to non-Cambridge subjects in his research, pursuing certain implications of Faraday's work. He met Kelvin about the time he was appointed to the Edinburgh chair, and by the early 1860s appears to have been well under his influence. In 1867, they published their *Treatise on Natural Philosophy*, a highly influential textbook that fully embodied energy theory. Upon coming to Edinburgh, Tait promptly moved the natural philosophy class (where the teaching had become somewhat outdated in Forbes's last years) into the modern world by making energy theory the centrepiece of the course. The subject for the prize-essay competition each year, for example, was usually on either the conservation, transformation or dissipation of energy. By 1870, Tait had emulated Kelvin both in opening a laboratory where students could voluntarily do experimental work themselves (as opposed to witnessing demonstration experiments) and also in establishing an advanced, more specialised class in mathematical physics.[9]

Hence, whereas Cambridge in the 1860s was much as it has been in the 1840s, Glasgow and Edinburgh offered their strongest students a combined experimental-mathematical study of *modern* physics, under two modern physicists of high reputation. As they usually do, however, things changed.

1870–1910

Various motives stimulated changes at Cambridge. Expansion of school education in Britain, with the increasing inclusion of science subjects, justified a more systematic science education for future schoolmasters or university teachers than had been available a few decades earlier. Thanks especially to Kelvin and Maxwell the subjects of heat, electricity and magnetism were now sufficiently mathematised to be included in the mathematical tripos. Moreover, the inclusion of these subjects heightened a long-felt need by some, that wranglers ought to be familiar with experimental work germane to their subjects. The Cavendish Laboratory was conceived mainly to meet this need. But it was also seen as relevant to another Cambridge examination, the natural sciences tripos which originated at mid century. This tripos had only marginally included physics before, but in the reforming spirit of the early 1870s experimental physics was added to help make it a comprehensive *experimental* sciences tripos. Finally, Maxwell became the Cavendish professor in 1871 and directed the Cavendish Laboratory from its opening in 1874 until his death in 1879. These reforms of the early 1870s had important short-term and long-term consequences.[10]

In the short term, Cambridge became the centre for Maxwellian research. Jed Buchwald has identified a group of thirty-three 'Maxwellians', most of whom were working in this area during the 1870s and early 1880s, well before Heinrich Hertz's experimental detection of electromagnetic radiation in 1887 that won Maxwell's theory general acceptance.[11] Two-thirds of Buchwald's Maxwellians had Cambridge connections, seventeen of them having taken the mathematical tripos and/or worked in the Cavendish between 1871 and 1880. Two of the Maxwellians succeeded Maxwell as Cavendish professor, Lord Rayleigh in 1879 and Thomson in 1884. Hence, the tripos's traditional attraction for mathematically-gifted young men, the introduction of electricity and magnetism into the tripos, the presence of the Cavendish, and three successive Maxwellians as Cavendish professors, all combined to thrust Cambridge to the forefront of research in modern theoretical physics from the 1870s at least to the end of the century. In the longer term, within this climate of strong theoretical physics, there emerged what became the British centre for experimental physics. Several factors contributed to these developments.

There had to be students. Under Maxwell, the Cavendish had been a place for voluntary research by Cambridge students and others. Under Rayleigh and Thomson, the Cavendish offered experimental courses for undergraduates: not, as originally intended, primarily for students preparing for the mathematical tripos, but for those intending to offer experimental physics in the natural sciences tripos. Thomson himself desired a combination of mathematical and experimental work for physics students and eventually, around 1890, fashioned such an education in the context of the natural sciences tripos. These students often became research students in the Cavendish after taking their degrees. Moreover, the new regulations of 1895 that brought Rutherford to Cambridge attracted many other non-Cambridge men as well. Especially from the mid-1890s, therefore, the Cavendish housed a strong and numerous corps of research students.[12]

Cambridge's staff of physics teachers, already much larger than Glasgow's or Edinburgh's, expanded significantly during this time.[13] Whereas Maxwell had had one demonstrator, by the 1890s Thomson had a staff of seven. Moreover, the new Cambridge chair of engineering was held during the 1890s by the physicist-engineer, J. A. Ewing; and Joseph Larmor, senior wrangler in 1880 and important Maxwellian, filled a new lectureship in mathematics from 1885 to 1903, when he succeeded Stokes as Lucasian professor. Even although Stokes' lectures as Lucasian professor in the 1890s were probably more directly relevant to the 1850s, yet in the 1870s he helped to shape the standard British view of cathode rays, which guided Thomson's research on the subject, and in the late 1890s formulated the most influential theory of the newly discovered X-rays. Thomson did not have a monopoly of Cambridge physics.[14]

As a new professor of *experimental* physics, the mathematical physicist Thomson needed an experimental research topic. He chose cathode rays and related matters. The research led to his famous discovery of the electron in 1897, the third monumental experimental discovery to have come in successive years, X-rays having been discovered in 1895 and radioactivity in 1896.

Thomson and his Cavendish researchers were thus ideally placed to investigate these interrelated discoveries and their implications for the structure of atoms themselves. Rutherford was able to determine in 1898 that at least two different radioactive radiations (called alpha and beta) existed and a few years later, at McGill, formulated (with the chemist Frederick Soddy) the 'disintegration' theory of radioactivity, according to which an atom of one element transmuted into one of another upon emitting an alpha or beta ray. It was Thomson and Rutherford who defined the mainstream of theoretical attempts to understand the configuration and activity of the atom's internal components. Thomson won his Nobel prize in 1904, Rutherford his in 1908.[15]

Thomson's and Rutherford's research programmes in the early years of the twentieth century depended on concepts from the much earlier Kelvin-Maxwell programme. Of course, all theories of atomic energies assumed the truth of the first and second laws of thermodynamics. The energy possessed by particles within the atom, before radioactive decay, had to be either potential or kinetic, and Thomson and Rutherford decided it was kinetic. The main thrust of electromagnetic research had shifted from Kelvin and Maxwell themselves to a newer generation, which included many mathematical tripos graduates of the 1870s and 1880s. But, more than any other one, it was Thomson who had brought that electromagnetic tradition to the Cavendish. Thomson and Rutherford assumed that part of an electron's mass was electromagnetic in nature, thus accounting for its increased mass at high speeds. They conceived their theories of atomic structure explicitly in the Kelvin-Maxwell tradition of model-building physics. The series of atomic models that they invented were, therefore, not necessarily true portrayals of nature but, as valid 'representations', were the best path towards true portrayals.

In the 1870s Cambridge appropriated not only Maxwell himself but also Kelvin's thermodynamics, Maxwell's electromagnetic theory, and their model-building approach to physical theory. These theoretical advances, allied to institutional expansion and further educational reform, allowed Cambridge to exploit developments in experimental physics more than any other late-Victorian or Edwardian university.

Meanwhile, in Scotland, after five decades in his professorship, Kelvin retired in 1899 and was replaced at Glasgow by his former student, Andrew Gray (1847–1925). In Edinburgh P. G. Tait completed four decades as professor shortly before his death in 1901, being replaced by his former student, James Gordon Macgregor (1852–1913). A central feature of Kelvin's later career was his rejection of Maxwell's electromagnetic theory of light,[16] scrawling in the margins of his copy of Maxwell's *Treatise* such judgements as 'wholly unacceptable'. Kelvin could thus hardly have inspired his Glasgow students to become Maxwellians, and in fact Buchwald's list of Maxwellians includes only one, W. E. Ayrton, who had attended University College, London, before being in Kelvin's class for the 1867–68 session.[17] Just as Kelvin had his own theory of electromagnetism, he also had his own theories of 'electrions', as he called them, and of atomic structure, which he presented in several papers from 1897 to 1907 in opposition to Thomson and Rutherford and their followers.[18] When an additional lecturer in natural philosophy was appointed at Glasgow in the 1870s, the position went to James Thomson Bottomley, not one of Kelvin's former students but his nephew, whose degree was from Queen's College, Belfast. Bottomley achieved only a modest research career and held his position until Kelvin's retirement.

Kelvin's successor, Andrew Gray, was however a former student (MA, 1876) and acted as Kelvin's personal secretary and official assistant for a decade, before becoming professor of physics at the University College of North Wales at Bangor from 1884 to 1899. Although he published a few papers on Maxwell's electromagnetic theory in the early 1890s, Gray was, as Buchwald has written, 'far from being on the leading edge of Maxwellian research'.[19] He neither contributed to nor, seemingly, was he even an enthusiast for, the new physics of the twentieth century, complaining in the 1921 edition of one of his textbooks: 'As it is, we have now an army of students and others talking glibly of Einstein and quantum theory, whose attention to the fundamentals of dynamics and physics has been woefully slight'.[20] Gray retained an enormous respect for Kelvin, patterning his lectures after Kelvin's and writing a biography of him.[21]

During his professorship at Edinburgh, Tait was highly regarded as a lecturer and author of textbooks on various branches of physics, while achieving significant research into the kinetic theory of gases and thermoelectricity. Kelvin's influence undoubtedly strengthened Tait's commitment to energy theory in the 1860s and directed Tait towards his later research topics. Indeed, Kelvin's theoretical ideas not only found their way into Tait's natural philosophy teaching, but appear also to have worked against Tait's accepting Maxwell's electromagnetic theory. Caught between the conflicting views of his two friends (and intellectual superiors) in an area outside his own expertise, Tait played down Maxwellian theory in both his lectures and publications. He regarded it as an important confirmation of the validity of field physics, but even in the late 1880s wrote that it was still in its 'infancy'. Only in the 1890s, after Hertz's experiment, did Maxwell's electromagnetic theory receive much attention in the natural philosophy classes at Edinburgh. Unsurprisingly, Buchwald's list of Maxwellians includes only one of Tait's students, J. A. Ewing, who had worked with Tait in the early 1870s and whose later experimental work on hysteresis was done within a Maxwellian framework.[22] Tait's successor, Macgregor, had studied with him in the early 1870s, having come to Edinburgh after taking a degree from Dalhousie College in Nova Scotia. He spent more than two decades as professor of physics at Dalhousie before replacing Tait, being selected in preference to Rutherford. Tait had directed Macgregor towards research on electrical conductivity in saline solutions, and this topic provided the main theme for the some twenty research papers Macgregor published. Macgregor contributed neither to the development of Maxwellian electromagnetic theory nor to atomic physics.[23]

Glasgow and Edinburgh thus differed from Cambridge in many ways. Stokes was the long-serving physics professor in Cambridge (1849–1903), but unlike Kelvin's and Tait's, Stokes's professorship was supplemented by others. In the Edwardian period, J. J. Thomson's prominence vastly exceeded that of Gray and Macgregor. Moreover, consider the students educated at the three universities from 1870 until 1913 (when Macgregor died). From the 1870s to the 1890s, Kelvin lectured in Glasgow to only two future fellows of the Royal Society in physics (Gray and Alexander Russell) while in Edinburgh Tait lectured to only three (Cargill Knott, Macgregor, and Ewing). Cambridge graduated nearly *forty*. From 1890 to 1935, section A (for mathematics and physics) of the British Association for the Advancement of Science had thirty-three presidents who were physicists, including Thomson who was president twice: of these nearly *two-thirds* had studied at Cambridge, seven came from Owen's College, Manchester, and one or two each from such as University College in London, Mason College in Birmingham, and the institutions in South

Kensington. There were two from Glasgow (Gray and Ayrton), none from Edinburgh. Britain produced ten Nobel prizewinners who were educated between 1870 and 1913. *Nine* of the ten had Cambridge degrees, five having previously studied at another university (three English, one Australian, one New Zealand) and one taking a DSc degree afterwards from University College, London. The one without a Cambridge degree, James Chadwick, took a degree in physics in 1911 at the University of Manchester, where Rutherford was professor. Becoming part of Rutherford's staff at Manchester in 1918, Chadwick went with him to the Cavendish the next year. None of the ten Nobel prizewinners had any of their education in a Scottish university.

These figures disclose something of the Victorian origin and growth of English universities, another factor in Scotland's relative decline. The South Kensington institutions that evolved into Imperial College; University College, London; and, especially, Owen's College (later University of Manchester); all became academic centres for physics education and re-search. When Arthur Schuster (who had received part of his education at Owen's, worked in the Cavendish for five years, and been a professor at Manchester since 1881) relinquished his professorship in 1907 to attract Rutherford, Manchester successfully made the transition from Victorian to modern physics.[24] When the young Niels Bohr visited England in 1911–12, for example, he divided his time between Thomson in Cambridge and Rutherford in Manchester. Rutherford published his theory of the nuclear atom in 1911, providing the basis for Bohr's quantum atom two years later. Bohr had little reason to visit Gray and Macgregor.

For the Scottish universities the heady days of the 1860s, and earlier, had run up against the reforms at Cambridge, which began in the early 1870s, and then the growth of other new English universities. Glasgow and Edinburgh would probably have been hard pressed to compete even without any of that stagnation that might be identified in their natural philosophy programmes. Both conceptually and institutionally, mid-century Scottish natural philosophy had been well anglicised by the Edwardian period.

Conclusion

How far does institutional policy explain the loss of stature of Scottish physics and the rise of English dominance in the period 1830–1910? True, Scottish universities did fail to find a long-term home for a Scot of genius such as Clerk Maxwell but, on the two occasions when his claims to appointment were overlooked, the correct decisions were probably made in the circumstances. Scottish professors lectured to large classes of non-specialists, and it is very likely that David Thomson at Aberdeen, and certainly Tait at Edinburgh, surpassed Maxwell at that task.[25] Nor can it be claimed that Cambridge's appointment of Maxwell was a case of astute foresight into the benefits of promoting Maxwellian electromagnetic theory; their first choice would have been Kelvin, but he wanted to stay in Glasgow. Even Stokes, with little accomplishment in electricity and magnetism, could probably have been appointed in Cambridge ahead of Maxwell, but Stokes had the wisdom and modesty to realise that he was not the right man. Nor should Kelvin and Tait be castigated too severely for de-emphasising Maxwell's theory in their teaching. Kelvin had his own insights into electromagnetism which had, after all, contributed greatly to the dramatic success of the Atlantic Cable in the 1860s. An objective observer could reasonably conclude during the 1870s and early 1880s that the exact fate of Maxwell's theory was undecided. In addition, it would be hard to fault Glasgow or Edinburgh for making appointments from their own former students at the turn of the century: arguably this policy had been successful for a century in both universities. There was no Glasgow graduate clearly superior to Gray in 1899. Of Edinburgh's graduates, only Ewing, who had been professor at Cambridge for a decade, might have been clearly preferable to Macgregor in 1901, while Rutherford was not nearly so prominent in 1901 as he was to become just a few years later.

Nevertheless, by 1913 the leadership of British physics had long since slipped away from Glasgow and Edinburgh. Both universities had done a respectable job, not only of providing a good education in physics but also by producing a reasonable number of respectable physicists; but at the turn of the century Glasgow and Edinburgh no longer defined the essence of academic physics to nearly the extent they had in the 1860s. Even (or especially) with professors of the stature of Kelvin and Tait, there clearly were potential disadvantages in a long-tenured professor intellectually dominating a small staff of relatives or former students, and then being succeeded by a former student in awe of the legend. From this viewpoint, Rutherford's disrespect for Kelvin, manners aside, contrasts refreshingly with Gray's adulation.[26]

Glasgow did change somewhat under Gray. Along with a new building, there was an appreciably expanded staff, filled however by recent Glasgow graduates. A second professorship was created in 1920, and it went to Gray's son, James Gordon Gray. James received his BSc in engineering from Glasgow in 1903, and served as lecturer in natural philosophy from 1904 until being appointed professor. Andrew Gray was succeeded in 1924 by H. A. Wilson, a product of Yorkshire College, Berlin University, and the Cavendish. But when he left after one year, Glasgow reverted to choosing former students, selecting Edward Taylor Jones, who had studied with Gray at the University College of North Wales, and, as Gray before him, was professor of physics there.[27]

The greater change occurred in Edinburgh. Under Macgregor there was a new laboratory and an expanded staff filled, as at Glasgow, by former students. Macgregor, however, was replaced by a non-Edinburgh man, Charles Barkla, who had studied at Liverpool and done research in the Cavendish. He received his Nobel prize in 1917, as an Edinburgh professor. Edinburgh's second professorship in natural philosophy came in 1923 with the appointment of C. G. Darwin, a graduate of the mathematical tripos who had also worked with Rutherford in Manchester. Moreover, another wrangler, E. T. Whittaker, became the Edinburgh professor of mathematics in 1912, using the position to promote mathematical physics. None of these — Barkla, Darwin, or Whittaker — had any Scottish education.[28]

There are signs, then, that Edinburgh — more than Glasgow — was attempting to rebuild its strength in physics by importing new blood from English universities. It was a far cry from the days when Edinburgh and Glasgow had dominated British physics.

NOTES

1. See D. B. Wilson, 'The educational matrix: physics education at early-Victorian Cambridge, Edinburgh, and Glasgow Universities', in P. M. Harman, (ed.), *Wranglers and Physicists: Studies on Cambridge Physics in the Nineteenth Century* (Manchester 1985), 12–48.

2. For discussions of Kelvin's and Maxwell's research in the context of nineteenth-century physics, P. M. Harman, *Energy, Force, and Matter: the Conceptual Development of Nineteenth-Century Physics* (Cambridge, 1982).

3. P. M. Harman, 'Mathematics and reality in Maxwell's dynamical physics', Robert Kargon and Peter Achinstein (eds), *Kelvin's Baltimore Lectures and Modern Theoretical Physics: Historical and Philosophical Perspectives* (Cambridge, Mass., 1987), 267–297.

4. P. M. Harman, 'Edinburgh philosophy and Cambridge physics: the natural philosophy of James Clerk Maxwell', in Harman, *Wranglers and Physicists*, 202–224. For the other view, George Elder Davie, *The Democratic Intellect: Scotland and her Universities in the Nineteenth Century* (Edinburgh, 1961), 191–197; Thomas K. Simpson, 'Some observations on Maxwell's *Treatise on Electricity and Magnetism*', *Studies in History and Philosophy of Science*, 1 (1970), 249–263; and C. W. F. Everitt, *James Clerk Maxwell, Physicist and Natural Philosopher* (New York, 1975), 50, 88, 102, 116.

5. Crosbie Smith and M. Norton Wise, *Energy and Empire: a Biographical Study of Lord Kelvin* (Cambridge, 1989), 182–184.

6. See Wilson, 'The educational matrix', 33–45.

7. For other discussions of the Scottish component in Kelvin's and Maxwell's physics, see Richard G. Olson, *Scottish Philosophy and British Physics 1750–1880: a Study in the Foundations of the Victorian Scientific Style* (Princeton, 1975), and Daniel M. Siegel, *Innovation in Maxwell's Electromagnetic Theory* (Cambridge, 1991), chap. 1.

8. Wilson, 'The educational matrix', 30–33; D. B. Wilson, *Kelvin and Stokes: a Comparative Study in Victorian Physics* (Bristol, 1987), 53–69; R. Sviedrys, 'The rise of physics laboratories in Britain', *Historical Studies in the Physical Sciences*, 7 (1976), 405–436; and M. N. Wise and C. Smith, 'Measurement, work and industry in Lord Kelvin's Britain', *Historical Studies in the Physical and Biological Sciences*, 17 (1987), 147–173.

9. D. B. Wilson, 'P. G. Tait and Edinburgh natural philosophy, 1860–1901', *Annals of Science*, 48 (1991), 267–87.

10. D. B. Wilson, 'Experimentalists among the mathematicians: physics in the Cambridge natural sciences tripos, 1851–1900', *Historical Studies in the Physical Sciences*, 12 (1982), 325–371.

11. Jed Z. Buchwald, *From Maxwell to Microphysics: Aspects of Electromagnetic Theory in the Last Quarter of the Nineteenth Century* (Chicago, 1985), 74. See, also, *idem.*, 'Modifying the continuum: methods of Maxwellian electrodynamics' in Harman,

Wranglers and Physicists, 225–241. Buchwald discusses the intricacies of Maxwell's theory and the ways it was transformed by his followers.

12. Wilson, 'Experimentalists'.

13. *Ibid.*; Paul Forman, John L. Heilbron, and Spencer Weart, 'Physics *circa* 1900: personnel, funding, and productivity of the academic establishments', *Historical Studies in the Physical Sciences*, 5 (1975), 1–185, especially the table at 18–19.

14. Wilson, *Kelvin and Stokes*, 41–53, 181–209; B. R. Wheaton, *The Tiger and the Shark; Empirical Roots of Wave-Particle Dualism* (Cambridge, 1983), 15–48.

15. On Thomson and Rutherford, see, for example: J. L. Heilbron's article on Thomson and Lawrence Badash's on Rutherford in the *Dictionary of Scientific Biography*; Thaddeus J. Trenn, *The Self-Splitting Atom: The History of the Rutherford-Soddy Collaboration* (London, 1977); and J. L. Heilbron, 'The scattering of α and β particles and Rutherford's atom', *Archive for History of Exact Sciences*, 4 (1967–68), 247–307.

16. Ole Knudsen, 'Mathematics and physical reality in William Thomson's electromagnetic theory' in Harman, *Wranglers and Physicists*, 149–179; Smith and Wise, *Energy and Empire*, 445–494.

17. Buchwald, *From Maxwell to Microphysics*, 74; Wilson, *Kelvin and Stokes*, 62.

18. Wilson, *Kelvin and Stokes*, 221–239.

19. Buchwald, *From Maxwell to Microphysics*, 39.

20. Andrew Gray, *Absolute Measurements in Electricity and Magnetism*, 2nd edn (London 1921), v.

21. P. I. Dee, 'Natural philosophy', in *Fortuna Domus* (Glasgow, 1952), 313–333; A. R., 'Andrew Gray — 1847–1925', *Proceedings of the Royal Society of London*, ser. A, 110 (1926), xvi–xix; A. Gray, *Lord Kelvin: an Account of his Scientific Life and Work* (London, 1908).

22. Wilson, 'P. G. Tait'; Buchwald, *From Maxwell to Microphysics*, 74.

23. James Walker, 'Natural philosophy', in A. Logan Turner, (ed.), *History of the University of Edinburgh, 1883–1933* (Edinburgh, 1933), 247–252; J. A. E[wing], 'James Gordon Macgregor, 1852–1913', *Proceedings of the Royal Society of London*, ser. A, 89 (1913–14), xxvi–xxviii; R. A. S., 'C. G. Knott, 1856–1922', *Proceedings of the Royal Society of London*, ser. A, 102 (1922–23), xxvii–xxviii. Knott wrote what is still the standard biography of Tait: *Life and Scientific Work of Peter Guthrie Tait* (Cambridge, 1911).

24. On Manchester, see Robert H. Kargon, *Science in Victorian Manchester: Enterprise and Expertise* (Baltimore, 1977).

25. R. V. Jones, 'James Clerk Maxwell at Aberdeen, 1856–1860', *Notes and Records of the Royal Society of London*, 28 (1973), 57–81; P. M. Harman, 'Introduction', in *idem.*, ed., *The Scientific Letters and Papers of James Clerk Maxwell. Volume I: 1846–1862* (Cambridge, 1990), 18–30; William Leslie Low, *David Thomson, MA, Professor of Natural Philosophy in the University of Aberdeen: a Sketch of his Character and Career* (Aberdeen, 1894).

26. On Rutherford, see A. S. Eve, *Rutherford: being the Life and Letters of the Rt. Hon. Lord Rutherford, O.M.* (New York, 1939), 29, 107–109.

27. Dee, 'Natural Philosophy'; *Glasgow University Calendar*.

28. Walker, 'Natural Philosophy'; *Edinburgh University Calendar*.

Part III
The Student Body
in the Scottish Universities

12

Discipline and Decorum: the Law-codes of the Universities of Aberdeen, 1605–86

Colin A. McLaren

Accounts of the changing nature of discipline in universities draw heavily upon *leges, statuta* and *instituta*, the codes of laws that regulated student life.[1] These set a standard of behaviour within and without the walls and prescribed the sanctions by which it was to be maintained. Amendments and additions, squeezed into and around the text, show how effective — or, rather, how ineffective — they were. In the course of the seventeenth century, the two universities of Aberdeen produced between them at least six codes, but they have hitherto attracted little attention.

Four related codes, in six versions, survive in the archives of King's College, and two discrete codes in those of Marischal. The codes of King's were published in the mid nineteenth century.[2] They were used briefly by P. J. Anderson, in his account of the arts curriculum, and sketchily by R. S. Rait and J. M. Bulloch in their quatercentenary histories.[3] The codes of Marischal remain unpublished. One was written in a register that lay, forgotten, in Edinburgh for much of the nineteenth century. The other was examined by William Knight, the college antiquary, around 1826, but found no place in his 'Collections'.[4] Both were known to Anderson, however, and would probably have featured in his projected selection of Marischal records, had he completed the book.[5] Rait and Bulloch, working mainly from printed or extracted material, ignored them.

The codes amended, extended and augmented the system of discipline incorporated towards the end of the sixteenth century in the New Foundation of King's and in the foundation charter of Marischal.[6] Under this system, students were to live, strictly secluded from the distractions and temptations of the town, in an atmosphere of piety, harmony, sobriety and docility; the bursars, especially, furnishing a model of humility and obedience in the performance of a variety of menial tasks. It was clear to the authors of both documents, however, that further legislation, matching new or changed circumstances, would be needed to keep the system intact. This they entrusted to the college principals: the codes of the seventeenth century were the result.

At King's, the first references to a code occur in the era of reform inaugurated by the chancellor, Bishop Patrick Forbes, in 1619. Amongst

128

other improvements, Forbes revitalised the role of the rector, making him responsible for maintaining standards of behaviour and discipline.[7] It was in this capacity, in 1634, that John Forbes, Patrick's son, reprimanded Principal William Leslie, for failing to read out to the students the laws concerning their private studies and discipline. The rebuke may refer simply to a sixteenth-century rule, that the foundation charter should be read four times a year;[8] or it may mean that a discrete code, based upon the charter, already existed. At all events, the rector ordered that in future the laws should be read before the entire college in the public school in December, and that the text should be produced by the principal, on demand, for revision and authorisation.[9] The latter requirement caused considerable trouble over the next three years. The principal was slow to provide the rector with a text, and attempts at revision, first by a small committee of staff, then by the staff as a whole, were something less than successful. In 1637 Forbes' successor threatened the principal with disciplinary action if he did not produce the text as ordered. The outcome is not recorded.[10]

The code that was the subject of these deliberations has not survived, but there are two versions of a text which must closely resemble it.[11] One is dated 1641 and can therefore be attributed to Leslie's successor, William Guild. There is no record of its promulgation, however, and no evidence to connect it with the transformation of the colleges into the Caroline University, which occurred around this time.

Guild's code repeated the provisions of the New Foundation against discord and violence but contained new laws designed to ensure that teachers and servants were treated with respect, to promote modesty in dress and civility at table, and to preserve the fabric from damage, defacement and dirt. It reasserted the restrictions of the New Foundation on students' visits to the town and exhorted them to avoid bad company. It referred briefly to their conduct on the three afternoons set aside for supervised sport — 'play days', as they came to be called[12] — and forbade them to make wagers. It dealt at greater length with their leisure, forbidding them to play cards and games of chance, prohibiting noise and disturbance around bedtimes, and imposing precautions against fire. As in the New Foundation, a high standard of conduct at a low level in the community was demanded from the bursars.

Two further texts have also been assigned to Guild's principalship,[13] although it is difficult to date them precisely.[14] They contain some 30 of the 44 laws from 1641. Among the new laws, several were designed to discourage disorder. In the first text, sacrilege and obscenity were punished along with swearing and cursing; those who went into town were ordered to return as soon as possible; and the organisation of roll-calls was tightened up. In the second, students were forbidden to wander round the college in an unruly manner, to meddle with the bells, or to commit excesses of any sort. This concern with disorder may have been simply a response to the turbulence of the times; it may also reflect growing indiscipline on the part of the students, as increasing numbers were housed inadequately at King's; and apprehension on the part of the staff, as relations with Marischal College declined. Among other additions in the first text were a law against laxity in dress and another compelling students to stay throughout the academic year. Among those in the second, there was a renewed emphasis on piety and reverence: a law by which students were examined on the Sunday sermon was revived as an old and praiseworthy custom, and they were ordered to read the Bible and pray in their rooms at bedtime; they were also instructed to bare their heads before the regents, in private and in public.

Guild was replaced in 1652 by John Row, who issued his own code in the following year and revised it at intervals until 1661.[15] He retained Guild's laws as a core but recast their order and elaborated their wording. Guild had protected from noise or interruption those who were asleep or studying: Row protected them from 'the sound of voices, resounding clamour, loud laughter, banging, crashing, uproar, musical instruments, immoderate and immodest promenading, dancing and running-around'.[16] Of the innovations in Row's code, the most significant was that against dissidence, unsurprising on the part of a staunch Cromwellian, during the early months of the pacification of the North. In addition, he constructed a detailed daily timetable; he proposed that Hebrew should be used, along with Latin and Greek, for conversation and recalled that French, too, had been advocated in the foundation charter; he prescribed study in the vacation — it was not, he said, a holiday; and he prohibited games like snowballing, handball and tennis, in order to protect the students — and the windows — from harm.

Row was, in turn, deposed at the Restoration, and in 1662 began the long rule of Alexander Middleton. Two years later, royal commissioners visited King's and examined the codes then in existence. They again made the revision of the laws the responsibility of the rector and demanded that they 'be reduced als neir as may be, according as the samen was practised in anno 1635'.[17] In the following year the rector dutifully called a meeting to carry out further revisions but, after a display of dilatoriness reminiscent of the 1630s, the staff reported that nothing more needed to be changed.[18]

The laws that were applied in Middleton's time may have been those contained in the second of the undated texts of the 1640s. It is amended in Middleton's hand and was reproduced almost verbatim, with his amendments and some of a later date, in the last of the codes to survive from the seventeenth century.[19] This was written out around 1686, probably on the initiative of Middleton's son George, who had become principal the previous year. The later additions were again primarily designed to prevent disorder, this time in the New Town. They restricted the students' visits there and forbade them to wander around or molest the townsfolk. They were the product of three decades in which hostility between the students of Marischal and King's had turned into spasmodic violence, spilling from the colleges into the streets.

Of the two codes from Marischal College, one is dated and attributed, the other is not. Unlike those of King's, they are not related: they do not refer to each other; and, echoes of the foundation charter and a few shared terms apart, their texts have little in common.

Gilbert Gray, second principal of Marischal, compiled his code in 1605.[20] Alone among the Aberdeen codes, it has a discernible pattern. Gray began with a brief preamble insisting upon the need for the rule of law 'in our republic of letters', and an oath of obedience to the code, which all the students had to swear. His first measures were designed to preserve harmony within the college, by prohibiting abusive language and the carrying of weapons. He dealt next with the students' demeanour inside and outside the walls, regulating their dress and their manner towards their teachers, their elders and the townsfolk at large.[21] He emphasised the seclusive nature of college life, confining the students within the walls at night and prohibiting outsiders from using college rooms; but he legislated, too, for the occasions when the students were, by design or default, in the public eye. He devoted particular attention to Sunday worship, when they attended the town church, prescribing how they should behave in the procession and during the services.[22] Back behind the walls, he set out measures to protect the fabric of the building and the furnishings of the students' rooms. Then he provided a timetable for the day[23] and a praxis for lectures, private study and the Saturday disputations.[24] From work, he turned to play and the thrice-weekly games of football on the Links,[25] regulating the organisation of the matches and the players' conduct on and off the pitch. He instructed the students in their attitude towards members of King's[26] and in their deportment in private houses; and he forbade them to drink in taverns, wander around the streets or play at cards in their rooms. Behind the walls once more, he described the duties of student censors[27] and listed the penalties for certain offences. Thereafter, he dealt with purely academic matters — the curricula of the four classes,[28] the form of examinations, the process of laureation and the payment of fees.

Gray's code shows a marked concern with the world immediately beyond the walls — distinctive, but hardly surprising. The college was, after all, only twelve years old, still seeking to establish itself in the town — in the very centre of the town, at that. Gray was determined that his students should learn to live in peace and charity with their hosts. A student who insulted the town worthies left a stain on his fellow-students that must be washed away by punishment.[29] He was equally concerned with the image of the college in the townspeople's eyes. Students were not to empty slops out of their windows or defile public places; nor were they to loiter outside the college gate on Sundays, when passers-by would expect them to be inside, studying.[30] Gray was also anxious to secure good relations with King's and insisted that the regents and students of the Old Town should be treated with respect. Nevertheless, he envisaged grounds — of virtue and honour — on which disputes might arise between the student bodies and ordained that such quarrels should be moderated by the regents, in order to avoid violence. He thus envisaged the hostility that ensued between the colleges; indeed, he seems to imply that it had already begun.[31]

The many flaggings, deletions and amendments that surround Gray's code show that it was revised several times. In the absence of any minutes of college meetings, however, there is nothing to say when this occurred. For the same reason, it is impossible to say when or why the other Marischal code was created. It was formerly dated, tentatively, around 1600.[32] Knight later suggested the 1640s, without explaining why, and his suggestion was adopted by Anderson.[33] The early ascription is questionable — surely, in the circumstances, Gray would have referred to the document somewhere; the later date raises a number of textual problems.[34] Until more is known about the organisation of the college in the first half of the century, it is unlikely that a firm conclusion can be reached.

The code is introduced by a grandiose preamble on discipline. No society can exist without men to admonish it and censure its behaviour; and young men, impetuous, inexperienced and pleasure-seeking, have particular need of them. They can be taught modesty and piety, but a sense of duty must be imposed through discipline which achieves, through the promise of rewards and the fear of punishment, what teaching and counsel cannot. This discipline must be applied not only to their work but to their private life inside and outside the college. The laws themselves deal for the most part with the curriculum, modes of study and the process of graduation. Towards the end, however, there are clauses on behaviour.[35] They are based largely on the provisions of the foundation charter; in addition, however, they enjoin students to respect their teachers as they would their parents, to keep the college clean and hygienic, and to abstain from games of chance. Three laws touch on relations with the town: the first implies that townsfolk could report students for wandering in the streets; the second penalises the injury of a citizen; the third involves the magistracy in the punishment of students who carried weapons.[36]

These, then, were the codes. How were they implemented and enforced? The key figure was the hebdomadar, the regent appointed on a weekly basis to supervise the students. His duties were established in the New Foundation and the Marischal College charter; they are mentioned in the codes of King's and are described in detail by Gilbert Gray.[37]

The hebdomadar's day began at five in the morning when he inspected the students' rooms, noting the names of any who were absent and urging the rest to their work. His arrival was evidently not welcomed by the occupants: at Marischal, an amendment to Gray's laws ordered them to obey him and not to give him any trouble. He then accompanied his charges to the common school for the first of four roll-calls and prayers. On play days he held a roll-call before leading the students out to the Links; he stayed with them for the requisite two hours, before bringing them back for yet another name-check. Two hours later, he supervised the evening roll-call, before taking prayers; and at nine o'clock he made another round of the rooms. He was evidently no more welcome at night than at dawn. At King's, William Guild ordered the students to open up as soon as he knocked; while the canny John Row decreed that the round should not begin until the college doors were locked and the key in the hedomadar's pocket, lest the students slipped out after his visit. He was to be on the look-out for anything unseemly, for the candle or ember that might cause a fire, and was to ensure that each occupant had performed his nightly devotions. On top of his daily rounds and roll-calls and his six hours on the Links, the hebdamodar at King's had the task on Fridays of checking the theses for the disputations the following morning, over which he presided; and on Sunday mornings he took round to the church door alms for the poor collected from the students.

It is doubtful if the regents faced their week on duty with enthusiasm. Nevertheless, their supervisory functions, at fixed points in the day, anchored the network of laws by which the students were confined. They were assisted by the eyes, ears and, ultimately, the tongues of the student censors.

The role of the censors at King's was described in the codes of the 1640s.[38] A public censor kept the roll, and a censor in each class was empowered to reprove classmates who committed minor offences, reporting serious infractions of the laws to the subprincipal on Monday mornings. There is some ambiguity in Guild's laws but the later codes show that class censors, at least, were chosen from the bursars. In Row's day, the censorial system seems to have been at its height. A censor accompanied the hebdomadar on the dawn patrol, to write down the names of absentees and late-risers; another, the 'censor corycaeus', was employed on play days to report those who went into town; and a third, the 'speculator', was sent out on 'unplay' days to check that no students were playing truant on the Links. Row also refers to 'clandestine' censors but for obvious reasons says nothing of their methods. The censors were themselves subject to discipline. Guild ordered them to be punished if they did not perform their office, especially if, by their own misbehaviour, they set a bad example. Row declared that their punishment should be double. His code laid down the standards to which they were to aspire: they were to act irrespective of persons, in a spirit of love, showing clemency and fairness. Delation was a fact of seventeenth-century life. At King's, it was not limited to the censors and the 'censure day'. If one student was attacked by another, he was to report the offence. The law was designed not just to impose punishment, but to forestall retaliation.[39]

The duties of the censors at Marischal are described in detail by Gray;[40] the office receives only a passing mention in the undated code. A public censor was appointed from the students each week to call the roll. He also reported to the principal, on Mondays or Saturdays, those who spoke in the vernacular instead of Latin or Greek, those who swore or caused quarrels, wandered around the college, or misbehaved in church. There were, in addition, class censors, reporting daily to the class regent those who chattered, were idle or caused a nuisance. In the regent's absence, they could give their classmates leave to go out of college.

What the hebdomadar found, what the censor saw, heard and reported, the principal and his staff punished. The codes of King's provide glimpses of the judicial process. On Monday mornings the subprincipal received a report from the public censor. He interviewed the offenders and decided which cases should go before the principal and his colleagues. The staff would then discuss the appropriate punishment: assessing compensation for damage to the fabric, for example, or deciding whether to expel a student for assault. Sadly, no records of such meetings survive.

William Guild graded the forms of punishment available to his staff: at the bottom of the scale was 'the prudent remedy of words'; next came 'the severity of the rod'; lastly, a combination of beating and expulsion.[41] The laws themselves, however, rarely indicated when these options were to be used, allowing regents some discretion in matching the punishment to the crime. Nevertheless, John Row specifically mentions beating as the penalty for those whose disputations overstepped the bounds of civility and for those who exposed the buildings to the danger of fire, by fetching live coals from the kitchen in tongs instead of a deep or covered pot.[42] Expulsion, too, was specified in several cases. It was the punishment for those who created discord, faction and dissidence; for those who uttered curses, sacrilege and obscenities; and, in some cases, for those who carried weapons. Students guilty of theft, fornication or drunkenness were expelled with hissing; if they spent their tuition fees on other things, they were cast out as thieves and their parents were informed of their crime. Expulsion was, finally, the punishment of the incorrigible.[43]

On one occasion, at least, an academic sanction was imposed. Fourth-year students who celebrated the end of their course with a feast forfeited their laureation. There was also a discrete set of punishments for bursars, described by Row in detail.[44] For minor offences, they were banished from the table or received three warnings, followed by expulsion; for major crimes, they were deprived of their bursaries — in effect, expelled.

Beatings and expulsion were likewise employed at Marischal, together with fines. Gray's code often says explicitly how and when. Beatings were administered for offences which involved violence — on the playing-field, for example; for escapades — like climbing the walls; and for misbehaviour in public — at the gates or in church. For serious crimes, like staying out at night, the beating was public. In one case, of repeated failure to learn lessons, it was to be administered by the principal. Students who were absent, swore or spoke in the vernacular were struck on the hand on the first two occasions and beaten on the third; but the minor strokes were later commuted to fines of a penny or twopence.[45] Fines were also imposed on students who mistreated the fabric or furnishings of the college and, subsequently, on those who returned late after the vacation.[46] Expulsion was reserved for the incorrigible. Students who carried weapons suffered their confiscation for the first offence, were punished in the public school for the second, and were expelled for the third. Those who played at dice or cards, wandered the streets at night or were caught drinking in taverns were given a warning on the first occasion and, if they disregarded it, were expelled.[47]

The college laws of Aberdeen depict a system of discipline imposed by regular supervision, maintained by public and secret delation and enforced by punishment, one that conformed closely to those in use elsewhere in Scotland and beyond. Hebdomadars were to be found in the other three Scottish universities. At Glasgow, institutes of 1580 assigned to the regents morning and evening inspections and the supervision of games, on a weekly rota; the title 'hebdomadar' itself was not used but occurs in institutes of 1645. At Edinburgh, according to the laws of 1628, the hebdomadar not only carried out a similar set of duties but hosted a meeting on Sundays to discuss the problems of keeping order. At St Andrew's in the 1690s, he led morning and evening prayers as he had done for over a century.[48] If the hebdomadar was a peculiarly Scottish figure, the censor had his counterparts almost everywhere: the 'explorateur' in the Paris statutes of 1601, the 'observator occultus' in the Dublin code of 1629 and the 'monitor', on a salary, in the Harvard laws of 1655.[49] As for punishment — evidently the rod was wielded as strenuously in Aberdeen as it was in universities and schools elsewhere.[50] Nevertheless, the amendments to Gray's code suggest that the fine was becoming an acceptable alternative, and by 1690, if not before, King's too punished some crimes 'by pecuniall mulct.'[51]

NOTES

1. E.g., Samuel E. Morison, *Harvard College in the Seventeenth Century*, 2 vols (Cambridge, Mass, 1936); Philippe Aries, *L'Enfant et la Vie Familiale sous l'Ancien Regime* (Paris, 1960) trans. by R. Baldick as *Centuries of Childhood (London, 1962, 1986);* John Durkan and James Kirk, *The University of Glasgow, 1451–1577* (Glasgow, 1977); James K. McConica (ed.), *History of the University of Oxford*, iii, *The Collegiate University* (Oxford, 1986); Lawrence W. B. Brockliss, *French Higher Education in the Seventeenth and Eighteenth Centuries* (Oxford, 1987).

2. Cosmo Innes (ed.), *Fasti Aberdonenses. Selections from the Records of the University and King's College of Aberdeen* (Spalding Club, Aberdeen, 1854), 33–40, 225–55 (hereafter Innes, *Fasti*).

3. *The Arts Curriculum* (Aberdeen, 1892), 7–8 (hereafter Anderson, *Curriculum*); Robert S. Rait, *The Universities of Aberdeen. A History* (Aberdeen, 1895); John M. Bulloch, *A History of the University of Aberdeen, 1495–1895* (London, 1895).

4. Aberdeen University Library, MS M 103, 113. All manuscripts cited hereafter are from AUL.

5. Anderson, *Curriculum*, 8–9; P. J. Anderson (ed.), *Fasti Academiae Mariscallanae, 1593–1860*, 3 vols (New Spalding Club, Aberdeen, 1889–98), 2, vii (hereafter Anderson, *FAM*).

6. The text of the New Foundation is discussed and translated by G. Patrick Edwards in D. Stevenson, *King's College, Aberdeen: from Protestant Reformation to Covenanting Revolution* (Aberdeen, 1990) (hereafter Stevenson, *King's College*). The foundation charter of Marischal is printed and translated in Anderson, *FAM*, 1, 39–77.

7. Stevenson, *King's College*, chap. 4.

8. Innes, *Fasti*, 263.

9. MS K 36, ff. 10v, 11v, 13v.

10. Ibid., ff. 14v, 17v, 18, 18v, 19v 21.

11. MS K 265/2, 'Leges Collegii Regii Aberdonensis 1641', 8 leaves, amended in at least two hands, one citing a visitation decree of 1650; MS K 256/3, untitled and

undated, endorsed 'Laws', 10 leaves. Innes prints K 265/3 in romans and variants from K 265/2 in italics; he entitles the texts 'Collegii Regii A⁾erdonensis leges veteres de novo promulgatae anno 1641', but the description does not appear on the documents; Innes, *Fasti*, 33–5, 225–31.

12. Innes, *Fasti*, 366.

13. MS K 3, 21–8, 'Leges Collegii Regii Aberdonensis', undated; MS K 265/1, 'Leges Collegii Regii Aberdonensis', undated, 6 leaves, additions in the hand of Alexander Middleton. The version printed by Innes, apparently composed indiscriminately from both texts, is entitled 'Leges Collegii Regii Aberdonensis post aliquot annos editae', but the description does not appear on the documents; its place in the edition implies a date before 1653; Innes, *Fasti*, 35–7, 232–9.

14. There is a reference in K 265/1 to a recent royal commission of visitation, but it cannot be identified with confidence.

15. MS K 3, 1–20, 'Leges Collegii Egii Aberdonensis promulgatae a Magistro Joanne Row Gymnasiarcha . . . 1653 [to] . . . 1661, holograph; Innes, *Fasti*, 240–55.

16. 'nemo voce vocali, et sonora vociferatione, cachinnis, strepitu, fragore, tumultu, musicis instrumentis, immodica et immodesta deambulatione saltatione aut discursatione, interpellato, impedito, disturbato . . . ; Innes, *Fasti*, 245, no. 26.

17. Innes, *Fasti*, 316, 318–20.

18. MS K 37, ff. 9r, 10r, 10v.

19. MS K 130, ff. 2–5, 'Leges et statuta Collegii Regii Aberdonensis', part of 'A double of the Mortifications, Rentall, and Statutes . . .', subscribed 1686.

20. MS M 2, ff. 170r–74v, 'Statuta accademiae Aberdonensis a Magistro Gilberto Graio gymnasiarcha . . . anno 1605 qui octavus est annus prefecturae eius'. Subsequent references cite the numbers added to the clauses in a later hand.

21. MS M 2, f. 170v, no. 5.

22. Ibid., f. 171r, no. 12.

23. Ibid., f. 171v, no. 19.

24. Ibid., f. 172r, no. 23.

25. Ibid., f. 172v, no. 24.

26. Ibid., f. 173r, no. 27.

27. Ibid., f. 173v, no. 29.

28. Ibid., beginning at no. 31.

29. Ibid., f. 170v, no. 5.

30. Ibid., nos. 6–8.

31. Ibid., f. 173r, no. 27.

32. MS M 391, 'Leges Novae Academiae Aberdonensis', 2 leaves, one incomplete, French pot watermark, undated but endorsed in 18th-cent. hand' (about 1600?)'.

33. See above, notes 3 and 4. The hand favours the early ascription; the evidence of the title and watermark is inconclusive.

34. E.g., the lack of references to institutions such as the Hebrew lectureship of 1617; the discrepancy between the fees ('didactri loco libellas tres' and 'locarii loco . . . marcam') and those of 1605 ('didactron quinque libellas' and 'locario marcam' altered to '20 ad minimum solidos'); and the reference to J. T. Freige, *Quaestiones physicae* (Basle, 1579), which is not listed as a course text in 1647/8; Anderson, *Curriculum*, 6–7.

35. MS M 391v, beginning at 5th para.

36. Ibid., 8th, 10th and 11th paras.

37. Innes, *Fasti*, 228, 233, no. 9, 235 no. 32, 236 nos. 38–40, 243 no. 22, 245 no. 24, 254 no. 5; MS M 2, ff. 171r, no. 18, 171v, no. 19, 172v, no. 24. His duties were also described at a Visitation of the colleges in 1690; Innes, *Fasti*, 366–7.

38. Innes, *Fasti*, 229, 236 no. 35, 237 no. 43, 238 no. 47, 241 no. 8, 243, no. 22, 244 no. 23, 245 no. 24, 247 no. 27, 254 no. 5.

39. Innes, *Fasti*, 227.

40. MS M 2, ff. 171r, no. 14; 171v, no. 19, 173, no. 29.

41. Innes, *Fasti*, 238 no. 45.

42. *Ibid.* 244 no. 22, 245 no. 25.

43. *Ibid.* 277, 228, 234 no. 22, 235 no. 32, 242 nos. 16 and 18, 247 no. 28, 248 no. 37.

44. *Ibid.* 248 no. 32; 230, 237 nos. 42 and 43, 238 no. 45, 246, no. 27, 254–5.

45. MS M 2, ff. 170r no. 4; 170v, nos 6, 9, 10; 171r, no. 12; 171v, no. 20; 173r, no. 26; 173v, no. 29.

46. Ibid., ff. 171r, no. 15; 173v, no. 32.

47. Ibid., ff. 170r, no. 4; 173r, no. 28.

48. Cosmo Innes (ed.), *Munimenta Alme Universitatis Glasquensis*, 3 vols (Maitland Club, Glasgow, 1854), 2, 47, 311; Marguerite Wood, *Extracts from the Records of the Burgh of Edinburgh, 1626 to 1641* (Edinburgh, 1936), 288; Ronald G. Cant, *The University of St Andrews* (Edinburgh, 1970 edn), 33, 84.

49. Brockliss, *French Higher Education*, 66, n. 41; John P. Mahaffy, *An Epoch in Irish History: Trinity College, Dublin, its Foundation and Early Fortunes, 1591–1660* (London, 1903), 348; Morison, *Harvard College in the Seventeenth Century*, i, 108.

50. Aries, *Centuries of Childhood* (1986 edn), 249–50; Samuel E. Morison, *The Founding of Harvard College* (Cambridge, Mass, 1935), 55, 232–5; Keith Thomas, *Rule and Misrule in the Schools of Early Modern England* (Reading, 1976), 9–11.

51. Innes, *Fasti*, 366.

13

The Scottish Universities and Women Students, 1862–1892

Lindy Moore

The first attempts made by women to gain admission to the Scottish universities were for the purpose of obtaining medical qualifications. Whereas women could become teachers or study subjects taught in the arts courses without attending university or graduating, after the Medical Practitioners Act of 1858 medical qualifications were controlled by examining bodies requiring the study of specific courses by approved lecturers. That women should wish to practise as doctors was a reflection of the growing women's movement of Victorian Britain. In the late 1850s and early 1860s there was much public correspondence and discussion about the social advantages and the personal justice of admitting middle-class women into paid employment. Even among social conservatives there was considerable support for the idea of medically-trained women, because it was thought they would provide an enlightened philanthropy and also hygienic and moral guidance for the working classes, especially working-class women; moreover it was felt more suitable for women and adolescent girls to be medically examined by women.[1] But those holding such views were concerned that the women receiving training in anatomy and physiology from men, and especially if they were to study alongside men, would themselves be morally contaminated. Among medical professors, some supported the first women candidates, seeing them as making a moral self-sacrifice for the sake of other women whom they could subsequently train; the personal distaste felt by others overrode all other considerations or rational argument. The universities became directly involved in this debate, gaining unwelcome publicity nationwide, firstly when Elizabeth Anderson applied to St Andrews in 1861,[2] and then during the better-known, bitter, and long drawn-out episode after Sophia Jex-Blake and others applied to enter Edinburgh in 1869.[3] On both occasions the universities initially gave permission for instruction, then had second thoughts, seeking legal advice when some of their professors objected.

The legal situation was confused. In 1862 the Solicitor-General thought St Andrews had no power to admit women, while the Lord Advocate thought the Senatus there had sufficient discretion to admit them to teaching, but was doubtful about them being allowed to graduate.[4] In 1872 a judgment in the High Court found that women had the right to attend university classes at

Edinburgh, but that the Senatus had no power to force professors to teach women nor power to appoint substitutes to do so. The complications which arose from this ruling were not widely understood and were to lead to more bad publicity for Edinburgh University when it decided to challenge the decision.[5] In 1873 the appeal was heard by the full Court of Session which, by a bare majority, decided against the women on both counts. The illegality of admitting women was thus definitely established; thereafter, the possible initiatives open to the universities were restricted. Nevertheless, the universities were quite happy to take dubious action in some situations. It was openly admitted that the local examinations and the higher certificates for women validated by some Scottish universities, and the LLA (Lady Licentiate in Arts) title conferred by St Andrews, were all probably illegal.[6] Legal difficulties only became an issue once internal organisational and institutional problems had arisen.

Following the adverse legal decision of 1873 a private member's bill was introduced in 1874 'to remove doubts as to the powers of the Universities in Scotland to admit women as students and to grant degrees to women'. Although introduced as a result of the experiences of the women medical students at Edinburgh University, this bill proposed to give each of the Scottish universities wide discretionary powers to admit women students to any of their faculties. Feelings ran highest at Edinburgh where the medical professoriate, the Senatus and the University Court all petitioned against the bill. This barrage of opposition centred on the influential figure of Sir Robert Christison, who was the queen's personal physician in Scotland and, significantly, a member of all three university bodies.[7] Afterwards, however, a larger number of Edinburgh professors individually signed a petition in support of the bill than had voted against the proposal in the Edinburgh Senate.[8] Glasgow University petitioned against the bill, but mainly on the grounds that it gave the (then unreformed) university courts too much power; yet Principal Caird's signature was one of the twenty-six signatures to the Scottish professors' petition in support of the bill.[9] Neither Aberdeen nor St Andrews Universities took official action, but three of the Aberdeen professors and eight of the fourteen St Andrews professors individually supported the bill.[10] The bill was debated in March 1875 and defeated by 194 votes to 151, much of the argument being centred on the teaching of medicine (particularly the experience of Edinburgh University), on the impropriety of mixed classes and otherwise on the impossibility of professors undertaking two parallel sets of lectures for men and women students.

Although Edinburgh University had said it would like a royal commission or some such inquiry on the question of women's admission, there was no complaint when the subject was ignored by the Scottish Universities Commission set up in the following year. When women inquired if the issue was part of the commission's remit, the matter was tossed back and forth between the government and the commissioners, the latter eventually deciding not to consider the question.[11]

Alongside the unsuccessful attempt to gain admission for women to university medical courses, various other efforts to promote the higher education of Scottish women were initiated from 1867 onwards, chiefly by local educational associations which were formed, not only to prod the universities into more systematic provision for women students, but equally to prod middle-class girls and their parents into an interest in academic education for women and into the belief that it was a socially acceptable and appropriate activity for them to engage in. There were three phases in the initiatives that were made.

First came the formation of ladies' educational associations at Edinburgh and St Andrews in the years 1867–69, and the start of university-style lectures under their aegis;[12] in Glasgow less formally-organised lectures were offered on an ad hoc basis by individual professors, which acquired a semi-corporate character from the active involvement of the university bookseller, James Maclehose.[13] During this period women were also admitted in Edinburgh to the Watt Institute and School of Art for the first time — as well as to the ill-fated university medical classes. The next phase, in the years 1876–77, saw a change in the constitution of the Edinburgh local association, which brought the more formal involvement in its activities of the Edinburgh professors; also, in both Glasgow[14] and Aberdeen[15] the formation of ladies' educational associations brought more systematic lecture arrangements; and, furthermore, a national initiative originating from Edinburgh for the support and promotion of a university local examinations scheme in Scotland,[16] and the start of the popular higher certificate for women by St Andrews with the award of the LLA (Lady Licentiate in Arts).[17] A series of public lecture courses open to women were given by St Andrews professors at Dundee, and the foundation of chairs of education in St Andrews and Edinburgh raised the issue of extending university education for women teachers. In the final phase, from 1883 to 1884, the University College at Dundee was opened, and admitted women;[18] and the Glasgow association incorporated itself into a limited company as Queen Margaret College. There was one missed opportunity, indicative of women's peripheral position, when the long-awaited Scottish universities bill of 1883 contained no provision for the admission of women students.

From its beginning in 1867, the pioneering Edinburgh Ladies Educational Association had restricted itself to providing courses given only by professors and lecturers at Edinburgh University, in effect to becoming an extra-mural arts department for women.[19] Its members disassociated themselves from the more contentious issue of studies which were oriented towards professional occupations, especially medicine; these were contended for by a separate but parallel association (though many individuals were members of both associations). The Edinburgh Ladies Educational Association influenced developments in other areas of Scotland but, whereas it restricted itself firmly to the promotion of higher education, the associations which were started subsequently at St Andrews, Aberdeen, Glasgow, Perth and Dundee became involved in movements to improve girls' schooling and in promoting various non-graduate tutorial, occupationally-oriented and further education schemes for women, as well as campaigning for the admission of women to the Scottish universities and for the interim establishment of university-approved lectures, not all necessarily offered by university teachers.

It was the intention that such lectures should be for academic audiences working towards examinations, and not merely for leisure-time entertainment value, something which distinguished them from the many earlier public lectures open to women given by Scottish professors. There were, however, varying degrees of success in achieving this aim. A co-ordinated scheme of lectures never materialised at St Andrews, and elsewhere many of those attending were older, married women with no interest in taking examinations. Aberdeen's scheme collapsed after its courses were increased to forty hours each, in an attempt to provide what was seen as sufficient content; six years after the Glasgow Association had been formed, two of its four courses were still less than twenty hours long.

The high point of such courses was the awarding, after examination, of university certificates of higher education, ostensibly of degree standard. In 1872 Edinburgh University approved a Certificate of Art in Literature, Philosophy and Science for women who, having previously passed the local examination's Senior Certificate, attended the association's lectures and passed the university's examinations in three subjects. The certificate was awarded for the first time in 1874. In 1876 it was suggested that St Andrews should introduce a different kind of diploma, which could be taken by any Scottish woman after private study, a proposal which was immediately taken up.[20] The Glasgow and Aberdeen associations were able to persuade their respective universities to introduce higher certificate examinations, and these started in 1881 and 1882 respectively. Both were to be adversely affected, however, by the competition of the already established St Andrews LLA, which offered the additional enticement of a university title. Between 1886 and 1896, as many as 1,867 girls who sat the St Andrews LLA had previously taken the Aberdeen, Edinburgh or Glasgow local examinations and then opted to be examined for the St Andrews award rather than for the higher certificates awarded by the other universities.

St Andrews was accused of 'poaching' students by the other universities but, despite petitions from the women's associations at Glasgow and Aberdeen,[21] neither university agreed to offer a title. These universities were afraid that the public would confuse the various titles, and would equate the university degree with the lower standard, relaxed time-scale and non-degree subjects of the higher certificates; there was also some anxiety that granting a title to students who had passed the higher certificate but had not been formally taught by university professors would weaken the universities' position in countering proposals then being made that they should become examining rather than teaching institutions. The St Andrews professors were accused by some of their counterparts elsewhere in Scotland of bringing the reputation of the Scottish universities into disrepute, and of being motivated by pecuniary objectives in setting up their scheme.[22] The St Andrews professors responded by insisting that they had done more for the higher education of women in Scotland than any of the other universities; and that the popularity of the LLA certainly proved it was meeting a demand.

The various higher certificate courses for women were supported both by 'separatists' who favoured a gender-differentiated higher education, and by those whose ultimate goal was the opening of existing universities to women, but who accepted the special examinations as an interim measure. Some Scottish professors thought there would always be a demand for both kinds of courses and examinations. Technical difficulties generally prevented the same examination papers being set for men and women students, although this did occur on occasion. As the standard of education rose and the number of subjects required for certification increased (initially it had been three), there was a move towards awarding special certificates to students taking the existing arts degree subjects, although only a minority ever did so. All the higher certificates retained a wider range of options — in addition to modern languages, for example, music and art were included at Glasgow and biblical criticism at Edinburgh — and so the separatists could also be satisfied. Meanwhile contemporary opinion was moving in favour of a wider choice of degree subjects for male university students, something not to be achieved until after the 1889 Act.

The Scottish professors became increasingly involved in the activities of the women's associations and in the administration of the higher certificates, often acting in a dual capacity — working with the female organisers to prepare initiatives, and then considering these recommendations in their capacity as members of Senatus. The ladies' educational associations were, however, in an impossible situation; not only were they dependent on the goodwill of individual professors, but they did not attract sufficient students to be able to act as separate institutions which could support parallel courses to those offered in the universities (and, indeed, it soon became clear that courses which did attract large numbers then created too much work for the professors). The associations frequently approached possible funding sources, but none had been established with their particular requirements in mind. Failing these, they looked to some form of relationship with the universities to provide the status which would give them access to financial support.

Separatists and the more uncompromising supporters of higher education for women differed on the appropriate institutional form this should take, depending on their opinions about the propriety of mixed classes and whether they felt higher education should be gender-differentiated in terms of content, time-span or compulsory examinations. The founders of the Edinburgh association aimed from the start at admission to the existing university — and to mixed classes.[23] As early as 1869 the Edinburgh Senatus had responded by proposing that the Edinburgh association should be affiliated to the university, but the University Court rejected this suggestion.[24] After the adverse legal decision in 1873, it became more difficult to arrange a symbiotic working relationship. An attempt to resolve the difficulty was made in 1883 in Glasgow, when the local association incorporated itself into a company, Queen Margaret College. But the offer of a building diverted the association from its prime objectives; thereafter it concentrated on fund-raising and began to aim at a separate, non-residential college for women which would be affiliated to the university. Many Glasgow committee members were disappointed by the subsequent legislation admitting women to the existing universities, because it forced them to give up their plans for affiliation, in favour of presenting the college to the university to enable teaching of an equal standard to be provided to men and women students in separate classes.[25] At Aberdeen, in contrast, there was evidence of support for co-education in university classes.[26] Meanwhile, with undergraduate numbers dwindling at St Andrews, outsiders suggested that the whole university should be turned into a women's college, serving all of Scotland. There is no evidence that St Andrews professors supported that idea, but they did argue that admitting women to their university would much increase its sphere of usefulness in the course of their campaign against the inclusion of a clause in the 1883 bill, which would have led to the dissolution of Scotland's oldest university.[27]

Not until the third draft of the Universities (Scotland) Bill was a clause providing for women's admission inserted. The final draft of the bill, passed in 1889, empowered commissioners who were to be appointed under the act to issue ordinances permitting any of the universities to admit women to graduation and/or to the teaching in any or all faculties. The commissioners originally intended only to empower the universities to admit women to the faculties of arts, medicine, science and music but, as a result of criticism from various quarters, the ordinance finally approved in 1892 permitted the admission of women to graduation and/or teaching in any faculty.[28]

This ordinance was enabling, not compulsory; and, despite the opposition of those who felt that the universities should teach all whom they examined, it made specific provision for the extra-mural education of women if required. Each of the universities thus had to decide, firstly, whether it would admit women to graduation and if so in which faculties; secondly, whether it would provide teaching facilities for them and if so in which faculties; and, thirdly, if the university was to provide teaching for women, whether this should be provided by opening the existing classes or by establishing separate classes for women. Furthermore, all professors appointed before the ordinance took effect had the right to refuse to teach women, and thus the outcome could be affected by the decisions of individuals as well as by the decisions of the constituent bodies of the universities. Practical considerations, personal inclinations and previous institutional developments combined to ensure that, although all four Scottish universities took advantage of the ordinance, their arrangements differed.

Glasgow University provided most of its initial teaching in the separate classes already established under the auspices of Queen Margaret College, where a medical school had been opened in 1890, although women later attended honours classes and some demonstrations at the university; and it made no provision for teaching women law or divinity. Edinburgh University immediately admitted women to mixed classes in the arts faculty but refused to provide any form of medical teaching, although it was prepared to recognise Dr Jex-Blake's Edinburgh School of Medicine for Women and the Scottish Medical School for Women as extra-mural institutions whose teaching qualified for graduation. Women were not admitted at all to the university's classes or degrees in law or divinity. St Andrews and its affiliated college at Dundee admitted women to its classes and degrees in arts, science and medicine, but again not to law or divinity, and it continued to promote its LLA scheme, seeing this as providing a less stressful alternative, with a wider choice, which could be combined with home life and therefore would be more suitable for the majority of women than any possible arts degree. Aberdeen also continued its higher certificate but, although it had made no objection to the subject restrictions of the original ordinance, it was the only university which immediately admitted women to graduation in all of its faculties; it deferred a decision to admit women to instruction in medicine until 1895, but immediately admitted them to all other classes, including those in law and divinity.

In 1895 Aberdeen had the smallest number and the lowest percentage of female students of the four Scottish universities. Edinburgh and Glasgow Universities had benefitted both from their proximity to more populous areas and also to the prior existence of comprehensive courses of higher education for women run in parallel with degree courses in the universities and of a standard which permitted some women to be awarded degrees retrospectively. Although St Andrews had had neither of these advantages, it had much the largest proportion of female students as a result of its well-publicised support for women's education and its LLA diploma. Aberdeen suffered by comparison with all three of the other universities, and had to start from scratch in its efforts to attract women students; most female medical students preferred initially to go to Edinburgh or Glasgow where there were separate training facilities, while the university's other radical move, the admission of women to the faculties of law and divinity, did not meet a felt need and did not attract women students.

Nevertheless, Aberdeen's arrangement of mixed teaching in all classes and in all subjects proved ultimately to be more satisfactory for women students and cheaper for the university than the arrangements at Edinburgh and Glasgow. By 1901 the Glasgow women were complaining of the lower teaching standards at the separate Queen Margaret College classes,[29] while the women's medical schools in Edinburgh encountered enormous difficulties in obtaining funding. In 1909, indeed, unlike the universities in Glasgow or Edinburgh, Aberdeen reported that it did not require any special financial assistance to provide for the teaching of female students.[30]

The relative attractiveness of the universities for women students depended partly on the physical facilities and social arrangements, and these in turn depended on previous developments. At Edinburgh the influential ladies' educational association had provided a social centre and had raised funds for residential accommodation,[31] these two facilities being amalgamated when Masson Hall was opened in 1897, with one of the first Edinburgh women graduates appointed as warden. At Glasgow, Queen Margaret College continued to act as the women students' centre, under the official but honorary supervision of Janet Galloway. At St Andrews, funds accumulated under the LLA scheme were used to establish residential accommodation supervised by a graduate lady warden; this residential scheme was unique in being owned and managed by the university itself. These facilities were popular, attracting wealthy English and Scottish students, and a separate women's college was even mooted. It was only at Aberdeen that the combination of shortage of funds, the earlier collapse of the ladies' association, and stronger support for co-education meant that there were no residential facilities, a half-hearted attempt to establish a modest scheme proving unsuccessful. However, the proportion of female students at Aberdeen was to increase faster than at the other universities. By 1907–8 women constituted 31 per cent of the student total at Aberdeen (4.5% in 1895–96), compared with 40 per cent (17.5%) at St Andrews, 24 per cent (9.1%) at Glasgow, and only 18 per cent (8.6%) at Edinburgh.[32]

NOTES

1. Letter to *Scotsman*, 20 June 1862; *ibid*, 20 June 1864; L. Moore, *Bajanellas and Semilinas: Aberdeen University and the Education of Women, 1860–1920* (Aberdeen, 1991), 21.

2. *Scotsman*, 4 Nov. 1862; *Fifeshire Journal*, 6 Nov. 1862; J. Manton, *Elizabeth Garrett Anderson* (London, 1965); L. G. Anderson, *Elizabeth Garrett Anderson, 1836–1917* (London, 1939).

3. M. Todd, *Life of Sophia Jex-Blake* (London, 1918); S. Jex-Blake, *Medical Women: a Thesis and a History* (Edinburgh, 2nd ed., 1886; repr. 1970).

4. Manton, *Anderson*, 137; Anderson, *Anderson*, 103.

5. L. Moore, 'Aberdeen and the higher education of women', *Aberdeen University Review*, 163 (1980), 286–8.

6. Moore, *Bajanellas and Semilinas*, 15–16; A. L. Turner (ed.), *History of the University of Edinburgh, 1883–1933* (Edinburgh, 1933), 219.

7. Edinburgh University Library [EUL], MSS, University of Edinburgh College Minutes 1872–1875, v, 28 Mar. 1874, 22 Apr. 1874, 27 Feb. 1875; Christison and Christison, *Life of Sir Robert Christison, Bart*, 2 vols (Edinburgh and London, 1886), ii, 43–50; Jex-Blake, *Medical Women*.

8. Twelve voted against the bill in Senate, thirteen signed the petition in support.

9. Glasgow University Archives, Minutes of Senate 1873–76, 27 Apr. 1874, 25 Feb. 1875; *Scotsman*, 27 Apr. 1874.

10. *Ibid*: five St Andrews's professors had signed Emily Davies' petition in support of higher education for women presented to the Taunton Commission in 1867.

11. *Sir Robert Christison*, 49–50; EUL, Edinburgh Association for the University Education of Women, box general 1977, letters to Miss Houldsworth from J. Muir dated 6 July 1876, from Lyon Playfair dated 31 Jan. 1877 and from Scottish University Commission dated 5 Feb. 1877.

12. K. Burton, *Memoir of Mrs Crudelius* (Edinburgh, 1879); 'University education for women in Scotland', *The Ladies Edinburgh Magazine [LEM]*, v, Nov. 1879, 517.

13. Letter from Dr John Young, in *Glasgow Herald*, May 1889.

14. *Report of the Glasgow Association for the Higher Education of Women, 1877–78* (Glasgow, 1878).

15. L. R. Moore, 'The Aberdeen Ladies' Educational Association'. *Northern Scotland*, 3 (1979–80), 123–57.

16. Burton, *Mrs Crudelius*; J. Menzies, 'On Local Examinations for Women', *LEM*, ii (Mar. 1876), 83–93; A. Dundas, 'Notes on the Edinburgh University Local Exams', *LEM*, iii (Oct. 1877), 305–309.

17. W. Knight, *History of the LLA Examination and Diploma for Women, and of the University Hall for Women Students at the University of St Andrews* (Dundee, 1896); R. N. Smart, 'Literate ladies — a fifty-year experiment', *Alumnus Chronicle*, 59 (June 1968), 21–31.

18. W. Knight, *Early Chapters in the History of the University of St Andrews and Dundee* (Dundee, 1903).

19. Burton, *Mrs Crudelius*, 26, 54, 198.

20. 'The higher education of women in Scotland: the St Andrews certificate', *LEM*, iii (Jan. 1877), 7–14.

21. Moore, *Bajanellas and Semilinas*, 14–5, 18; GUA, MS 20481, 'Petition to the Senate for a University Title for Women'.

22. Moore, *Bajanellas and Semilinas*, 15–16; A. Mackie, 'The Higher Certificate for Women', *Educational News*, 11 (13 and 20 Nov. 1886), 803–4.

23. Burton, *Mrs Crudelius*, 81, 130.

24. EUL, Edinburgh Association for the University Education of Women, box General 1977, MS letter from Alexander Grant to Mary Crudelius, 25 Dec. 1871; Edinburgh University Senatus Minutes, 2 Apr. 1869.

25. J. Campbell, 'The rise of the higher education of women movement in Glasgow', *Book of the Jubilee, in Commemoration of the Ninth Jubilee of the University of Glasgow 1451–1901* (Glasgow, 1901), 137.

26. Moore 'Aberdeen and the higher education of women', 289–92; *Bajanellas and Semilinas*, 135.

27. Moore 'Aberdeen Ladies Educational Association', 147n, 153; Scottish Record Office, MS ED26/7, Universities (Scotland) Bill 1883: Memorial by Professors of United College of St Andrews.

28. Moore, *Bajanellas and Semilinas*, 39.

29. I. Elder, *Statement as to Questions which have arisen in Connection with the Transfer of Queen Margaret College to the University of Glasgow* (Glasgow, 1910).

30. Committee on Scottish Universities, *Minutes of Evidence taken before the Committee on Scottish Universities, with Index* (HMSO, 1910, Cd. 5258), paras 50, 224, 672, 982–1036, 1108–1105.

31. J. B. Watson, *Edinburgh Association for the University Education of Women 1867–1967* (Edinburgh, n.d.).

32. The Edinburgh figures exclude female medical students.

14

The Challenges and Rewards of Databases: Aberdeen University Students, 1860–c 1880

Marjory Harper

Methodology

The study of Aberdeen University's student population in the nineteenth and early twentieth centuries is an integral part of the Quincentenary History Project, honouring the university's quincentenary in 1995. The major long-term aim is to construct a computerised database of records relating to students who attended Aberdeen University from 1860 to the 1920s, but also subsequently to computerise the older, more complex, and fragmentary records of King's and Marischal Colleges. The union of these two independent universities in 1860 resulted in a standardisation and improvement of student records, and this provided an obvious starting-point for an investigation which, at the time of writing, has been taken as far as 1879–80 in each of the four faculties in the university.

The major challenge lay in devising a system flexible enough to cater for the needs of a variety of users. Its primary function is to act as a repository of information about the student body, storing that information in a medium which permits rapid retrieval and rigorous statistical analysis of large quantities of data. In addition, by assembling material from a range of sources, the database is intended to be a useful tool for the university archivist, providing a comprehensive dossier of information about individual students at the touch of a button. The availability of such a database should also facilitate the researches of scholars investigating different aspects of university life, such as the effect on study patterns of changes in the curriculum, or the overseas connections of Aberdeen students.

With these diverse functions in mind, a ready-made computer programme, Cardbox-Plus, was purchased, which allows information to be entered into a mechanised card-index system. Separate versions of the database were created for each faculty, with fifty-two fields (categories of information) available within each version. Most fields were indexed for rapid retrieval, sorting and analysis, with miscellaneous information being entered into an unindexed appendix to each 'card'. Three broad categories of data have been sought, in order to allow both minute documentation of individuals and global analysis of changing patterns of geographical and social mobility among the student population as a whole. Approximately sixteen fields are devoted to biographical and background information, including dates of birth and death, place of origin and father's occupation. A further twenty-one fields are concerned with the student's university education and experiences, including period of study, classes attended, degree(s) obtained (at Aberdeen and at other universities), and the location of lodgings. The third major area of investigation is the student's post-university life, incorporating information on locations, careers, and civil, military and academic honours and awards. The remaining fields are allocated to identifying sources of information, primarily the manuscript matriculation registers, used in conjunction with the published *Rolls of Graduates*[1] and supplemented by other manuscript sources such as bursary lists and class records.

The four versions of the database contain information by faculty on 4,678 students who appeared in the university's matriculation registers between 1860–61 and 1879–80. Yet the number of *individuals* who studied at Aberdeen University in that period was considerably smaller, only 3,794. This is because students who matriculated in more than one faculty — a common occurrence — have been entered in each version of the database, in order to represent correctly the total composition of each faculty and thus ensure that each faculty can be studied autonomously. Duplicate and triplicate entries must be discarded, however, in order to establish the total number of individuals who passed through the university in the period under review, and to permit uncorrupted analysis of the entire student body.

Inconsistencies and omissions within the manuscript registers, particularly in the recording of dates of birth and the spelling of surnames, have posed a few problems. In the earlier entries, fathers' occupations are rarely noted, and students' Aberdeen addresses, unless they lived at home, have been entered consistently only in the medical faculty registers. Different faculties registered students in slightly different ways, arts, science and divinity students being recorded in a single entry, whereas the careers of medical and law students have to be traced through a series of entries, one for each year of study. The lack of indexing in the registers is felt most acutely when dealing with medical students, whose patterns of study were extremely complex, and often involved both repeated years and gaps of a year or more in the student's attendance. Yet most of the problems associated with the source material are not insurmountable — merely time-consuming. Discrepancies within registers and between registers and *Rolls* are infrequent, and do not invalidate the overall soundness of the data.

Analysis of the Database

The university's average annual intake was 233 students, almost fifty per cent of whom went into the arts faculty, the core of the university. A further forty per cent went into medicine, which had an average annual intake of ninety-four, but the faculties of divinity and law took in totals of only 334 and 157 students respectively during the whole period under review. The average age of students was nineteen, although those in the arts faculty tended to be younger than their medical, theological and legal counterparts. Indeed, the youngest arts student in the sample, William Douglas from Aberdeen, was only eight years old when he first appeared in 1862. Having taken no classes or examinations in that session, he reappeared in the following four sessions, during which he followed the full arts course, failing in only one examination. He then took a summer session in medicine in 1867, but did not graduate in either faculty.

The example of William Douglas illustrates two significant features of student life in this period. Arts students tended to be younger because the faculty was the first resort, and the main common denominator, for the many individuals who took courses in more than one faculty. Thirty-eight per cent of all arts students between 1860 and 1880 undertook further studies in another faculty, 598 of them in medicine,[2] 219 in divinity, and sixty in law. Secondly, William Douglas was by no means unique in his failure to graduate. Since the matriculation registers, unlike the published *Rolls*, list *all* matriculated students, not simply those who subsequently graduated, it is possible to detect the high proportion of students who did not graduate, fifty-three per cent of the overall sample. There were no law graduates, as the BL degree was not instituted until 1894, and only forty-five of the 334 divinity students graduated in that faculty. Although most law and divinity students would have undertaken their initial studies in the arts faculty, even there only 950 of the 2,312 students took the MA degree.

In some cases failure to graduate was probably due to poor examination performance, particularly among students who had spent three or more years in the arts faculty.[3] But this was not the only reason for non-graduation. Since several professions still accepted evidence of attendance at university and did not require the possession of a formal qualification, students often enrolled in the arts faculty with no intention of graduating, even if they pursued the full course of study. Men intending to enter the church, for instance, were expected to complete a full arts course, though not necessarily to graduate. Most of the non-graduates, however, appeared for only a single year, or part of a year, including all fifty-five 'private' students. Medical students, who were required to take some courses in arts before being admitted to the medical faculty, usually pursued these preliminary studies for two years.

The highest proportion of graduates was produced by the Medical School. Fifty-eight per cent of the 1,875 medical students in the sample took a medical degree, although there were marked dissimilarities in the study patterns of students from different areas. Whereas most Scottish students spent four or five years in the medical faculty, English, Welsh, Irish and overseas students were much more likely to graduate after only one or two years' study at Aberdeen, presumably because they had begun their medical training elsewhere and were simply completing their degrees. For example, seventy-six per cent of English students graduated after only one or two years, compared with sixteen per cent who stayed for four or five years. Similarly, sixty-seven per cent of overseas students graduated after one or two years, and twenty-three per cent after four or five years. On the other hand, only twelve per cent of students from north-east Scotland graduated after one or two years, compared with the seventy-seven per cent who attended for four or five years before taking their medical degree.

Another aspect of this varied study pattern was that some medical students, instead of taking a summer session in the university, spent the summer working as medical officers on board local whaling ships, which went to Greenland and generally left north-east Scotland in February or March. A total of thirty-eight students in the sample spent a session in Greenland, mainly in the 1860s, the largest contingent (eleven) leaving in 1861. Most went on to graduate in medicine, and four subsequently became naval surgeons, including William Gordon Stables who went to the whaling in 1861 and was later better-known as a novelist and author of boys' adventure stories. David Cardno, a Peterhead whalerman and veteran of numerous Arctic expeditions, recalled in the 1920s that most of these adventurous young medical students had 'revelled in the opportunity of getting an interesting sea voyage . . . [and] did much to enliven things on board'.[4]

Most of the men who went to Greenland came from Aberdeen and its hinterland, reflecting another significant feature of the student body as a whole. The vast majority of students in the overall sample came from the North East — the counties of Aberdeen, Banff, Kincardine, Moray and Nairn, and included the second largest intake, from the city of Aberdeen itself. The rural north-east of Scotland accounted for 1,676 students (forty-four per cent of the total student body) and Aberdeen city for a further 646 students (seventeen per cent). It was generally accepted that students from the city and region should attend their 'local' university, which was therefore clearly identified with its hinterland, to a greater extent than the other Scottish universities of St Andrews, Glasgow and Edinburgh.[5] A greater proportion of the remaining students came from England (fourteen per cent) than from other counties of the Scottish lowlands (eight per cent) or the Highlands and North (seven per cent), and a further seven per cent of students was of foreign origin.[6]

Although local students were predominant throughout the university, the extent of their numerical superiority differed from faculty to faculty. Only fourteen of the 157 law students did not belong to the North East, as might be expected from a body of men who were mainly part-time students, working in legal offices in Aberdeen. Seventy-six per cent of divinity students were also local, with the rest coming mainly from the Highlands, again a predictable emphasis, given the limited relevance of the training to those who did not intend to go into the ministry or teaching in Scotland. Only two divinity students were of English origin and one of foreign origin, and all three were in fact resident in Scotland by the time they came to Aberdeen University.

Three-quarters of arts students also came from Aberdeen and the North

East, and a detailed study of their origins shows interesting links between particular parishes and the university. Most of the sixteen non-city parishes which supplied twenty or more students to the faculty — places like Peterhead, Huntly, Keith and Elgin — contained towns with sizeable populations and, predictably, the largest numbers of students were supplied by the most populous urban parishes of Old Machar (262) and St Nicholas (157) within the city of Aberdeen. The exception, remarkably, was the large but thinly populated upland Banffshire parish of Kirkmichael, which sent twenty-six arts students to Aberdeen University between 1860 and 1880.

Under the terms of the Dick Bequest, an early nineteenth-century endowment, parish schoolmasters in Aberdeenshire, Banffshire and Morayshire were rewarded for high academic qualifications and for their ability to teach classics.[7] The appointment of university-trained men to parish schools had a positive impact throughout the region, particularly in Kirkmichael, where both the parish school and the village school at Tomintoul benefited from the appointment of a succession of Aberdeen graduates, who successfully prepared boys for the Aberdeen University bursary competition. Kirkmichael's connection with Aberdeen University in our period was established by Alexander Cameron, a native of Tomintoul, who, after being educated locally, completed his schooling at Aberdeen Grammar School before entering King's College on a bursary in 1844. When only a year into his arts course he was appointed schoolmaster in his native parish, a post which he held for over a decade. During this period Cameron sent several pupils to the universities in Aberdeen, and maintained his own links with King's College when in winter 1851 and 1852 he was appointed temporary assistant to the elderly and frail professor of Greek. Cameron was succeeded briefly at Kirkmichael by his brother Robert, who had also studied at King's College, and he in turn was succeeded by another local man and King's College graduate, Donald Robertson. When Robertson left to become minister of Daviot, Aberdeenshire, the post went to yet another local man, Charles Innes, a graduate of Aberdeen University, who in turn was succeeded in 1876 by yet another Aberdeen graduate, William Johnstone from Inverurie.

But perhaps the best-known of the Kirkmichael schoolmasters was Dr James Grant, who served in the village school at Tomintoul for twelve years, from 1859 to 1870. During that period he devoted himself to preparing suitable pupils for the Aberdeen bursary competition, producing twenty successful candidates. According to one of his former pupils, writing in 1924, Grant's fame spread well beyond the village of Tomintoul:

Many of his Glenlivet pupils followed him to Tomintoul and took lodgings in the village. Many more from surrounding parishes and farther afield lodged in Tomintoul that they might attend Mr Grant's school, as his fame as a teacher got to be more and more known. He was most successful in preparing young lads for the bursary competition at Aberdeen University . . . Perhaps 10 or 12 pupils went straight from Tomintoul almost yearly, and in 99 cases out of 100 gained a bursary.[8]

Grant was succeeded at Tomintoul by Robert Dey, a former pupil and subsequently a graduate of Aberdeen University, who was in turn succeeded by another Aberdeen graduate, John Henderson Fraser. The efforts of these teachers, and the academic attainments of their pupils, were highly praised in contemporary reports by HM Inspectors, and in a later observation by the Director of Education for Moray — himself an old Tomintoul pupil — who in 1920 remarked of his native parish, that 'one of its few products was its annual output of boys for the University'.[9]

Despite the local origins of medical students who went to Greenland, a far smaller proportion of all medical students came from north-east Scotland than was the case in any other faculty. While forty-seven per cent of the medical intake came from the North East, England (which supplied very few students to the arts faculty) accounted for twenty-five per cent, and overseas locations accounted for a further eleven per cent, no doubt attracted by the high reputation of medical training at Aberdeen. Indeed, if it had not been for the Medical School's increasingly strong tradition of southern and overseas recruitment, non-Scottish students would have constituted a negligible part of the total student population.

Overseas medical students were drawn from a much greater variety of countries than their counterparts in the arts faculty, and by no means all were the sons of expatriate Scots. Although the majority, as in the arts faculty, came from India, Ceylon and other East Indian locations, at least twenty-five of these 111 individuals had native names, or, in the case of those from Ceylon, names which reflected the 150 years up to 1802 when the island had been under the control of the Dutch East India Company. South Africa was also well-represented, with twenty-two students, followed by the West Indies (twenty-one), Australasia (twenty), North America (nine) and Europe (nine). Unlike the East Indian recruits, most students with African or West Indian origins seem to have been expatriate Britons. The best-known — if not immediately obvious — exception was Christopher James Davis, a black student from Barbados, who graduated MB CM in 1870, after only two years' study. Before the end of that year he had died of smallpox in France, where he had gone to help casualties of the Franco-Prussian War, and he was accorded detailed obituaries in the *British Medical Journal*, *The Lancet* and the *Aberdeen Free Press*. He was best-known in the Aberdeen area not for his medical skills, but as an early advocate of the doctrines of the Christian Brethren, and he established an Exclusive Brethren Assembly in New Deer in the 1860s.[10]

Students' termtime addresses were recorded consistently only in the medical faculty registers. A total of 392 students (twenty-one per cent of the sample) lived at home, all but fourteen of them for the entire duration of their course. The remainder usually lived either with family friends or in lodgings in the city, often changing their lodgings each session. Throughout the period under review, the most popular area of first residence was George Street and its surrounding streets, such as Schoolhill, Broad Street, the Gallowgate, Charlotte Street and John Street, all within easy reach of Marischal College where the medical classes were held. This area accounted for 259 students, fifty-five of whom lived in George Street itself. Also popular was the Crown Street area, which attracted 238 students, followed by the city centre (157), Gilcomston (150) and King Street (106). Old Aberdeen, which was probably popular with arts students because of its proximity to King's College, was less convenient for medical students, and only seventy-seven took their first lodging there, most of them in the 1860s. By the 1870s other areas of the city were becoming popular, such as Causewayend, Rosemount and Woolmanhill, and particularly Rosemount which attracted fifty of its sixty-three medical students in only five sessions, from 1875 to 1879.

While information about students' backgrounds and university experiences can be obtained from the matriculation registers, subsequent career details are generally found only in the *Roll of Graduates* and are therefore available just for the forty-seven per cent of students who took a degree. Information from this smaller sample confirms that the traditional outlets of the church, teaching and medicine continued to absorb the majority of graduates in the period under review. Careers in business, the civil and diplomatic services, and the armed forces were also popular, but virtually no graduates from the sample went into engineering or other branches of applied or pure science, perhaps a reflection of the paucity of science teaching in the old curriculum.

As might be expected, the greatest range of occupations was found among arts graduates. Thirty-five per cent pursued careers in the churches, slightly less than half after undertaking further study in the divinity faculty. Teaching, at various levels, accounted for a further thirty-two per cent of arts graduates, although nine of these individuals later relinquished teaching for a career in farming, and others became involved in journalism, librarianship, bookselling and publishing. Legal and business careers together accounted for 102 arts graduates, twenty-nine of whom subsequently studied in the law faculty. Thirty-four men went into the civil or diplomatic service, twenty-nine into the armed forces and twenty-six into farming.[11]

Medical careers were taken up by approximately eight arts graduates per year, in many cases after further studies in the medical faculty.[12] Yet even here, where the least diversity of occupation might have been predicted, by no means all the graduates followed orthodox medical careers. Arthur Culver James from Middlesex, who graduated MB CM in 1874 and MD in 1877, became an actor; and two other English medical graduates became London barristers. Others followed non-medical professions after working for a time as doctors, or combined their medical careers with a variety of other enterprises. Robert Gibb from Roxburgh, for instance (MB CM, 1872) became a farmer at Lauder, Berwickshire, after serving as medical officer of health for the county of Berwick; a further three doctors who gave up medicine for a farming career were all emigrants.

Various careers were available within the medical profession itself. Service in the Indian Army was particularly popular in the 1860s, among both Scots and those who had been born in India.[13] Apart from the Indian Army, military service attracted ninety-six medical graduates, fifty-nine of whom went into the army and thirty-seven into the navy. At least ninety-five doctors went into hospital work, including thirty-nine who specialised in the (often lucrative) care of the mentally-ill. Nine graduates became medical officers of health, and seven — all Scots — became medical missionaries overseas.[14] Most medical graduates, however, became general practitioners in a wide variety of locations and, indeed, information on their *place* of employment was often the only career information given in the *Roll of Graduates*.

Geographical mobility, not just of doctors, but of the whole graduate sample, is another phenomenon revealed by global analysis of the database. While north-east Scotland clearly provided most entrants to the university, a high proportion of graduates subsequently left the area and even the country. England was the favourite destination; forty-six per cent of graduating students in the integrated database spent at least part of their working lives south of the border, and at least twenty-eight per cent of these men worked in London. Overseas opportunities attracted 458 graduates at some stage of their careers. Most went to India, where seventy-seven served in the Indian Army, fifteen were engaged in missionary activity, and twelve were civil servants. Ceylon, which had strong business links with north-east Scotland, and whose coffee and tea plantations were being developed largely by Aberdeenshire exiles, attracted twenty-two graduates; other popular destinations were Australia with eighty-eight graduates, and South Africa with sixty-two.

Certain localities can be linked with certain occupations. It is not surprising, for instance, that the Highlands, with no industrial base, provided opportunities in little more than standard careers in the churches, teaching and medicine. Conversely, graduates who wished to take up careers in fields such as engineering, stockbroking or diplomacy had to go south, to Glasgow, Edinburgh, London or overseas. While seventy-six per cent of those who became teachers spent at least part of their working lives in the North East, and the vast majority of ministers and lawyers remained in Scotland, the distribution of medical graduates — like their origins — was much more widespread.

The Ongoing Investigation

The compilation and analysis of the database are by no means complete, and this paper reflects only twenty years of university life. Bursary lists, not yet utilised, should yield information not only on the bursary competition, an institution which remained a central part of preparation for university life well into the twentieth century, but also on the preliminary schooling of the students. As the matriculation registers themselves become more detailed and consistent, term-time accommodation patterns can be more rigorously examined, while the systematic inclusion of parental occupations will permit the analysis of patterns of social mobility throughout the student population.

New themes which will be investigated, as the database is extended chronologically, include the impact of major academic and social changes

— notably the broadening of the curriculum in the late 1880s and 1890s, the introduction of taught honours degrees, the creation of a separate faculty of science, and the appearance of the first women students from 1894. Finally, the extension of the database into the 1920s will permit an investigation of the impact of the First World War on various aspects of the university's academic and social life.

NOTES

1. Nineteenth-century graduates are listed in W. Johnston, *Roll of Graduates, 1860–1900* (Aberdeen, 1906) and those who survived after 1900 often reappear in supplements to later volumes of the *Roll*: T. Watt, *Roll of Graduates, 1901–1925* (Aberdeen, 1935), J. Mackintosh, *Roll of Graduates, 1926–1955* (Aberdeen, 1960).

2. Twenty-six of the 598 arts students who went on to medical studies also appear in the divinity faculty registers.

3. Only the arts matriculation registers record examination results in this period. Among those who were registered for three or four years, seventy-one and seventy-eight per cent respectively either failed examinations or did not submit papers.

4. Aberdeen University Library, MS 3090/9, p. 3: Diaries and papers of David Cardno, Arctic Whaler, 1866–1917; see also Marjory Harper, 'Arctic Adventures' in *Aberdeen Leopard* (Dec. 1989), 24–7.

5. See Angus MacIntyre, 'A Time of Change' in *Alma Mater*, lxxxii (1961), 13.

6. 526 students in the integrated database came from England, 311 from non north-eastern and non-Highland counties in Scotland, 267 from the Highlands and North, 263 from overseas, thirty-six from Wales and thirty-three from Ireland. Thirty-two were of unknown origin, and fourteen were born at sea.

7. Marjorie Cruickshank, *History of the Training of Teachers in Scotland* (London, 1970), 66.

8. Quoted in William Barclay, *The Schools and Schoolmasters of Banffshire* (Banff, 1925), 195.

9. *Ibid*, 18.

10. For further details of Davis, see Napoleon Noel, *History of the Brethren* (Denver, 1936); *Lancet*, (10 Dec. 1870), 830, (24 Dec. 1870), 904; *Aberdeen Free Press*, 9 Dec. 1870; and A. T. Schofield, *The Good Black Doctor* (Kilmarnock, n.d.).

11. Only seven arts graduates went into farming as their initial occupation.

12. In fact, a total of 358 men from the arts faculty ultimately became doctors, but 185 went into the medical school at Aberdeen without having first taken their MA.

13. Seventy-nine men in the sample joined the Indian Medical Service, eleven of them in 1865 alone.

14. A further seven men with arts degrees studied medicine without graduating before becoming missionaries, but it is unclear from the *Roll* whether any of them subsequently used this medical training.

15

The 'Lad o' Pairts': a Study of the Literary Myth

David A. R. Forrester

Contemporary educational policies are contrived from many strands and sentiments, some denying and some relying on the state. Since the era of the Prussian victories of 1871, a universal and largely non-fee-charging provision of education has been urged as a prime duty of the nation-state. In Scotland, the land-owning heritors had been responsible for the provision of churches and for appointing or at least recommending the appointment of ministers and teachers in each parish. After the Disruption in 1843 patrons, heritors and the Established Church assemblies and presbyteries faced the problem of filling pulpits and manses, and parochial schoolmasterships, from which Free Church adherents had withdrawn.[1] The Free Church also had its problems in attracting candidates for the ministries of often poorly subsidised congregations and teachers for schools which could not always match the stipends of the old parochial schools.

Faced with such difficulties, Free Churchmen seem to have revelled in tales of simple rural life disseminated by writers of the so-called 'Kailyard School', whose tales ignored the problems of immigrant groups[2] and urban industrial parishes, featuring instead the social stabilities of rural Scotland and the opportunities there for low-born students to rise in society through their educational prowess. They featured an egalitarianism to be found in rural schools, which was to be blended uneasily with favouritism for the gifted, and with something like adulation for the ordained minister.

In elucidating this argument, it will be helpful to concentrate largely on one parish and on one literary school. Education at all levels in Victorian Scotland has recently been widely studied,[3] and we can therefore highlight just one author, 'Ian MacLaren'. This was the pseudonym of the Rev John Watson whose first parish was that of Logiealmond outside Perth; it is on his period there as the Free Church minister and on the major figures in his first publications that we shall concentrate — Domsie, the teacher, and Geordie Howe, the lad o' pairts. This will allow me to throw a clear light on the characteristics of our educational system which could lead so readily from local school to university, and this at a remarkably young age. Such a study may allow us better to judge whether in the Free Church there existed — in contrast to a *sponsored* upward mobility available in the

Established Church — a rather harsher 'contest-orientated' education for social advancement.[4]

Ian MacLaren's *Beside the Bonnie Briar Bush*, published in 1894, sold three-quarters of a million copies, and was based on stories he had been invited to contribute to *The British Weekly*. The editor of that nonconformist journal was William Robertson Nicoll, who was recognised in the later nineteenth century as the literary strategist of Scottish dissent; in 1908, indeed, he was to write a biography of Ian MacLaren. It was the bucolic verses prefixed to MacLaren's book which gave the name of 'kailyard' to a group of writers including J. M. Barrie and S. R. Crockett, who wrote in similarly glowing terms about Scottish rural life.[5]

John Watson served as Free Kirk minister at Logiealmond from 1875 to 1878, a parish where one of his uncles had been the first incumbent after the Disruption. Watson himself had been born in England but was schooled in Stirling before going on to the University of Edinburgh. It was through his family connections with Logiealmond and also with the rougher farm life of Blairgowrie that he had first hand experience of rural Scotland.[6] Watson had moved, firstly to a congregation in Glasgow and then to a large presbyterian church in Liverpool, before he achieved his literary successes.

His tales recalled wider events and more distant times than those directly associated with his few years in Logiealmond; nevertheless that parish seems to have remained as his first love, and was to be sentimentalised for his many readers as 'Drumtochty'. The stories that reflect that locality served it and his parishioners well; for he made humane and humorous, in a characteristically ironic vein, what must have often been coarse, drunken, bigotted and unidyllic. Thus, the farmers of Drumtochty are described as self-reliant and prosperous but during the decades of the two Watson ministries Logiealmond farms were being merged, and were mainly leased to Established Church supporters,[7] in a form of lowland clearances which isolated tenant-families and led to conflicts such as those described later in George Douglas Brown's *The House with the Green Shutters* or Ian MacPherson's *Shepherd's Calendar*. From such unhappy rural isolation and Oedipean structures (notably *not* featured by MacLaren) the path from school to college offered an obvious and attractive escape. MacLaren's sketches were not painted true to life.

The 'revolution' of the coming of the regime of school boards after the Education (Scotland) Act of 1872, with their formalising of school provision and school management is described whimsically in the first paragraph of *Beside the Bonnie Briar Bush*. Its first victim in Logiealmond was Alexander Robb, who had taught there from 1858 and had to go to law — right up to the Court of Session — to obtain a retirement allowance from the local school board.[8] It is as a belated compensation for the rough treatments meted out to teachers by the new boards that

MacLaren presented Domsie, the dominie of his tales, as a model of self-sacrifice and devotion. Yet the virtues ascribed to this paragon cannot disguise the partiality in his teaching methods and in his treatment of his pupils.

The most suitable teaching methods for parochial schools had been long discussed. Single-teacher, multi-class and multi-ability schools presented evident challenges, and offered a contrast to that individual tuition which had been generally preferred, in earlier ages at least, for the children of the wealthy. The necessary group-teaching in such schools had advantages in encouraging intra-group rivalry or in Adam Smith's words, in stimulating emulation between those sharing sympathies.[9] But Domsie had a dominating goal: he was a coach, and hunted for those capable in Latinity as for fine gold, with little care for those pupils who were otherwise gifted. When he found such educable talents, he was unremitting; and is presented as blind to all ambitions or vocations, even in those from humble homes, other than for careers which required boys to proceed to college and then the church ministry, regardless of all costs. These priorities ignored, of course, all less academically-oriented vocations: it was Domsie's pride that he had sent forward to college seven ministers, four school-masters, three civil servants and a professor (who he considered was equal to an earl at the very least); others (less able or ambitious?) had gone to mercantile pursuits. Nevertheless the professional goals and rankings were no more important to him than the competition by which they were achieved — not only in academic trials but even in games and other past-times.[10] Domsie selected and coached the Drumtochty protagonists against the sore competition which could be expected from the town schools, and looked like Simeon whose eyes had beheld the coming of his Lord when Geordie Howe came home with class medals. Surprisingly, educational competitiveness was not always materially rewarded and the selection of pupils and their subsequent successes were separable from the financing of their studies. Those perplexed by today's problems of student finance may examine closely how sponsorship was obtained for Geordie Howe, in an age when bursaries were often distributed on bases other than success in examinations.[11]

For the voluntaryist Free Church, devoted giving had to be encouraged since little or no support could be expected from the state or landlords. Rules for private sponsorship or charity were developed, including total secrecy, although individual beneficences might be revealed at the sponsor's death. By Watson's account of his kail-yard community, everyone in Drumtochty had two faces — Hyde outside and Jekyll within, one might say. Society and the minister could work on that hidden conscience which had great and charitable urges (to be contrasted with those uncovered by Freud in Vienna). So it was that in *The Bonny Briar Bush* Domsie appeals to a laird, Drumsheugh, who was widely reputed to be a miser, to support Geordie Howe's education:

I tell ye man, a'm honourin ye and giving ye the fairest chance ye'll ever hae o' winning health. Gin ye store the money ye hae scrapit by mony a hard bargain, some heir ye never saw 'ill gar it flee in chamberin and wantoness. Gin ye had the heart to spend it on a lad o pairts like Geordie Hoo, ye wad hae twa rewards nae man can tak from ye. Ane wud be the honest gratitude o a laddie . . . and the second wud be this — anither scholar in the land; and I'm thinkin with auld John Knox that ilka scholar is something added to the riches of the commonwealth.

Thus the sponsoring of a scholar is presented as giving a better return to the donor and the country than merely passing on wealth to an heir.[12] But the trick was not accomplished by words only. The text tells us that Domsie was so intoxicated, 'but not with strong drink', that he suggested to a passer-by that Drumsheugh had a Latin style like Cicero's, and would still be a credit to them.[13] Neither the parochial schools nor the universities, still under the aegis of the Establishment were denied to those who supported the Free Church, yet Free Churchmen stretched their voluntary giving to provide not only churches, manses and schools but also three colleges where their ministers were trained. Keeping alive the myths and ideals was necessary in order to keep flowing both the recruits and the finance they needed.

'Geordie Howe' was immortalised by MacLaren as the *lad o' pairts*, someone selected, coached and financed, to be triumphant at college and soon to be dead of an illness acquired in the city, another sentimental twist to the tale. MacLaren's popularisation of the lad o' pairts in the 1890s had a precedent in Lyon Playfair urging, at a Newcastle meeting of the Association for the Promotion of Social Science, that presbyteries should select and finance the university studies of lads of 'pregnant parts' — a phrase borrowed from Matthew Arnold's poem of 1853 about a scholar gypsy:

The story of the Oxford scholar poor,
Of pregnant parts and quick inventive brain,
Who tired of knocking at preferment's door,
One summer morn forsook
His friends and went to learn the gipsy-lore . . .

Arnold suggests here the thwarting of attempts at social climbing which gave way to a romantic flight to the country: did such compensation in nostalgia prove particularly attractive for Free Churchmen who had forsaken established securities at the Disruption? But what did this lad o' pairts find awaiting him at the university he had so striven to reach?

Except for students who could live at home, there was increased isolation and weakening of communal life even if improved transport meant that the numbers of commuters to classes would grow. For most students, however, the life-line of supplies to and from distant homes was probably not strengthened. Older system of 'common tables' had by mid-nineteenth century long disappeared, and there was little community-life in the Scottish universities until the 1880s, when there developed the unions, 'common dines' athletic clubs, and other societies which both MacLaren and George

Douglas Brown chose to ignore. Such developments did not serve the fancy of writers who wanted to stress the loneliness of the rustic student who competed in class-room and also in the tavern. Patrick Geddes in 1887 had secured accommodation in a hall for a very few students in Edinburgh and the universities in Scotland turned slowly towards providing some form of collegiate and boarding residence for their students — a kind of accommodation associated in Scotland with English-type 'public schools' such as Fettes and Glenalmond. It was paradoxical that the cloisters of Glenalmond should offer an alternative ideal to that of Watson's kailyard, for they were located only a mile to the south of Logiealmond and 'Drumtochty'.

In MacLaren's tales, competition and the rewards of competition were continually stressed: within many diverse and changing environments, institutional and individual excellence could still be demonstrated, especially excellence in class. Before the introduction of classified Honours degrees or before even graduation was common, outstanding performance in class could be measured somewhat arbitrarily by the award of medals; and in some Scottish universities the system of reckoning merit was very destructive:

> In the competition for prizes, which were monetary and sometimes relatively valuable, decisions as to the order of rank in class often lay not with the professor but with the vote of the class . . . assessing the competence of their fellows in standing up to the professor's questions.[14]

This 'contest' structure would be complemented by the written exams for the East India Company and also by the sometimes exhaustive exposure which could face competing candidates for a congregation, after 1874 in the Established Church as well as in the other Scottish presbyterian churches. Competition at school leading to selection and coaching for university entrance, competition for bursaries, the typically competitive university classes, all emphasized this contest ideal. Not many became 'scholar gipsies' and refused the contests, in the outcome of which families and neighbourhood were so interested. Rustic neighbourliness, indeed, could promote individualism against those who were preaching class solidarity and widening access to such benefits as sponsored education.

Socialist solidarity may be contrasted with both personal pietism and ambition. And, yet, it appears that MacLaren is a sentimentalist rather than an individualist. Drumtochty is presented less as a plurality of souls than as a mutually inter-dependent 'civitas dei' or godly commonwealth. If there were no equality of gifts or equality of opportunity to leave the glen, then a more just dispensation still applied to all: for all were catechised and all had access to the communion table. At that sacrament, a class-free society gathers, more evident there than at Domsie's discriminating school. Educational disadvantage was marked — if less clearly so in rural Scotland than in other cities.[15]

This search for a specifically Scottish exemplification of vertical social mobility through education has focussed not on particular groups or classes but on an ideal type. The 'real' lad o' pairts had a long ancestry in parish schools, before being idealised and popularised in 1894 in the first pages penned by Ian MacLaren. There is irony disguising sheer sentiment when MacLaren presents to his readers a teacher who was devoted to teaching the classical languages rather than the wider range of subjects which were very generally taught in parochial schools. And there is farce in the description of how Domsie obtained financial sponsorship for Geordie Howe's progress to university. Whereas it may be argued that patronage and sponsorship characterised the Established Church and its agencies (the parochial schools and the universities) until 1843, thereafter competition was increasingly accepted. Standards were increasingly set and raised for entry to university; the contests for classwork-medals were given great importance, not least by families at home; the taking of degrees, and later competition for classified Honours, shifted the competition to final examinations for graduation. In church and state, appointments were awarded to those lads with 'parts' or abilities who had demonstrated their worth in public competitive examination. Yet writing in the 1890s and later, the kailyard authors ignore the arrival of women as students in the Scottish universities — another signal of the selective reality which they were in fact offering their readers.

NOTES

1. See an account of the parish of Moneydie, adjoining Logiealmond, in H. Lehnemann's 'Exercise of patronage in the Established Church of Scotland after the Disruption', a prize-winning essay in ecclesiastical history, submitted in 1990 at New College, Edinburgh University.

2. Acceptance and mobility had to be sought by Irish Catholic immigrants from the 1840s and by East European Jews from c 1900 AD.

3. Notably by G. E. Davie, *The Democratic Intellect* (Edinburgh, 1961); and by R. D. Anderson, *Education and Opportunity in Victorian Scotland* (Oxford, 1983) and 'In Search of the Lad o' Pairts', *History Workshop*, 19 (Spring 1985).

4. The alternative models of contest and sponsorship are featured in eg R. H. Turner, 'Modes of social ascent' in A. H. Halsey (ed), *Education, Economy and Society* (New York, 1968); see also K. Hope, *As Others See Us: Schooling and Social Mobility in Scotland and the United States* (Cambridge, 1984).

5. See George Blake, *Barrie and the Kailyard School* (London, 1951): on occasion, we will describe Drumtochty/Logiealmond as the Kailyard. The most recent study of the Kailyard is by Gillean Shepherd in Douglas Gifford (ed.), *History of Scottish Literature: vol iii, Nineteenth Century* (Aberdeen, 1989), 309–320.

6. W. R. Nicoll, *Ian MacLaren* (London, 1908), *passim*.

7. See D. M. Forrester, *Logiealmond: the place and the people* (Edinburgh, 1944) 150.

8. *Ibid*, 169.

9. David Hamilton traces class-room theory and practice from Erasmus almost to the present day in 'Adam Smith and the Moral Economy of the Class-room System', *Journal of Curriculum Studies*, xii (1980), 281–298.

10. Forrester, *Logiealmond*, 167.

11. See Anderson, *Education and Opportunity*, 233.

12. Heritable wealth without conflict could produce decadence according to many Victorians. Moreover Smith in *The Wealth of Nations* (1776) I, x, iii, suggested that sponsorship would glut professions and reduce the individual rewards.

13. Here we have some justification for the *laird* o' pairts mentioned in Emma Letley, *From Galt to Douglas Brown* (Edinburgh, 1988) 232.

14. Davie, *Democratic Intellect*, 15 et seq.

15. Anderson, *Education and Opportunity*, 150.

Part IV
Distinctiveness and Diversity in University Systems

16

Federal Universities and Multi-Campus Systems: Britain and the United States since the Nineteenth Century

Sheldon Rothblatt

In Presbyterian Scotland references to the Old Testament are assuredly in order. Moses's father-in-law, Jethro, finding the prophet weary from days of adjudicating disputes among the tribes, suggested that a system of courts be instituted to spread the juridical burden, 'for the thing is too heavy for you; you will not be able to perform it yourself alone.' We must conclude that Jethro did not believe that his system of judgeships would necessarily dispense justice more equitably than the great but harried statesman — indeed, how could he? — but presumably he anticipated gains in productivity and scheduling.

From that episode it is perhaps only a step to the truism that the appearance of new social problems requires new organisational models for coping with altered or strange circumstances, and those models reflect a rationalising mentality or outlook characteristic of all societies at virtually any time. This tempting conclusion — to find the systematising human intellect at work at particularly interesting moments in the organisational history of institutions — is, from an historian's perspective, greatly oversimplified. One obvious objection is that the existence of a rationalising mentality does not in itself predict the exact form a particular organisational change might take. For that we would have to look elsewhere, possibly within the host culture or in its pre-existing institutional disposition. Another caveat is that organisational innovation or complexity can rarely be attributed to a single motive or source. One generation's rationalising is not always another's. Because present-day societies appear to be interested in some form of 'efficiency,' or in productivity gains or 'coordination' or 'accountability' — the terms which we use to explain and justify the bureaucratic introductions of modern societies — hardly proves that the same impulse was at work in the past. Innovation may be the result of ideology, or problem-solving, or accident or a conjunction of events.[1] It may arise from certain identifiable cultural inclinations on the part of a society, or it may well be a combination of more than one variable, which is the more likely explanation, especially as we move forward in time to societies with many political actors and numerous decision-making centres. The value of an historical view of the origins and rise of complex institutions lies in

164

emphasising circumstances specific to time and context; and this in turn leads to wider conclusions about the nature and meaning of innovation.

These opening remarks have their own historical context. As we close the twentieth century there exists an unusual amount of international interest in devising and expanding the organisational forms of higher education. Indeed, this interest is already embodied in a great number of experiments and revisions, some of which result from the internal differentiation of higher education institutions in response to changing external circumstances and some from less evolutionary and more dirigiste or ideological causes, as in the university reforms undergone in Sweden in the late 1960s and now in the process of radical revision once again.[2] The prospect of a forthcoming united Europe has understandably awakened considerable thought about how nations based on different linguistic and cultural inheritances might combine their resources, encouraging an easier movement of students, researchers and teachers across the boundaries of national sovereignties. Experiments along such lines are already well advanced, most notably in programs like ERASMUS, and both market and étatist possibilities, as well as partnerships between public and private sectors, are actively discussed.

But also within nations there exist new interest and energy in breaking down or in challenging historic conceptions of institutional autonomy and academic frontiers hitherto zealously guarded. Some of these fall into the category of programmes affording greater academic mobility to student populations, and they do not exactly directly affect the overall administration or control of separate participating institutions. The Polylink arrangements within the polytechnic sector as centred at Newcastle in England is one example. There is, especially in countries like Australia, a policy of central government-mandated amalgamations, usually between technical colleges or teacher-training institutions, and these mergers could take many forms, from simple combinations leading to the disappearance of smaller and more vulnerable institutions to new organisations with expanded hierarchies. At the University of New England in Armidale, a local educational college has been combined with the university's school of education, increasing the size of the teaching staff and producing (so I understand) a tension between teaching and research and the value assigned to each.[3] At Brisbane, a number of city colleges have been joined with the local technological institute — an MIT or Imperial College — to produce a new system. The resulting organisational difficulties, compounded by geography, are a headache for the vice-chancellors.

Experiments with organisational groupings and inter-institutional cooperation have characterised American higher education, both public and private, since the nineteenth century. These have taken a number of primary forms, of which just a few will be mentioned here. Since the Progressive Era of the first decades of the present century, when modern theories of scientific management and time and motion studies were first popular, Americans rationalised the propensity of students to move at will from institution to institution into what today amounts to a national system of student exchanges. Called 'articulation' (the word also appeared in the Progressive Era) or transferring, the habit of students to wander doubtless originated long before. Articulation consisted of voluntary agreements between institutions freely entered into — although, since no action is truly 'free,' market discipline can certainly be listed as a form of coercion. That articulation was not to every institution's liking is evidenced by the fact that the higher education institutions in the United States which participated least in these exchanges of students are the highly-endowed, elite prestige colleges and universities, those most resistant to consumer pressure.

Transfer students have a direct affect on the administration and even the organisation of American universities. They require special administrative and record-keeping units, special admissions policies and the adjustment of academic standards, insofar as no national standard of achievement exists. And transfer students affect the control that American universities have over their curriculum and degree qualifications, for in accepting articulating students, American colleges and universities agree to accept course work done elsewhere, as well as months or years invested in that work, thus effectively reducing the time to complete the degree at their own institutions for twentieth-century scholar gypsies. Such considerations will arise, or have already arisen, with ERASMUS and similar intra-European exchanges.

But whereas articulation may directly affect the curricular autonomy or admissions policies of individual institutions, it does not directly affect governance. Nevertheless, other forms of inter-institutional cooperation may well do so — federations for example. In an article published in 1987, I defined multi-campus or multi-institutional clusters as parts relating to a centre, with the centre responsible for some major function.[4] I noted that the centre could be strong or weak. I cited the collegiate structure of Cambridge University as the oldest example in the English-speaking world, Cambridge rather than Oxford because at an early date — somewhere around the middle of the eighteenth century — the introduction of the tripos gave the university, as distinct from the colleges, a new role in education. As a modified version of the Cambridge model, I cited the creation of the examining University of London in 1836, with its metropolitan jurisdiction broadening fairly rapidly to include national and imperial responsibilities; and then, on the London model, again with modifications, federal universities in other parts of England, Ireland and Wales. Scotland did not have a federal system, having five universities of a unitary kind until a merger reduced the universities to four in 1860; but Scots had long debated among themselves the creation of some form of national higher education system incorporating the considerable sophistication of their school feeder system. It is true that some collegiate differentiation did exist within the Scottish universities, principally, I understand, as a device for supplementing the incomes of the teaching staff before about 1820.[5] However, undergraduates at new Scottish colleges founded later in the nineteenth century, like that at Dundee, read for the London degree. In my article I traced recent arrangements for degree-taking in the polytechnics through centralised bureaucracies like the Council for National Academic Awards back to Victorian innovations. One could also cite the local examinations of the last century as conceived in the same spirit, the top (or a perceived top such as Oxford or Cambridge) pressing down upon, and setting standards for, the developing sectors of state and private schooling. The first unitary university to be created in England was Birmingham less than a century ago. The University of Durham, founded in the 1830s, was devised on the collegiate model.

The precise origins of the Royal University of London of 1836 are obscure. Daylight and champagne discover not more. The historiographical literature dealing with its beginning generally accepts London University's organisation as a given, simply a fact of history or a happenstance. While it is true that the origins of the first University of London of the 1820s, subsequently called University College, London, makes sense in a familiar English context — the rise in numbers, wealth and influence of the Dissenting community, the growth of London to metropolitan stature and its bursting demography, the expansion of the professions, especially medicine — the origins of the Royal University of London 1836 makes almost no sense in the context of the 1830s; for to term it a compromise, which it unquestionably was, does not at all explain why it was that particular kind of compromise, or who thought of it, or where exactly its philosophical origins lay.

Consequently, the historian must and should remain surprised and puzzled, but also delighted, by the creation of the examining University of London, by its sudden or apparently sudden fabrication, by the minds who created it and the reasoning behind it. The delight derives from encountering an institution which appears wholly or nearly wholly new, thus representing an historical and intellectual conundrum in need of solving. The story of the founding and history of the examining university of 1836 may also be one of those instances in which the offshore observer can be useful — that is, the observer whose own national educational institutions do not include the conception of an examining university; for although nineteenth-century Americans certainly knew of London's existence, and here and there founding bodies of new institutions remarked upon the idea, and were here and there attracted to it, no such institution was created or evolved south of the Canadian border. And the reasons are not difficult to adduce. No national conception of university education existed in the United States once the followers of Alexander Hamilton in the Early Republic were defeated in their scheme to establish a federal university in the District of Columbia. The states of the Union feared the influence that a concentration of intellectual resources might have on American pluralism. The federal constitution prevailed, and the separate states retained their monopoly over public-sector higher education. But in England — and one might add Scotland, where the state as well as the idea of the state appears to have been less feared in the nineteenth century than in England (or so Robert Anderson has cogently argued) — a national conception of higher education was entertained by intellectual and governing elites and put into practice in the mild form, the only form which would have been acceptable in the 1830s, of a degree-granting monopoly whose authority, nevertheless, could not touch the established institutions of Oxford and Cambridge but did, for the briefest imaginable time, a year or less, touch the Anglican, collegiate university of Durham.

Unable to locate the deliberations of the Privy Council that may have cast light on the origins of 1836, I have tried to consider the foundation of the University of London in the more general historical context of the changing religious and political configuration of the 1820s and 1830s and to view the outcome as the result of a series of trade-offs rooted in England's culture. Broadly, the creation of the London federal university was an attempt to cope with several important emerging problems or questions, foremost among them being the definition of a university. It should not exactly surprise us to learn, but in some fashion it may well do so, that it was precisely the controversies over the meaning of a university engendered by the first London University that excited and angered John Henry Newman and led in a direct line to the writing of those discourses, some thirty years later, that remain the most stimulating attempt to define a university in the English language.

Discussion over the definition of a university had actually been going on ever since the newly-founded quality periodical, the *Edinburgh Review,* pitched Scotland against England in the earliest part of the nineteenth century by questioning the value and nature of the education acquired at Oxford.[6] The debate effectively forced argument along three lines:

— What is a university? How does it differ from a college? What are its distinguishing features? What is its purpose? Is there a legal definition of a university? These questions involve the critical dimensions of curriculum, access, financing and the organisation of teaching.

— Is there a distinction between a private educational institution and a public one?

— In what body or authority should control of a university be invested? in the Church? in the state? in a legal trust, and if so, are the trustees to be drawn from laymen or from the academy? in the professions? or, effectively if not legally, in the operations of a free market, implying the sovereignty of the consumer?

The context in which these questions must be understood has to be the 1820s and 1830s. In these two decades — actually the crucial answers are given in less than one decade, from 1828 to 1836 — the context was being altered. Quite suddenly the legal status of Dissenters and Roman Catholics was transformed. Their disabilities were removed, at least respecting public life, and they became citizens at last. This in turn implied a change in the future social and class composition of Parliament, the Cabinet, the departments of state and the Privy Council, although the change was delayed far longer than anyone initially expected, Parliament changing before the Cabinet and the various departments at differential rates into the twentieth century.[7] Also, in educational matters, market discipline was instrumental. As Margaret Bryant has shown with respect to the London area before about 1860, consumer demand had resulted in the creation of a substantial number of varied secondary schools, from private to proprietary,[8] and both of the new London university colleges represented the play of market forces, unlike, I believe, Durham, which appears to have been a defensive operation to stave off an attack by political radicals on the surpluses generated by Durham Cathedral's ownership of coal mines.[9]

Very generally, the 1830s was a period in which the division of national feeling was acute. The reform of parliament encouraged the Dissenting community and all those who were anxious for radical reform. Radical reform there was, in municipal government, the poor laws, the law of tithes, and perhaps less radical, in the provision for popular education. Reform parties had been forming at Oxford since the 1820s. Newman excoriated the Noetics at Oriel and other academic liberals in his *Apologia;* but, if one examines the history of academic and curricular innovation at both senior universities, it is apparent that reform could come from either end of the political spectrum. In the 1820s and 1830s entrenched and vested interests — the older liberal professions, especially the London-based physicians, the Church, and sections of the aristocracy — were eager to hold on to some historical advantages.[10] The creation of the University of London was a comprise between these contending forces, a trade-off between a metropolitan or centre culture which we can in cultural terms call 'aristocratic,' and a provincial or peripheral culture which we can term 'liberal'.[11] The former embodied the idea of taste, or a standard imposed from above, excellence by consensus on high. The latter embodied the principles of diversity, variety, plurality, or excellence through individual competition. The former realised its idea in the formation of an examining university which alone could award degrees. The latter realised its aims through the establishment of colleges. Some of these were secular, some religious, some interdenominational, some devoted to the liberal arts, others (for example, Mason College, Manchester, as yet to come) to the sciences. The definition of a college could also be revised to mean institutions that could be non-residential rather than upscale boarding establishments or professorial rather than tutorial — drawing, therefore, from the substantial Scottish inheritance which had such a great impact on the curricular and organisational structure of University College, London, as well as on the entire range of systems of American colleges and universities developing from colonial times onwards.

As I have stated the situation, the cardinal principle of the metropolitan culture appears to have been the idea of measuring academic achievement by using a separate central authority. The specific model or forerunner of this notion was the Cambridge Senate House examinations which had appeared sometime in the middle of the eighteenth century.[12] The exact origins of these are as vague to us as the exact origins of the Burlington House, University of London examinations, but the evidence suggests that the tripos and Honours schools at Oxford (established first in 1800) had what may be broadly called political origins and were thought of as instruments for maintaining discipline.[13] What made the tripos distinctive — different, let us say, from the scholastic or public disputations which still existed when the new mathematical honours examination evolved in the later eighteenth century — was its written nature, the first such examination in England, and the order of merit. Written examinations were regarded or came to be regarded with considerable justification (given the historical context) as more rigorous, more demanding, more accurate and consequently of a higher level than oral examinations, where candidates could be led or coaxed into acceptable answers. When speed and endurance were added to the examination formula, many Victorians believed that they had created the perfect instrument for choosing the leaders of an evolving liberal democracy and imperial kingdom. The order of merit in mathematics at Cambridge was a further refinement. Candidates were ranked twice: once according to category — first-class, second-class, etc — and again according to absolute rank: senior wrangler downwards.

Yet to describe examinations as a metropolitan/aristocratic principle presents certain difficulties, most conspicuously because aristocracies do not enjoy competing for distinction, especially with outsiders, and a governing class does not like to be publicly humiliated. Yet it was not only members of landed elites who disliked competitive assessments. Resistance to the coming and the spread of examination-fever at Oxford and Cambridge in the early nineteenth century was widespread, taking the form of an elaborate counter-culture celebration of failure and a repudiation of success as measured by examinations. Matthew Arnold and other humanists who associated themselves with the metropolitan culture continued to question the value of examinations, although from a less apologetic perspective, finding them narrowing, denaturing and mechanical, and a positive hindrance to creating a higher type of national character. Yet other, equally serious members of the reformed and reforming university culture, both students and junior dons, embraced the new definition of success as measured by competitive examinations, and played a major part in transforming the internal academic culture of the senior universities of England long before direct state intervention commenced in the middle decades of the nineteenth century.[14] A bifurcation of academic culture was already in place in the first half of the nineteenth century, taking the form of the serious 'reading man' and the old-fashioned Regency 'buck' or 'pickle,' but this division certainly became even more pronounced in the second half of the Victorian era, after the numerous reforms conferred greater legitimacy on the schemes and proposals of the reforming party.

While I believe that the London University idea of an examination has a strong connection to the metropolitan culture, I also accept the usual assumption that it was related to the liberal individualist culture of the periphery and endorse the less common assumption that it was connected to the liberal professional culture of the capital. It was a combination of ideals, a fusion of different value systems, not unlike the other cultural and institutional combinations giving us Victorian culture which was both retrospective and forward-looking at the same time. The very idea of measuring worth by competitive examination represents yet another area of Victorian or proto-Victorian compromise, or a special amalgamation of metropolitan ideas of the importance of a centre with a standard and a liberal idea of the significance of competition in achieving that standard. One can, after all, have competition without a standard, winner take all, but winning against a standard provides an independent measure and a more lasting basis of comparison, and reduces the market and the idea of the market, where competition prevails, to a subsidiary position.

What gave these ideas of competition and a standard both substance and influence was their adoption, and therefore sanctioning, by the elite institutions of England, by the ancient universities and the public schools, and by the civil service, all of which underwent significant reform by the middle decades of Victoria's century.

The Royal University of London, then, as well as the other federations that sprang from its inspiration, were mechanisms for achieving what Cambridge and Oxford had achieved, or were claiming they had achieved, for by 1836 reading for Honours examinations was an activity still only favoured by a few. Federations had the further advantage of being inexpensive, for their sole function was to set and mark examinations and award first degrees, and frugality was also a principle of the periphery in mid-Victorian England. But I would like to suggest that federations were widely acceptable, at least to begin with, not so much because they embodied the contradictory principles of merit selection and the idea of a metropolitan standard and culture but because the burden of sitting examinations was regarded as essentially optional, a matter of choice and hence uncoercive, and therefore well in keeping with nineteenth-century liberal conceptions of freedom and initiative.

Degrees were for those who wanted them. Dissenters might want degrees because they had some value in medicine or, more broadly, because they were indicative of citizenship status and were the symbolic counterparts of the vote. But apart from this special consideration, degrees were not important in the 1830s. The aristocracy and gentry at Oxford and Cambridge had not necessarily taken degrees. Intending clergy took degrees because bishops required them for ordination, and Oxbridge colleges usually required them for fellowships. Even in medicine as practised in England, entry into the profession lay through the teaching hospitals and medical societies, not through universities, although a first degree cleared the way for election to a fellowship in the Royal College of Physicians. Being called to the bar also did not require a university degree, and practice as a solicitor certainly not. From the standpoint of King's College and University College in London, federation through the form of an examining university may have severely compromised their curricular autonomy and educational flexibility, but only if degrees were sought. And federation, at least to begin with, did not really threaten existing professional monopolies.

In Scotland by contrast, efforts to tighten standards and raise the level of the degree had met with keen resistance, for many undergraduates considered the

Scottish universities to be a form of extra-mural teaching, rather than a total way of life. Intending clergy and ministers took degrees. The few who would become professors or college and public school teachers took degrees; but in general the degree had not risen to the position it holds today. Federations, whatever principles of merit selection they may have embodied, were directly proportional in value to the degrees that were sought. And degrees were sought when aristocratic patronage and other forms of sponsorship waned, and when an urban professional culture began to challenge an entrepreneurial one, as Harold Perkin has discussed at great length in his studies of the coming of a service culture to Britain.[15]

Not to draw the contrasts too sharply, but to allow for other slow developments contributing to the enhanced respect for selection by merit, I would point out that in a modest way the career open to talent had been evolving in government since the eighteenth century. The relatively weak character of Cabinet government contributed to the evolution. In the absence of strong political parties, ministers of the crown were sufficiently independent to exercise their own judgment and patronage, and in certain departments of state, notably the Victorian ministry concerned with education, some staff were being hired on meritocratic criteria.[16] Indeed, it was this existing practice which undoubtedly led to the Northcote-Trevelyan recommendations, not so much as a wholly new idea as the wholesale advocacy of a new practice and its elevation into principle.

At present the usual reasons offered for the creation of federal systems of higher education involve the rationalization of resources in the interests of some form of efficiency or productivity, involving lower costs in the unit of resource or coordination or accountability, with accountability leading to outside or ministerial control of systems and budgets in countries like present-day Australia. I hardly struggle with myself to include in such a list of reasons, knowing full well that it is frivolous, the pleasure taken by some in the creation of organisational charts and management models and what is thought to be a superior way of handling complexity. By complexity, the sociologists of higher education mean social and cultural pluralism as represented by demands for access, curriculum reform, affirmative action, articulation, and accountability. A standard and important work on multi-campus systems in the United States refers to 'the promotion of "intentional change" through academic planning', budgeting and programme review as 'the heart of system activity.'[17] But none of these contemporary management ideas helps us fully to understand the origins of Victorian federations. They were not created to rationalise a system in terms of expenditures, growth, admissions, and planning, nor to advance productivity targets and improve efficiency, nor yet to stimulate creativity. They also were not created to manage complexity or introduce diversity — objectives which appear in today's American multiversities. Such objectives were in Victorian times relegated to market forces, which many Victorians respected but hardly all, especially those who identified with the metropolitan culture. The Victorian federations were established as forms of quality control, as mechanisms for guaranteeing the value of the degree against its expected debasement in the marketplace. What is even more special about this development is the means chosen to support the degree, namely a system of examining that featured written examinations, blind marking and the total separation of the act of teaching from the act of examining, leading to the development of the system of external examiners, a system barely recognised in the United States. In this last respect, the divorce between teaching and examining, London even went beyond Cambridge, Burlington House beyond the Senate House, for on the Cam there were indeed written examinations and blind marking, but teachers also examined.

The metropolitan ideal was also embodied in another Oxbridge innovation, perhaps not so thorough-going if we consider the hybrid curriculum called *literae humaniores* installed at Oxford in the early nineteenth century, but thorough-going enough; and that was the elevation of the single-subject examination above the more general examination (with a modified version in Scotland) on the grounds that specialisation also promotes rigour. Here too, as in so many other instances, Americans and British parted company. The American undergraduate university curriculum, truer perhaps to its Scottish roots, continued to broaden in the course of the nineteenth and twentieth centuries. The safeguarding of quality became less important than providing for options and electives, and when Americans did discuss quality — which of course they had to do — the public discussion was and is normally centred on programmes of study, the curricular 'canon,' and the availability of resources. So the history of federation in Victorian Britain is also the history of the triumph of a particular kind of examining system and equally the triumph of faith in that kind of examining, in its accuracy and as the best means for both producing and recognising a 'first-class' mind.

The question of the standard of academic achievement in Scotland was really at the heart of the inquiries conducted by the Royal Commission on the Scottish Universities of 1826–30, the very first royal commission on universities to be appointed in the nineteenth century. The commission proposed the introduction of an Honours degree, amongst other considerations, as a means of encouraging rigour and competition. The opposing sides took shape immediately. There were those who agreed with the commissioners and were willing to be guided by 'English' sentiment. And then there were the Scottish nationals who adhered to older (shall we call them 'democratic'?) policies and who were willing to trade off high student drop-out rates for relatively open admissions. At mid century a proposal was circulated for a single board of degree examiners for all of Scotland, but this was beaten back.

Let me take this analysis one step further. The history of federation in Victorian Britain is also the history of faith in science, by which I mean that the reaction to the older, that is to say, aristocratic forms of networking was so strong that the search commenced for a means of objectively assessing worth, a means independent of the widespread belief in the value of 'character' summed up in the eighteenth-century tag, 'men and manners.'[18] The federal principle challenged this older conception of worth, which was closely related to style, to the ability to present oneself publicly, or to what may also be called 'acting.'

The aristocratic culture of the eighteenth century was strongly influenced by Italian models of civic conduct. It was openly social and as such heavily theatrical. Aristocratic leaders were public figures and continually on view, and Georgian principles of town planning, derived from Italian models, featured the open square which encouraged visibility and display. The square was supported and reinforced by the promenade and the 'parade,' which likewise encouraged strolling but also the new habit of window shopping. The novelist Henry Fielding described the great wen of London in 1749 as a place in which style and street commingled.[19] The extravagant dress of London men and women of fashion derived from the same spirit of openness. The theatre itself was immensely popular in the Georgian period, partly, as we know, in reaction to puritan dislike of the stage. It had moved out of the court into the new London playhouses, where high and low mixed, if literally not on the same levels. The Georgian theatre attempted to become yet more popular by becoming respectable. Playwrights displayed a great variety of virtuous as well as fatuous types on the stage as examples to be emulated or avoided. Nevertheless, the anti-theatrical bias which Jonas Barish has traced back to Plato was sufficiently strong, especially during the evangelical revival of the early nineteenth century, to call spectacle and performance into question and to continue the bias against acting as no more than a form of deceit and dissimulation, as likely to fool the performer as it was the audience.[20]

The federal principle was therefore a profound attack on a hallowed theory of liberal education which equated manner with education. At the older universities of England the theory did not immediately disappear. There the division between college and university allowed for the simultaneous existence of the older conception that style makes the man[21] and the newer one emphasising more cerebral or intellectual qualities. (Something of the former still lingers in the noted American liberal arts colleges, where student-oriented learning and 'moral' education remain ideals.) The conflict between the two conceptions was sharp, if mitigated in practice. For example, in the older version of liberal education, failure was a moral or personal failing, the result of not working sufficiently hard. The stigma of failure could therefore be eradicated by applying oneself in some recognisable way, either through reading hard or rowing hard. But insofar as the examination system emphasised qualities of mind, the results of Judgement Day could not be easily eradicated. Once posted on the noticeboards outside the Senate House, the tripos results became a fact of history. Furthermore, re-trial was made difficult or even impossible. Undergraduates who missed examinations, or performed badly because of illness or circumstances beyond their control, lost the chance to become first-class men. Examinations were the Victorian side of Dr Johnson's belief in the utility of caning. He accepted caning because it settled an issue at once. (Hanging, he might have noticed, accomplished the same end.) Examinations, too, were final and decisive. They erased any lingering doubt as to intellectual worth. It is hardly an accident that eugenics, the measurement of cranial capacity, and the efforts to define 'intelligence' all appear at approximately the same time as examination fever takes hold in Britain.

The federal principle represented the separation of mind from style or personality, and the latter were to be replaced by a less flexible conception of character, which Lionel Trilling calls 'authenticity' or 'sincerity'. Trilling notices national differences in expressing individual sincerity or authenticity. Thus in France sincerity consisted in revealing oneself truthfully, but in Britain (or England) a national reticence required a veil to be drawn over matters intimate, leaving sincerity to mean deeds, actions or forthright communication. In either case, the relationship between individuals and social institutions shifted; for once it was accepted that the members of a particular culture act sincerely or authentically as a matter of course, breakdowns in moral behaviour have to be attributed to less personal causes. They become the fault of institutions and social systems.[22] Not to exaggerate the point, the logic of the argument suggests that if examinations do in fact reveal one's 'true' intellectual qualities (and perhaps moral ones as well — for example, self-discipline, responsibility, diligence, a capacity to plan), the only way in which a 'second-class mind' can improve is for an examination system to be changed or its results de-emphasised. This was the strategy adopted by Victorian humanists and critics — a strategy that failed.

Interestingly enough, the distinction between college and university in the federal systems did not produce a partition between character-formation and mind-training. In fact, federated colleges were not so much Oxbridge colleges as "university colleges," smaller versions of universities without degree-giving powers. Possibly the reason lay in the fact that professional even more than liberal education was the raison d'etre behind University College, London. It was King's College, London, which actually had the honour of introducing the first school or department of engineering into English university education, although the first chair was established at the rival college in 1841.[23] One of the continual complaints of undergraduates at London but especially at the redbricks founded later — complaints that go well into the twentieth century — was the relative absence of style with its glittering past associations.

The examining university derived its authority and legitimacy from three sources. The first was the slowly-growing prestige of the degree as a validation of competence. The second was simplicity in coping with complexity. Almost no bureaucracy was necessary, expenses were customarily met out of fees — at worst, only a tiny state subsidy was necessary. Throughout the Victorian period, government resisted pressure from below to bail out or finance federal systems, except on a one-time basis, but that was before the incorporation of big science into the universities. The dominant Victorian belief was that teaching, which also included professional teaching, could be met out of a combination of endowments, gifts and fees.

The third source of legitimacy for the federal universities was their royal origins. That is, they were agencies of the state. This might appear to us ludicrous, since the London University of 1836 consisted of a miniscule staff, technically a committee of the Treasury. The premises were maintained by the Office of Works. But, however odd this first bureaucratic system might appear to us today, it held two contradictory principles in easy tension. Both have been mentioned. The first was the metropolitan or centre culture, here represented by the prestige of the state, and the second was the principle of liberty. The state was present, if just barely; but a precedent had been laid down, to be used if ever necessary.

The comparative case, referred to thus far only in passing, can now be examined in more detail and perspective. Federalism in the form of multi-campus academic systems has been called 'one of the most extensive and significant developments in university organisation in the past quarter century' in the United States.[24] It is mainly a twentieth-century phenomenon. Adumbrations existed as early as the Federal period following Independence, however, and are probably traceable to the rising competition for resources and market shares by institutions as varied as schools, academies, colleges and universities. Concern over the rampant proliferation of teaching institutions is the origin of the famous Yale Report of 1828 bemoaning the cheapening of education through the creation of fly-by-night opportunists.[25] In other words, in America as in England, the existing elite sectors of what we today might call 'higher education' but then less specific and layered, were concerned about the rise of new institutions without standards; but federal systems were not created to promote a standard of culture as expressed through a particular kind of examining system. The centre of a federal system did not and does not 'examine.' It does not embody an 'idea' in the European sense, Humboldtian or Newmanesque, although such ideas flowed into American universities in the course of the nineteenth century, and have never departed. But, however much lofty ideas or special conceptions of a university may have influenced and inspired individual teachers or presidents, they never succeeded in fastening upon universities a single conception of their role in society, their duties or their historical legacy.[26]

Nor did the multi-campus system come into being to protect the word 'university' as properly belonging only to a particular type of superior higher education institution. 'University' had come into use in the late eighteenth century at Harvard to describe a single institution with more than one college or 'school' attached to it — in this case, a medical school or department — but no reference was made to degrees or examinations. A university was a form of organisation.

Yet there are exceptions even if they prove the rule, the rule being the inability of American universities or university elites or the centre to monopolise a particular conception of a university by denying use of the word to other and usually newer institutions, or to those regarded as inferior in status or quality. Thus alongside state universities there arose in the United States a second tier of state-supported institutions, usually or often normal schools in origin, which in time, particularly during the extraordinary higher education expansion following the Second World War, grew into large-scale bodies with high aspirations. Among those aspirations was access to the name 'university,' which implied 'higher' tasks such as educating future members of the liberal professions and the granting of doctorates of philosophy. Insofar as these educational missions had acquired prestige in American society, the title of university was coveted. The older or original state universities wanted to hold the line at both title and mission, but lobbying efforts with legislatures usually came to nought. Losing title, the older institutions usually retained mission, but the word university was degraded even further, acquiring a wholly neutral and almost meaningless connotation in the American context. The contrast with London University could not be greater.

A multi-campus, federal system became the basic type of university for state-supported higher education in the United States. The word university, with its European echoes and ancient legacies, symbols and rituals, was asked to accept as partner a neologism which disturbed all those who recoiled at the vulgarities of modern, mass higher education culture, a neologism which carried none of the antique meanings but suggested a bureaucratic or technocratic or managerial culture. That neologism was of course the 'multiversity' (or 'pluriversity' as it was sometimes known in the Britain of the 1960s), which implied a certain size and complexity. (Although writers sometimes distinguish between multiversities and multi-campus systems, for present purposes the two will be conflated.) From that followed a classificatory lexicon of a technical character. Consequently present-day authorities on the subject of American academic federalism distinguish between two types: the first is called 'segmental,' a grouping of campuses with similar functions, as in the case of the nine-campus University of California under a president (although the San Francisco campus is exclusively a medical school). Another Californian segment is the California State University and College system — about half a dozen campuses with four- and five-year degree programmes similar in function to British polytechnics; and a third public segment is composed of some hundred, two-year community colleges, whose chancellor sits in the state capital, Sacramento. Occasionally the private colleges and universities are loosely termed a 'segment,' but only as a semantic convenience. The Claremont colleges in Southern California are an example of a private federation consisting of colleges and graduate schools of independent origins retaining some of their former identifying characteristics.

The second kind of federal system in existence in the United States is often called 'comprehensive.' American comprehensives come in all shapes and sizes, but are characterised by the great variety of institutional forms which they encompass. The constituent institutions range from community colleges to research and professional schools. Examples are the City University of New York (CUNY) and the State University of New York (SUNY). The London University, with its present collection of schools, colleges and hospitals, is of this nature, but with a weak centre and with legally independent colleges and schools which have their own governing boards. It is, therefore, rather a confederation than a federation. California supports a tripartite federated system surmounted by no single authority. Illinois has another version of this. Texas supports no fewer than thirty-seven public senior universities under fifteen different governing boards, six of which govern systems. About one third of the states have created single systems with a single state governing board.[27]

Although I cannot speak for all the state systems of higher education, I can hypothesise that many of the systems, at least the earlier, famous ones, were built from the inside out rather than from the outside in, being created, as at the University of California, by innovative academic leaders winning the support of key government officials. But other systems were undoubtedly created at the initiative of government officials themselves, as Burton Clark has noted, in order to simplify the difficulty of choosing between a large number of public institutions clamoring for funding and attention, lobbying and in other ways attempting to seek favors and privileges.[28]

For what reason or purpose? I doubt very much if we could say that Californians or Americans generally have an in-built liking for systems. Certainly the American professoriate is either mildly hostile or indifferent, but more the latter because the teachers find in general that the 'system' does not really impose upon them all that much — although I am sure that this generalisation would have to be highly qualified according to types of systems. Boards of trustees and regents may well impose upon teaching staff, but that is a different point. The ostensible or manifest function of American higher education federations lies in the familiar bureaucratic notions that I mentioned at the outset: overall planning, to include resource allocation and priorities, something called efficiency, the avoidance of duplication, accountability, 'coordination' — another wonderfully confusing word — and, a contrast this with the Victorian British federations, quality control, which in the American context usually means minimal not optimal standards.[29] Even more so, as I mentioned in passing, it usually means programme evaluation, which is a far less invidious method of assessment than measuring the intellectual quality of teaching by some external yardstick. When such a yardstick is applied, Americans prefer that it be done through peer review or by 'voluntary' accrediting agencies which lack the authority to implement findings and recommendations. It is difficult to find in the United States the kind of central assessment of disciplines and departments introduced by the University Grants Committee in its final years, and indeed American institutions would fear the ramifications of such an assessment by a powerful arm of the government, whether in the nation's Capitol or in the state houses. With their national ideology of opportunity for individuals, their commitment to social mobility and their perennial optimism, not to mention the populism that is generally available for use, Americans do not like to embarrass institutions by pointing to defects that may not be correctable if subjected to an elite standard.

But the latent function or hidden agenda of American federations, which has just now been hinted at, is far more interesting as a comparison to British university history than their apparent or manifest functions. The hidden agenda of federated systems in the United States is to minimise the intrusion of government into everyday decision-making and to reduce externally-mandated policy decisions to the broadest and most innocuous level of generalisation, so that the business of research, teaching, consultation and public service may continue with a high level of de facto independence. Federalism is also a means for encouraging a tolerance for ambiguity — ambiguity in the relations of heads of systems to heads of constituent campuses or indeed throughout the system's functionings.[30] So strongly is this the American — or Californian? — position that I note with some satisfaction that the American rationale for federation is provided in a March 1989 report on London University commissioned by the vice-chancellor and prepared by two Californians. Among the statements about the virtues of federation we find the need for an enhanced central administration in order to facilitate planning in an era of growing demands and complexity (these demands and complexities being manifest in school-based or decentralised degree-giving and an increasing number of modular courses. Indeed, the Murray Committee of 1972 had mentioned something of the same sort). Another statement quietly suggests that greater attention to the federal organisation of the London University would better prepare the institutes, university colleges, medical and other specialised components to meet the challenge of Westminster, Whitehall and the Universities Funding Council — in other words, provide London with a greater capacity for fighting back, anticipating outside reform, mediating and negotiating.[31]

Segmental federal systems have another, not quite so latent, function which at first glance appears un-American. It is to prevent the dilution of mission that occurs or can occur in the comprehensive systems or that exists or can exist under conditions of unfettered institutional competition. Market discipline either forces competition along the same route or leads to wholly new directions as institutions attempt to find a special niche for themselves, a place in the consumption structure that provides unique opportunities. Segments try to prevent 'mission creep' by formalising boundaries and having them recognised by state legislatures, and by being vigilant in protecting monopoly functions, for example, research or medical education. Or the 'mother' campuses of federal systems may object to the establishment of new sites on a variety of grounds, snobbery or financial fears, as the campus at Berkeley and Northern Californians generally objected to the creation of a southern branch, now the University of California at Los Angeles, in the 1920s.[32]

Throughout the 1980s the University of California system fought off the claims of the California State University system, which through its chancellor tried to leverage its component campuses into the high-status research market and attract the substantial resources that accompany 'upward academic drift'. Here and there such inroads have in fact been made at the disciplinary level; but on the whole, the intrusions have been resisted, and the formal boundaries have held, probably because the process of upward academic drift brings different funding formulae into play and immensely increases the cost of higher education. American state governments, then, in the name of diversity and access, have resisted applying the Robbins principle to new or ambitious higher education institutions and have instead adhered to the practice of differential segmental financing.

Establishing bulwarks against intruders from 'below,' and appealing to the authority and assistance of government in doing so, appear to resemble the British desire to preserve the standards and definition of a university, and it would be foolish to deny the imputation. American universities and colleges belong to a reputational or status system. Prestige drives many of the hiring and admissions policies of higher education institutions in the United States.[33] It may in particular be argued that prestige is all the more important as a regulator of American colleges and universities precisely because few outside high-status institutions exist with which higher education institutions can associate, deriving their prestige from a halo effect. The United States never had a national church, a landed aristocracy, a governing elite (after about 1820), a highly-regarded civil service, or a 'state' representing the nation in its 'noblest' and most idealised guise, as in France, Sweden, or Germany. The liberal professions in America come closest to possessing a traditional status. Perhaps that, as well as the antiquity of the association, is why the ties between universities and the professions are close. Otherwise, it is the colleges and universities of the United States that help to create status distinctions in the United States, rather than merely reproducing such distinctions as European universities are sometimes charged with doing.[34]

But it is still the case that prestige cannot rest upon the authority of state governments to establish mission boundaries and funding differentials between public-sector institutions. A prestigious private sector stands outside state higher education legislation; and furthermore, the public legitimacy of all higher education depends upon its accessibility to students. This especially applies to the public elite sector, which must pay attention to the transfer process, even at the cost of lessening institutional control over the degree. Consequently, however much federal systems may attempt to protect the characteristics of their satellite campuses, the essential point is that they do compete against one another for talent, resources and status advantages in their own and against other states, and against the private sector, in a bewildering array of leagues, circles and other groupings. That competition includes what to Europeans must and does appear a baffling amount of fuss over intercollegiate athletics in a highly commercialised form, and other activities not historically associated with universities. Furthermore, since the centre of the federal system in many state multi-campus arrangements does not even supply the bulk of the total operating and research budget to its constitutents, corporate raiding can and does occur within systems, and lures are dangled before undergraduates and postgraduates. Ultimately, no federal system can claim the loyalty of its colonial dependencies and academic faculties, which remain wholly attached to their outlying disciplinary fiefs and tribal territories, a fact of life made famous in different words by the chief architect of one of the celebrated multi-campus systems.[35] Whether or not individual universities (wherever they are) will lose their 'soul' in the future service of multiple clients, as one recent writer suggests,[36] it is certain that the federal university in America never had one.

In a sense then — and to repeat — the Royal University of London, the Victoria University, the University of Wales and so on, and the American segmented systems, have had a common objective in the preservation of a particular kind of monopoly through constraint of market competition. In the British case, the monopoly was the degree. In the American one, it was the mission, to which degrees may be attached (for example, the Ph D). The similarities are always interesting, but the differences are what really matter. In England, the task of preserving or establishing a monopoly was a task that fell to central government at precisely the moment when the higher education system in England began to expand and the market began to play an important role in the provision for post-secondary instruction.

A further essential point is that government in Britain could exercise its authority over both the public and the private sector because fundamentally there was no conception of 'society' such as had developed in the United States, by which I mean no legitimate source of authority to appeal to beyond the prerogative state, beyond the crown in parliament. In America an inherent distrust of political authority made itself felt at the time of the Revolution and just afterwards, as manifested in the intense dispute between Jeffersonians and Hamiltonians. The result was a weakening of central power, an increase in states' rights and, more importantly, a conception of 'society' or 'public opinion' as being above and beyond government, both morally and legitimately. One can see this very clearly in the debates over the privileges to be accorded the University of California at the time of the Second Constitutional Convention in 1878. Efforts by the highly organised populist farmers' and urban workers' movements to use government to force the university into a heavily utilitarian and vocational curriculum were defeated by a widespread distrust of state power in the regulation of educational matters, and the result was the relatively autonomous position which the university enjoys in the Californian Constitution today.[37]

The ability of American universities and colleges to appeal over the heads of politicians to a conception like 'society' has, over time, produced a special definition of American freedom. Customarily — and Max Weber's famous essay warning about the intrusions of the German Imperial State fed American fears — academic freedom in the United States is defined as being outside political interference, both in the running of universities and in attempts to influence the subject matter of teaching. In earlier periods, as American colleges and universities were breaking away from religious ties and affiliations important in their founding, academic freedom was also described in the language of religious freedom. 'Society,' regarded as antithetical to government possibly because it was plural and hence divided, was looked upon more as an ally than a threat; and to this day university presidents in the public sector will campaign against impending legislation considered inimical to university interests. It is only recently that threats to academic freedom have been seen as emanating from sources internal to the universities themselves, sources representing radical student movements or teaching staff with specific ideologies.

By contrast with an American concern for the independence of universities and colleges as expressed in conceptions of academic freedom, there is very little literature on the subject in writings on the history of British universities, and no single comprehensive work such as Richard Hofstadter and Walter Metzger have produced for the United States.[38] State or religious interference in the running of British universities is a well-established historical fact, and the revolt against religious orthodoxy at Oxford and Cambridge that marked the middle decades of the nineteenth century is not an exception to that remark but a confirmation of it. The dons who advocated religious toleration in undergraduate admissions, the receipt of degrees and the appointment of fellows did not really mind if the state replaced the Church as the primary influence on the ancient universities. Indeed, it was the academic Tories, the clerical dons, who worried most about the intrusion of state power and who resisted the demands and initially refused to answer the questions of royal commissioners appointed to inquire into the running of their colleges.

But I have stated the problem incorrectly. Where Church and state are one, embodied in the person of the crown, and where the crown's prerogative, as expressed through the Privy Council, remains legitimate, and where universities identify completely with the state and Church establishments, the word 'interference' is misleading. The polarities which Americans take for granted as an essential part of their institutional history, leading to shifts from consensus one day to litigation the next, do not exist to the same degree in Britain. A fortiori, when Victorian dons wanted to protest against the intrusion of outside influence into university affairs, they frequently spoke of standing up to 'public opinion'. What they feared was the unfettered consumerism of Victorian liberal society. An historian like Edward Gibbon might well write in his autobiography a propos the successful sale and reception of his *Decline and Fall of the Roman Empire* that 'the public is seldom wrong'.[39] But that is because he was an Augustan who felt liberated from patronage by his success in the market place. The situation was perceived differently in the different value system of the nineteenth century.

Do these sketchy remarks account for the comparatively weak responses by British universities to government policy in the 1980s, or are we also to attribute the relative calm or sense of defeat to the absence of effective institutions for channelling protest, such as law courts, constitutional rights with regard to tenure, an independent or private sector of higher education, a conception of society as distinct from government? Perhaps so — if the Charter 88 movement is to be taken seriously.

Whether public or private, American institutions of higher education attempt to preserve their independence by acting as if they were private, by automatically, as it were, conducting their affairs as if they possessed natural rights. Although today only the University of Buckingham is considered to be a private university in Britain, not answerable to the Universities Funding Council, the conception of a private higher education was actually very prevalent in the 1830s. The private sector in Britain consisted of the new London colleges of King's and University, and as the century progressed other private colleges were formed. But actually, the private sector also included the ancient colleges of Oxford and Cambridge, for the definition of a college had been greatly clarified by the decisions of 1836 to invest the word 'university' with a special definition. It was the academic Tories who took the lead in defining a college as a private body owing its origins 'not to Kings or Parliaments, but . . . to the piety and benevolence, and enlarged and far-seeing liberality of private individuals'.[40] While a 'college' could be a university college or a type of school — the College at Eton, Bedford College for Women, or in our time, Carmel College — it could also have a private identity allowing it to decide upon its own curriculum, admissions policies and religious affiliation or leanings. Colleges could be non-denominational, even secular, even in some respects atheistic, or, as in the case of King's College, they could be Anglican. At Durham, the colleges were regarded as private — hence religious subscription could be required of matriculands.

However, the University of Durham (as distinct from its colleges) was public, and its lectures were consequently open to all comers. By contrast, the word 'university' belonged to the public sphere of higher education. Because of the London compromise of 1836, a university was a public entity, beholden to the state, since the state had declared its interest in upholding qualifications as represented by the degree. The university was public, its lectures consequently open to all comers. The private/public distinction in the United States had nothing to do with the type of institution or mission or degree-granting capability. The distinction existed because in the early nineteenth century the State of New Hampshire was prevented by the courts from taking over Dartmouth College, one of the seven colonial colleges which the state had hitherto supported as a kind of state-supported college. But if one of the states was prevented from exercising control over a college for which it had once had some degree of fiscal responsibility, in a deeper sense the distinction between private and public in the United States is misleading. Both sectors emulate one another because they are competitive. Both appeal to the same sources for financial support (the private sector has access to all kinds of federal dollars), and both are beholden to 'society' and claim to be serving the general public.

Victorian Britain, as a liberal society albeit with a prerogative state, had a number of features in common with the world of twentieth-century America, but the differences are always more striking. The metropolitan culture captured the degree examinations and made them into an effective instrument for imposing curricular control from above, waiting patiently for degree demand to build up. Federal university systems in the United States did not attempt to impose quality control, beyond some minimal regulation, because federal systems in the United States looked outward as much as inward, generally alert to the enemies lurking beneath the walls. Even within segments, serious differences have existed and continue to exist on the constituent campuses with respect to admissions, curriculum and the recruitment of academic staff and students, not to mention athletic programmes and solicitations for private funding. In fact, as I have noted, it is precisely the preservation of differences that public segments desire, differences which define their identities and independence but do not restrict their ability to compete against other similar segments or the independents outside the federal system.

To be sure, it is not always easy to notice the differences. One might be just as much astonished by the homogeneity of American universities, and wonder whether their claims to being unique are rhetorical rather than actual market hype rather than reality, a part of the recruiting game and self-advertisement that is especially conspicuous at the moment as higher education costs mount furiously. All American universities or colleges, beyond a handful, are divided into teaching departments based on disciplines. All feature modular course structures, offer credits or units, and combine teaching with examining. All claim to be 'diverse' — a word rapidly becoming a cliche. The differences are quite probably not so much differences of aim and organisation, but differences in intangibles, depending upon geographic location, urban or small-town settings, the composition of the student body, their prior schooling or family culture or ethnicity, the early history and prestige of the institution, or the national and international reputation of the academic staff.

But whether the differences are actual or only a matter of emphasis, or whether they are created as marketing strategies, many American university teachers and administrators think they need to be preserved and legitimated against the homogenising tendencies of a populist culture which every now and then arouses itself against the suggestion of elitism in any form — this is perhaps easiest to resist in some of its political forms than in its social forms. Segments and systems have large bureaucracies. Martin Trow has pointed out that the answer to big government is an equally big university-based bureaucracy, which speaks the same language as the civil servants in the state capitals and the 'pols' in the state houses and keeps them well supplied with a himalayan quantity of facts, figures, phone calls and legislative appearances.[41] Burton Clark has suggested that a similar stand-off is produced through voluntarism, pre-emptive strikes taken with the assistance of a network of interlinked self-help associations of universities, colleges, graduate schools, governing boards and other Washington-based organisations acting as a kind of larger federal centre. These associations 'nationalise' the higher education system, lobby for it and keep it in touch with a very broad range of public opinion. Clark has also noted that it would be a mistake to think that the creation of numerous public or quasi-public coordinating agencies and councils at governmental levels really means coordination. In the American context it means rather the protection of diversity and differentiation within a segment. As he says, it is essential to divide power, support variety and legitimate disorder.[42]

These examples, historical as well as more recent, establish, I believe, that there exist and have existed a great many different federated academic communities, certainly in Britain and the United States, serving quite different and often enough quite contrasting purposes. Those purposes also probably underwent periodic changes of emphasis or possibly transformations which a more detailed examination might reveal. In any case, the different uses of federation are undoubtedly worth bearing in mind as in the 1990s the nations of Europe set about creating a federated system of sometime sovereign states and experience inter-institutional arrangements well below both political initiative and political control. Even where bureaucratic agencies appear to resemble one another, they are not necessarily driven by the same mental laws (as a Victorian philosopher might say). Civil servants abound in the United States, but they are not necessarily dirigiste in outlook. While they 'coordinate' and recommend, their decisions also reflect the intricate system of checks and balances, of trade-offs and conceptions of spheres of autonomy and independence that pervade American legal and political life in a nation that has remained peculiarly loyal to its special Enlightenment roots.

NOTES

1. See the famous debate of the 1960s over the origins of public intervention in England as started by Oliver MacDonagh, *A Pattern of Government Growth, 1880–1860* (London, 1961).

2. An account of recent events is provided by Peter Scott, *Higher Education in Sweden — a Look from the Outside* (London and Lund, 1991). I am also greatly indebted to forthcoming work by Aant Elzinga of the University of Gothenburg.

3. See Grant Harman and V. Lynn Meek (eds), *Institutional Amalgamations in Higher Education, Process and Outcome in Five Countries* (Armidale, New South Wales 1988). Also by the same editors, *Australian Higher Education Reconstructed? Analysis of the Proposals and Assumptions of the Dawkins Green Paper* (Armidale, N.S.W., 1988).

4. Sheldon Rothblatt, 'Historical and comparative remarks on the federal principle in higher education,' in *History of Education*, 16 (1987), 151–80; also 'London: a metropolitan university,' in Thomas Bender (ed.), *The City and the University* (Oxford and New York, 1988), 119–149.

5. For these facts and others about Scotland, I am indebted to conversations with Donald Withrington and to Robert Anderson, *Education and Opportunity in Victorian Scotland* (Oxford, 1983).

6. See the *Edinburgh Review* articles by John Playfair, (xi, Jan. 1808, 249–284); Richard Payne Knight (xiv, July 1809, 429–441); and Sydney Smith (xv, Oct. 1809, 40–53, and xvii, Nov. 1810, 122–135). These essays were published anonymously. The famous Oxford rebuttal is by Edward Copleston of Oriel, *A Reply to the Calumnies of the Edinburgh Review against Oxford Containing an Account of the Studies Pursued in the University* (Oxford, 1810).

7. The best source for this is W. L. Guttsman, *The British Political Elite* (London, 1963).

8. Margaret Bryant, *The London Experience of Secondary Education* (London, 1986).

9. Alan Heeson, *The Founding of the University of Durham* (Durham, 1982); C. E. Whiting, *The University of Durham, 1832–1932* (London, 1932).

10. The early controversies surrounding the first London university are detailed in H. Hale Bellot, *University College London 1826–1926* (London, 1929).

11. My use of words like 'metropolitan' or 'peripheral' is obviously indebted to Edward Shils's well-known essays appearing in *Center and Periphery: Essays in Macrosociology* (Chicago, 1975), but also to the writings of Lawrence Cremin on the history of American education.

12. Negley Harte, *The University of London, 1836–1986* (London, 1986), 73.

13. John Gascoigne, 'Mathematics and meritocracy: the emergence of the Cambridge mathematical tripos,' in *Social Studies of Science*, 14 (1984), 547–584; Sheldon Rothblatt, 'The student sub-culture and the examination system in early nineteenth-century Oxbridge,' in Lawrence Stone (ed.), *The University in Society* (Princeton, 1974), i, 247–304.

14. Sheldon Rothblatt, *The Revolution of the Dons, Cambridge and Society in Victorian England* (Cambridge, 1981).

15. Harold Perkin, *The Origins of Modern English Society, 1780–1880* (London, 1969, repr. 1972); and *The Rise of Professional Society, England since 1880* (London, 1989).

16. See, for example, George Kitson Clark, 'Statesmen in disguise: reflections on the history of the neutrality of the civil service,' reprinted in Peter Stansky, *The Victorian Revolution: Government and Society in Victorian Britain* (New York, 1973); and Franklin B. Wickwire, 'King's friends, civil servants, or politicians,' *American Historical Review*, 71 (Oct. 1965), 18–42.

17. Eugene C. Lee and Frank M. Bowen, *The Multicampus University: a Study of Academic Governance* (Berkeley, 1971), 215.

18. Stefan Collini takes education for character formation into the Victorian era in 'The idea of "character" in Victorian political thought,' *Transactions of the Royal Historical Society*, 5th ser., 35 (London, 1985), 29–50.

19. Mentioned by Richard Sennet, *The Fall of Public Man* (Cambridge, 1977), 64.

20. Jonas Barish, *The Antitheatrical Prejudice* (Berkeley, 1981).

21. Does this apply to women? Insofar as character formation was thought to be the peculiar virtue of a collegiate education, the answer may be no. Many late Victorian dons thought that collegiate life was especially suited to men students and not to women, because only men by their nature and their public destinations were able to profit from the kind of interpersonal communication characterised by residence in a college. I am indebted to conversations with my student Monica Rico for these thoughts.

22. Lionel Trilling, *Sincerity and Authenticity* (Cambridge, 1973), 10, 14, 58.

23. F. G. Brook, 'The early years of London University — its influence on higher education and the professions,' *Universities Review*, 33 (1960), 12.

24. Lee and Bowen, *Multicampus University*, 1.

25. 'Original papers in relation to a course of liberal education', *The American Journal of Science and Arts*, 15 (Jan. 1829), 297–351.

26. Sheldon Rothblatt, 'The idea of the idea of a university and its antithesis', in *Conversazione* (La Trobe University, Australia, 1989).

27. Information on the variety of federal systems is taken from a draft article by Eugene Lee on the subject of multicampus universities, prepared for the forthcoming *Encyclopaedia of Higher Education*; see also Lee and Bowen, *Multicampus University*, chaps 2 and 3.

28. I am referring specifically to the recollections of Clark Kerr, President Emeritus of the University of California, as contained in an unpublished paper entitled 'The California master plan of 1960 for higher education: an ex ante view', written in 990–91; see also the draft article by Eugene Lee, where Clark is cited.

29. Eugene C. Lee and Frank M. Bowen, *The University of London: an American Perspective* (Working Paper 89–3, Institute of Governmental Studies, University of California, Berkeley, March 1989), list 'quality control' among the general missions of multi-campus universities, but they almost immediately temper this object with another, 'the promotion of differential dimensions of quality' — a very different purpose.

30. *Ibid.*, 14.

31. *Ibid.*, 10.

32. Remarks made by Julie Robinson during discussion at the University History Seminar, Center for Studies in Higher Education, University of California, May 14, 1991.

33. Martin Trow, 'Analysis of status', in Burton Clark (ed.), *Perspectives on Higher Education: Eight Disciplinary and Comparative Views* (Berkeley and Los Angeles, 1984), 132–164.

34. As in Detlef K. Muller, Fritz Ringer and Brian Simon (eds), *The Rise of the Modern Educational System: Structural Change and Social Reproduction, 1870–1920* (Cambridge and Paris, 1987). The editors have included critiques of reproduction theory, but see also Sheldon Rothblatt, 'Supply and demand: the "two histories" of English education', *History of Education Quarterly*, 28 (1988), 627–644.

35. Clark Kerr, *The Uses of the University* (Cambridge, Ma, 1963). For disciplinary and professional attachments, Tony Becher, *Academic Tribes and Territories, Intellectual Enquiry and the Cultures of Disciplines* (Milton Keynes, 1989).

36. Scott, *Higher Education in Sweden*, 21.

37. Peter Van Houten, 'The Development of the Constitutional Provisions Pertaining to the University of California in the California Constitutional Convention of 1878–79' (unpublished Ph D dissertation, University of California, 1973).

38. Richard Hofstadter and Walter Metzger, *Academic Freedom in the United States* (New York, 1955).

39. Edward Gibbon, *Memories of My Life* (Harmondsworth, 1984), 163.

40. Sir Robert Inglis, *The Universities* (London, 1850), 54.

41. In conversation with Martin Trow.

42. Remarks made at a *Conversazione* held at the University of California at Berkeley, 21 and 22 May 1990 on the report, *A Review of Higher Education Policy in California* commissioned and released by the Organisation for Economic Co-Operation and Development, Paris, in 1989. The word conversazione to describe the Berkeley meetings was inspired by the Conversazione that Claudio Veliz has held for many years at La Trobe University, Australia, and which he has now expanded to include Boston University and Oxford University.

Index